Digital photography with your computer

Other Computer Titles

by

Robert Penfold

Digital photography with your computer

Robert Penfold

Bernard Babani (publishing) Ltd
The Grampians
Shepherds Bush Road
London W6 7NF
England
www.babanibooks.com

Please note

Although every care has been taken with the production of this book to ensure that any projects, designs, modifications, and/or programs, etc., contained herewith, operate in a correct and safe manner and also that any components specified are normally available in Great Britain, the Publisher and Author do not accept responsibility in any way for the failure (including fault in design) of any projects, design, modification, or program to work correctly or to cause damage to any equipment that it may be connected to or used in conjunction with, or in respect of any other damage or injury that may be caused, nor do the Publishers accept responsibility in any way for the failure to obtain specified components.

Notice is also given that if any equipment that is still under warranty is modified in any way or used or connected with home-built equipment then that warranty may be void.

© 2003 BERNARD BABANI (publishing) LTD

First Published July 2003
Reprinted April 2004

British Library Cataloguing in Publication Data

A catalogue record for this book is available from the British Library

ISBN   0 85934 537 8

Cover Design by Gregor Arthur
Printed and bound in Great Britain by Cox and Wyman

Preface

It is not that long ago that there was no such thing as digital photography. Progress was actually quite slow when digital cameras first started to appear, with one or two false starts. It was probably the mass demand for cameras capable of producing images for web pages that finally launched the digital revolution. These early cameras did not have sufficient resolution to produce anything more than tiny "thumbnail" prints, but they could produce instant images for use in web sites.

Digital cameras have kept getting better since then, and even the budget models of today will produce good quality postcard size prints. The more upmarket cameras can produce prints up to about A3 size, which is more than sufficient for most users. In fact mid-range models capable of producing prints up to about A4 size are perfectly adequate for most people. The reducing cost and increasing quality of inkjet printers has certainly played a key role in the popularity of digital photography. With digital photography you are no longer at the mercy of commercial photographic labs, and you can print good quality colour prints exactly the way you think they should be. No more washed out sunsets or lobster red skin tones.

One slight problem with the upsurge in the popularity of digital cameras is that you are spoiled for choice. A vast range of cameras is supported by an even vaster range of printers and accessories. There is no shortage of computer software to help rescue poor photographs, make good pictures even better, join several photographs into one outsize picture, and so on. Choice is a good thing, but it confuses matters for beginners. With digital photography you are in danger of "having too much of a good thing"

The first three chapters of this book cover the basics of digital photography, explaining camera and printer specifications, the different types of memory available, the amount of memory needed, and so on. The remaining chapters cover the techniques for dealing with the photographs once you have loaded them into a PC. Sloping horizons can be straightened, dull pictures can be made to sparkle, slightly fuzzy pictures can be made sharp, red eyes can be made blue again, and unwanted objects can be made to miraculously disappear. You can even put together images using bits of photographs. Amaze your friends with a photograph of you collecting an Oscar or an Olympic gold medal!

No photographic expertise is assumed, other than knowing which part of the camera to look into and which bit to aim at the subject. Experience with image editing software is not required either, but it is assumed that the reader knows the basics of using a PC. Anyone new to computing would be well advised to spend a little time learning the fundamentals before trying to use any applications program.

Robert Penfold

Trademarks

Contents

1

The same but different 1

What is it? 1
Editing 3
Pixels 4
Minimum resolution? 7
How much memory? 8
Compression 11
Connections 12
USB 13
TWAIN 14
TWAIN importing 16
Output 19
Formats 19
Jpeg or Jpg 20
GIF 21
Png 21
TIFF or TIF 21
EPS 22
BMP 22
PDF 22
PICT 22
PCX 22
RAW 23
PSD 23
Layers 23
Which format? 25
Points to remember 27

2

Pros and cons 29

Advantages 29
Speed? 30
Convenience 31

Battery drain 32
In the real world 32
Cost 33
Overall cost 34
If at first... 35
Biggest advantage 37
Camera never lies? 38
Through the lens 45
Drawbacks 45
Powerful computer? 46
Developing technology 48
Quality 48
Longevity 49
Points to remember 51

3

The right equipment...................... 53

Which computer 53
Storage 54
Printers 55
Dots per inch 55
Colour 56
Speed 58
Running costs 59
Paper 60
The camera 61
Lens 62
F numbers 66
Speed rating 67
Flash modes 68
Automatic 68
Always off 68
Always fires 69
Macro 72
Batteries 75
Integral monitor 76

LCD 77
Software 78
Image editing 80
Getting information 82
Points to remember 85

4

Basic editing 87

Why process? 87
Photoshop Elements 88
Screen layout 90
Sizing up 91
Pixel count 92
Resolution 93
Image quality 94
Pixel boost 96
Glitches 98
Rotation 98
Crop tool 102
Cropping 104
Marquee 106
Correcting perspective 108
Stretching 114
Alternatives 115
Flipping 116
Hard copy 117
Points to remember 123

5

Colour mixing 125

Mixing it 125
Colour models 126
RGB 126
CMYK 128

HSB 129
Greyscale 131
Bitmap 133
Indexed Color 136
Greyscale to colour 140
Swatches 141
Wrong colour 142
Alternative picker 143
Points to remember 145

6

Colour and contrast 147

In control 147
Enhance menu 148
Variations 148
Shadows and highlights 151
Saturation 152
Clipping 154
Histogram 154
Auto Contrast 157
Auto Levels.. 159
Levels 160
Brightness/Contrast 165
Hue/Saturation 167
"Red-eye" removal 169
Saturation 172
Single colour 172
Fill Flash 173
Adjust Backlighting 177
Alternatives 177
Replace Color 179
Points to remember 181

7

Making selections 183

Getting choosy 183
Difficulty factor 184
Multiple selections 185
Style 188
Deselection 189
Lasso tool 190
Polygonal Lasso tool 192
Magnetic Lasso tool 196
Options 198
Magic Wand tool 199
Settings 202
Contiguous 204
Anti-aliased 205
Selection menu 206
Grow 209
Similar 210
Inverse 211
Masks and selections 214
Getting creative 215
Copy and Paste 217
Stitching 218
Stitching methods 219
Automation 221
Points to remember 224

8

Using brushes 227

Brush off 227
Getting artistic 231
Cloning 234
Tricky situations 238
Expanding images 241

Duplicate flaws 243
Alignment option 245
Layers 246
Mode menu 249
Dodge and Burn 250
Sponge tool 254
Pressure sensitive 255
Selection Brush tool 256
Paint Bucket tool 259
Graduation tool 262
Points to remember 269

9

Filters 271

What is a filter? 271
Artistic filtering 273
Preview 275
Editing 282
Oversize printing 288
Blurring 289
Gaussian Blur 294
Soft focus 298
Smart Blur 302
Sharp filtering 305
Options 307
Unsharp Mask 310
The rest 312
Points to remember 315

10

Adding text 317

Text and layers 317
Text options 318
Adding text 322

Drop shadow 323
Opacity 324
Selection 327
Rasterizing 328
Captions 329
On the cards 332
Finally 333
Points to remember 334

Index 335

The same
but different

What is it?

I would guess that most people in the UK have loaded a camera with film, taken some photographs, and then had the film developed and printed. Probably many fewer have taken photographs using a digital camera and then printed them. Digital photography is very popular, and increasingly so, but it is relatively new and unfamiliar to many. The obvious starting point is to go through the basic steps involved in producing a photograph via the digital route. It is possible to produce digital images from film by scanning a print, transparency, or negative, but the purely digital method will be described here.

Clearly the first requirement for the all-digital approach is a digital camera, and one that suits your intended use of digital photography. Digital cameras come in a variety of shapes and sizes, most of which have direct equivalents in 35-millimetre film photography. My first digital camera was an Olympus SLR having non-interchangeable lenses, which was more or less a digital equivalent of their popular 35-millimetre SLR cameras of the period. This type of camera is now produced by other manufacturers, and they are still produced by Olympus. Figure 1.1 shows the desirable Olympus E10 digital SLR camera, which is the modern equivalent of the first digital camera I used. Figure 1.2 shows a Canon Ixus 400, which is very much a digital equivalent of Canon's film compact cameras.

Digital cameras look very much like film cameras, and they have many of the same controls such as a shutter button and a control for the flash mode. In general, taking a photograph using a digital camera is not much different to taking the same shot using a film camera. Adapting to a digital camera should be quite easy if you are experienced with conventional cameras. However, there are also some huge differences between the two types of camera and the ways they are used. The most

*Fig.1.1 The Olympus E10 is a digital SLR having a non-
interchangeable lens*

obvious one is that a digital camera does not use film. Instead, it has a
built-in electronic sensor that converts the image into electronic data.
When a photograph is taken, this data is stored in memory circuits that
are sometimes built into the camera. In other cases the memory is in the
form of small cards that can be fitted into a slot in the camera, and in
other cases there is built-in memory and a slot for memory cards.

I suppose that memory cards are the nearest equivalent to the film of a
conventional camera. A film only lasts for so many photographs, and
the same is true of memory. Unlike film though, the memory is reusable.
You can take out one memory card, insert another, and carry on shooting,
much like changing films. Once you have finished taking photographs it
is time to download the data from the memory and store it on a computer.
Computer hard disc drives are not infallible, so it is then a good idea to
make at least one backup copy onto a CD-R disc. The data can then be
erased from the memory cards, which are then ready for a fresh set of
photographs to be taken.

Editing

With the image files in the computer it is possible to view them on the monitor. If necessary the brightness, contrast, and colour balance can be adjusted, and many other types of processing can be applied to the images. This processing requires photo-editing software, which is often supplied with the digital camera. There are good low-cost image editing programs available if suitable software is not supplied with the camera, or it is but you are unhappy with the supplied program.

Figure 1.2 The Canon Ixus 400 is a very compact digital camera

Many of the advantages of digital imaging are due to the power of modern image editing software, so it is worthwhile having software that is powerful and user-friendly.

Some of the bundled software is quite good, but much of it is pretty basic. This type of image editing software provides an easy introduction to the subject, and in fairness that is all it is designed to do. It is worth using a basic image editing program initially, as it will get you "up and running" straight away. Before too long you will probably wish to move on to something more potent though.

Many digital images are taken specifically for use in web pages or in other applications where printed images are not required. Most users will require at least some prints though, and there are two basic options available. Many photographic processing labs can now produce prints from image files stored on floppy discs or CD-ROMs (including CD-Rs). Results should be excellent, but the cost tends to be relatively high unless only a few prints are required from time to time. Maybe the economics will change in due course, but at present it is generally much cheaper to produce your own prints using an inkjet printer. Figure 1.3 shows an inkjet printer from the popular Epson range. I would not wish to give the impression that producing your own prints in this way is cheap in absolute

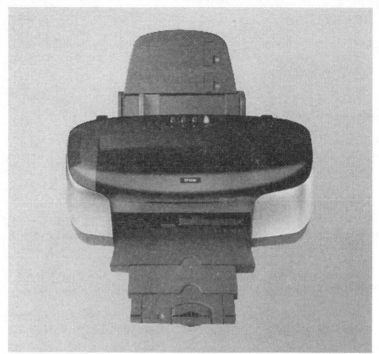

Fig.1.3 An inkjet printer such as this Epson model is the most popular method of producing colour prints

terms. The costs involved are reasonable though, and being able to produce prints as and when needed has the advantage of convenience. The fact that you are in control of the process and can produce prints exactly the way you require them is a major plus point.

Pixels

A digital image of the type produced by scanners and digital cameras is comprised of dots, or pixels as they are termed. The maximum number of pixels per image is something that is usually at or near the top in digital camera specifications, and it is often alluded to in the names of cameras. I suppose that one day camera technology might advance to the point where there is no point in producing cameras having more pixels than their predecessors, but we are not yet at that stage. As things stand, it is definitely a case of the more pixels the better.

*Fig.1.4 This photograph of Tower Bridge is just about recognisable,
but a lack of pixels produces a lack of detail*

*Fig.1.5 There are about 100 times as many pixels in this version of the
photograph, which gives plenty of detail*

The greater the number of pixels that a camera can produce, the greater the practical range of uses there are for that camera. The maximum print size that can be produced is directly related to the number of pixels in the image. There is actually more to picture quality than the number of pixels, and there are other factors such as lens quality. However, all else being equal, the camera that has the highest pixel output will provide the best picture quality. Figures 1.4 and 1.5 show the importance of having a sufficient number of pixels for a given print size.

In Figure 1.4 the picture has just 60 by 88 pixels, and there are two obvious problems. One is simply that the pixels are so large that they are clearly visible; giving a sort of mosaic effect that is known as pixilation. The second is an obvious lack of definition, with no detail in the picture at all. In Figure 1.5 there are nearly 100 times more pixels, giving a lot of detail. Also, the pixels are no longer big enough to be seen individually. They merge together to produce a proper image having nicely graduated tones. The subject of the picture is sufficiently famous that most people could probably guess that the version of Figure 1.4 was a picture of Tower Bridge, and this type of picture can be visually pleasing.

Apart from the use of low resolution as a special effect though, a large number of pixels are needed in order to produce satisfactory results. Although the examples of Figures 1.4 and 1.5 are greyscale images, the same is true of colour images. Too few pixels still give inadequate detail and a mosaic effect.

Minimum resolution?

It would seem reasonable to ask the minimum acceptable resolution for a digital camera, but this is very much a "how long is a piece of string?" style question. If the camera will only be used for producing web images, then a relatively low resolution will probably be adequate. Most images used on the web are quite small at around 300 by 200 pixels, but larger images of about 640 by 480 pixels are sometimes used. High resolution images tend to produce large image files that take a long time to download. Small images have the advantage of speeding up the download times for web pages, and are usually perfectly adequate.

Even the cheapest of digital cameras has sufficient resolution for producing web images. However, there are now some good low-cost cameras that have higher resolutions. Unless you are working on a very tight budget it is probably best to opt for one of these. The higher resolution enables prints of a reasonable size to be made should you wish to do so, and it is quite likely that you will wish to do so before too long. Most digital cameras have low resolution modes for producing web images, but the resolution of an image is easily reduced using any photo-editing software.

The minimum acceptable resolution for producing prints, or DTP where the final document will be printed, depends on the final size of the image. To some extent it is also a subjective matter, and it depends on the minimum acceptable image quality. It also depends on factors such as the type of image and the printing process used. There is no "hard and fast" figure at which resolution becomes inadequate. In general, most people are reasonably happy with photographic images having a resolution of 200 pixels per inch, but notice graininess or even the individual pixels at a resolution as low as 150 pixels per inch.

The minimum acceptable resolution for most people is therefore somewhere between these two figures. Note that you have to be careful with the resolution of a digital image whether it is built up from scratch, scanned, or loaded from a digital camera. Whatever the source, the same rules apply. If the resolution is too low the individual pixels will be visible.

If you take the middle of the range figure or 175 pixels per inch (about 70 pixels per centimetre) as the minimum acceptable resolution, the required number of pixels for a given print size can then be calculated. Suppose that you require a maximum print size of 10 inches by 8 inches. This requires a resolution of at least 1750 by 1400 pixels, which works out at 2.45 million pixels. Of course, the resolution of the camera would ideally be somewhat greater than this, and one having a resolution of about three million pixels would comfortably handle 10 inch by 8 inch prints. One having about 2.2 million pixels might be able to produce acceptable prints of this size, but this would be stretching things to the limit.

How much memory?

Images are stored in memory until they have been successfully downloaded, and then they can be erased so that a new batch of photographs can be taken. The memory can be built into the camera, but even if there is some integral memory it is usually possible to use plug-in memory cards as well. In many cases the memory is only provided by plug-in cards, but at least one card of reasonable capacity should be supplied with the camera. There are three types of memory card in common use with digital cameras, and these are Smartmedia, Compactflash (versions 1 and 2), and Sony's Memory Stick. Figures 1.6

and 1.7 respectively show 32 megabyte Memory Stick and Compactflash memory cards. Incidentally, memory cards are used for other portable electronic gadgets such as organisers, and they are not exclusive to digital cameras.

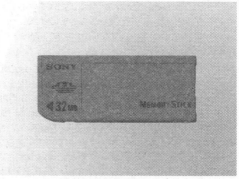

Fig.1.6 *This 32 megabyte memory card is a Sony Memory Stick*

The memory cards fit into compartments right inside the body of the camera, and once inside they are covered by a door. Figure 1.8 shows a Compactflash card fitted into a camera. Some cameras can take more than one card, and some can even take more than one type of memory card. In most cases though, only one card at a time and only one type of card can be used. Memory cards are reasonably safe when inside a camera, but they need to be treated with due care when outside a camera. They should be kept away from direct sunlight, moisture, and high temperatures. It is best not to touch any

Fig.1.7 *Compactflash cards are the most common type of memory for cameras*

exposed metal on connectors as this could give poor electrical connections. Due to their small size and thinness it is inevitable that memory cards are not very tough, and care must be taken to avoid physical damage.

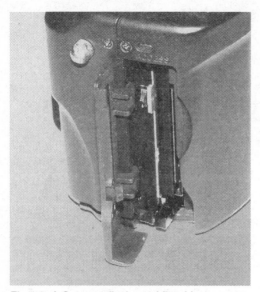

Fig.1.8 A Compactflash card fitted in a camera

The amount of memory required per picture is dependent on several factors. One of these is the number of pixels per image. One byte per pixel is sufficient for greyscale images, and this gives black, white, and 254 shades of grey. Good quality colour images require more bytes per pixel, and quite good results are obtained using two bytes. The most popular system uses three bytes per pixel, with one byte being used for each primary colour. This gives 256 levels per primary colour, and a total of nearly 16.8 million colours. A camera that has a maximum resolution of 3.3 million pixels will therefore produce almost 10 million bytes of data per colour picture, which gives about 12 or 13 pictures on a 128 megabyte memory card. A megabyte is just over one million bytes incidentally.

At one time memory cards were expensive and their capacities were quite low. Technology has moved on and prices have fallen. Also, memory cards having capacities into the hundreds of megabytes are now available, and there are minute hard disc drives that can provide cameras with massive amounts or data storage. Thus it is possible to shoot dozens of pictures at 10 or 20 megabytes a time and store them until you get home and upload them to a computer. It is not a particularly cheap way of doing things though, and cameras have the option of compressing images so that more images can be stored in a given amount of memory. It is for this reason that the specifications for digital cameras list various image quality settings, some of which have an identical image resolution. The higher quality setting has little or no data compression while the lower quality setting uses large amounts of it.

Compression

There are actually two distinctly different types of data compression. Computer programs are often supplied on CD-ROMs and floppy discs in compressed form, but when the data is uncompressed it is exactly the same as the original. It has to be, because programs will not work properly if there is even a single byte that contains an error. This type of compression can be used with images, but the reduction in file sizes it provides is relatively modest. The 10 megabytes of data in our previous example would be reduced to about 3 to 5 megabytes using this type of compression. Such a reduction is certainly useful, but it would still not permit many images to be stored on a cheap 32-megabyte memory card.

The other type of compression works in much the same way as the type used for compressing programs and other critical data. The basic technique is for the compression program to look for occurrences of the same series of bytes. It then stores this series of bytes, together with the position of each occurrence. Apparently, even in a random set of data there are numerous series of bytes that occur over and over again. Hence, with some refinements, this system can significantly compress real world data. The compression systems normally used with images operate in a similar fashion, but they will settle for something less than exact duplications. The more compression that is used, the more approximate the program becomes when looking for recurring patterns.

In practice this means that it is possible to obtain quite high degrees of compression, but that the image quality tends to deteriorate at the highest compression ratios. So how much compression can be used before the image degrades noticeably? It depends on the type of image and how carefully viewers will scrutinise it. Having tried various cameras and levels of compression, ratios of up to about 8 to 1 have always provided very good results. Ratios of 10 to 1 and greater start to produce a noticeable loss of quality, and usually add what are generally termed artefacts. In other words, the compression adds spurious details and objects that were not in the original image.

Figure 1.9 shows a couple of icons on the Desktop of my PC, and this image has been saved using a high degree of compression. The "clean" version of Figure 1.10 shows the same two icons but with the image saved using minimal compression. In Figure 1.9 some loss of accuracy is apparent in the icons, but the most noticeable problem is all the rubbish that has been added into the plain areas around the icons and the text. With high degrees of compression it is often the added artefacts rather than missing detail that reduces the quality to an unacceptable level.

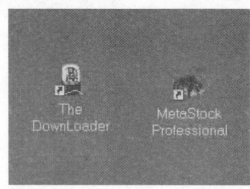

Fig.1.9 A large amount of compression has produced artefacts

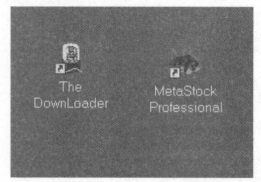

Fig.1.10 The "clean" version of the image

Using a compression ratio of between 5 to 1 and 8 to 1 is sufficient to reduce our example 10 megabyte files down about 1.25 to 2 megabytes. This equates to about 25 images on an inexpensive 32-megabyte memory card, or around 100 on a 128-megabyte card, which is more than adequate for most users.

Connections

In the early days of digital cameras an RS232C serial connection was the most common means of uploading data from the camera to the computer. This was convenient as most PCs had at least one spare serial port, but normal serial ports are notoriously slow. Taking a normal PC serial port to its limits still gives a transfer rate of only about 0.5 megabytes or so per minute. This gave long uploads times with the relatively low resolution cameras of the day. With a modern camera fitted with a 32-megabyte memory card it could take about an hour to upload all the images. Uploading all the images from a practically full 128 megabyte card would take several hours! A fast connection to the computer is not so much desirable as essential with modern cameras.

A few digital cameras use a Firewire interface. This is a high-speed serial interface that was designed to permit Macintosh computers to handle digital video. Some PCs are now equipped with a Firewire port,

*Fig.1.11 A USB link is the most common method of connecting a
digital camera to a computer*

and it is a feature that can be added via an expansion card. In theory
anyway, all the data could be uploaded from a full 32-megabyte memory
card in a second or two via a Firewire interface. With high speed interfaces
it pays to bear in mind that some PCs are not fast enough to fully utilize
the available bandwidth. This type of interfacing is mainly used with
upmarket "professional" cameras, so it is unlikely that you will use it
unless you also use a digital video camera.

USB

These days the most common way of uploading images from a digital
camera to a computer is to connect the camera to a USB port on the
computer. Any reasonably modern PC will have at least a couple of USB
ports as standard, but USB ports are easily added to a PC using an
expansion card. Note that Windows 98 or later is needed in order to
utilize USB ports. A camera that uses this method of connection should
be supplied with a suitable data cable. The smaller connector fits into
the camera and the larger one plugs into the computer (Figure 1.11).

The connectors are polarised, so it is only possible to plug them in the right way round.

Normal USB ports can transfer data to and from a single device at up to about 0.6 megabytes per second, which gives reasonably short upload times. The more recent USB 2.0 ports can transfer data at similar speeds to those obtained using a Firewire interface. Note though, that the port on the camera and the one on the computer must both be USB 2.0 types in order to obtain the high transfer rate.

The camera will also be supplied with a CD-ROM containing the necessary driver software to permit the camera and the computer to communicate. With luck there will also be some other software such as a library program and photo-editing software. Getting the software installed on the computer is usually very straightforward, and there is often an automatic installation program. Make sure that the driver software is installed exactly in accordance with the manufacturer's instructions. It is often necessary to install the software, then connect the camera, and finally reboot the computer so that the installation can be finalised.

There are two basic approaches to uploading images to the computer. Some digital cameras are supplied with download programs that place the images onto the hard disc drive in a standard image file format such as JPEG. The images can then be imported into practically any image editing program, as well as desktop publishing programs, word processors, and so on. Most of these programs also have database and preview facilities that make it easier to find the required image file. Finding the right image might not be difficult initially, but it can certainly become an issue when there are hundreds or thousands of them stored on your hard disc drive. It pays to get things well organised right from the start.

TWAIN

Practically all imaging devices, including digital cameras, are supplied with a TWAIN driver in addition to any download and preview software. A few cameras are only supplied with one or the other, which limits your options. However, the equipment is usable provided one of these methods is supported. The TWAIN option is probably the more popular method of downloading files from an imaging device, particularly among professional users. TWAIN is supposedly an acronym for "technology without an interesting name", but this is explanation is far from universally accepted. It is probably derived from the saying "never the twain shall meet". The purpose of the TWAIN driver is to ensure that the twain (meaning two) shall meet, and the two that must be brought together are the imaging device and the computer.

TWAIN drivers tend to confuse the uninitiated, because having loaded the drivers onto the PC there is no obvious way of downloading images. The all-important point to keep in mind is that the TWAIN drivers provide a link to other software, and also

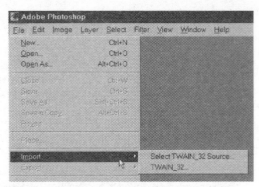

Fig.1.12 It might be necessary to select the correct TWAIN source

provide additional features when using that software. These features enable the user to view "thumbnails" of the pictures stored in the camera, select the images to download, and so on. However, the TWAIN drivers are not standalone applications programs.

In order to use the TWAIN drivers you must have applications software that can utilize them. Most imaging programs, including the "cheap and cheerful" variety, do support TWAIN drivers. The method used to access the TWAIN facilities vary somewhat from one program to another. In addition, the facilities offered by the TWAIN driver vary considerably, and have to be tailored to suit the particular hardware in use.

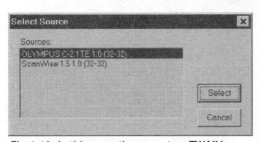

If you use two or three imaging devices with your computer, each device will require its own TWAIN drivers

Fig.1.13 In this case there are two TWAIN devices to choose from

to be installed. These are often loaded automatically when the installation program for the camera or scanner is run. When loading the TWAIN drivers is optional, it is advisable to select this option even if you have no immediate use for them. The drivers will take up little space on the hard disc, and it is likely that you will wish to use them before too long.

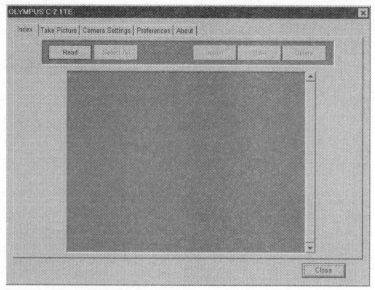

Fig.1.14 This window enables images to be selected and loaded from the camera

TWAIN importing

The exact method of importing images into an application via the TWAIN route varies from one program to another. It might be necessary to delve into the Help system or the instruction manuals to find the correct menu options, but a little delving into the File menu will usually bring them to light. Here a couple of examples will be considered, starting with Photoshop. The process is exactly the same using lower cost version, Photoshop Elements, which is sometimes bundled with cameras and scanners.

With Photoshop the TWAIN option is accessed via the Import option of the File menu (Figure 1.12). One option enables the source to be selected, but this is only relevant if more than one TWAIN compliant device is used with the PC. The PC used for this example has two TWAIN compliant peripherals, which are a digital camera and a scanner. Left-clicking on the Select TWAIN_32 source option produces the small window of Figure 1.13, and the required source can then be selected.

Images from the camera or scanner can then be downloaded by returning to the File menu, selecting the Import option, and then selecting TWAIN_32 from the submenu. The window that appears next depends on the source in use. Figure 1.14 shows the window that appears with the Olympus digital camera used as the source. This provides full control over the camera, but in most cases it is only needed to download the

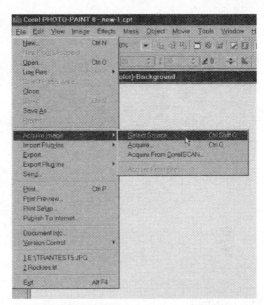

Fig.1.15 The TWAIN devices are accessed via the Acquire Image submenu

images stored in the camera's memory. This is achieved by operating the Read button, which results in "thumbnail" pictures being downloaded and displayed in the window. The required images are then downloaded by selecting the corresponding "thumbnail" images and operating the Import button. The images are then downloaded from the camera and loaded into the graphics program. Here they can be edited, printed, and saved to disc, just like any other images.

Corel Photo-Paint 8 is used for the second example of importing images from a TWAIN source. This time the Acquire Image option is selected from the File menu, and this leads to three choices that are available from the submenu (Figure 1.15). As before, one of these enables the source to be selected via a small window   (Figure

Fig.1.16 Two TWAIN devices are available

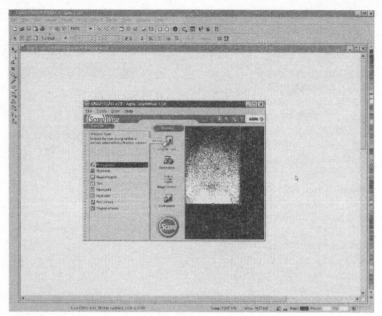

*Fig.1.17 The scanning utility runs from within the main application,
and loads the images straight into that application*

1.16). The other two options enable images to be downloaded from the
current source, either into Photo-Paint 8 or into the CorelSCAN utility. It
will usually be the direct route that is needed, and selecting this option
results in the required utility being run from within Photo-Paint 8 (Figure
1.17). This utility program is then used to make the scans or download
the images from the camera. Either way, they are loaded into Photo-
Paint 8 where they can be used in the normal way.

In menus, the TWAIN option may be referred as just plain TWAIN or
something like TWAIN32 or TWAIN_32. The "32" simply indicates that
the driver is for a 32-bit version of Windows, which means Windows NT,
Windows 95, or any later versions. These days it is not of any practical
significance. Some graphics software lacks any means of using TWAIN
drivers. If a search of the menus and the Help system does not reveal
any means of directly downloading images into the program, this feature
is probably unavailable. Generally, only older and very simple graphics
software has this shortcoming.

Output

I think it is worth emphasising again, that having uploaded the images by one means or another it is a good idea to make at least one backup copy onto a removable disc such as a CD-R. You are then ready to go through the images, doing any necessary tinkering to them using the image editing program. With the original images safely stored on a disc you have complete freedom to alter the images. You can alter the contrast, change the colours, crop the edges, copy bits from one image to another, and so on, until the images are exactly as required. It does not matter if you make a complete hash of things because it is always possible to return to the original images and start again.

With images that are required for the Internet it might be necessary to alter the size (in pixels) so that the image fits the page correctly, although it is often easier to do this from within the web page creation program. If prints are required, the physical size of each image is set and then it is printed out on what will usually be an inkjet printer. A big advantage of the digital method is that you can print the images small, medium, large, or not at all, depending on their merits. There is no wasted film or money spent on prints of failed shots.

The process described here is the normal one for digital photography, but there are numerous variations on this basic scheme of things. The images can, of course, originate from a film camera with a scanner being used to produce the digitised images. There are gadgets for uploading memory cards to a PC, and printers that can operate direct from memory cards, with no PC being required. The basic method described here is the most common approach. Printing direct from memory cards has its attractions for those of a non-technical disposition, but all or most of the power of digital imaging is lost using this method. In order to get the most from digital imaging it is essential to master and use a good image editing program. Practically anything is then possible.

Formats

When dealing with digital cameras you will soon encounter various file formats such as Jpeg and Png. What is a file format, and why are there so many of them? A file format is simply a standard way of storing image data so that various devices and programs can handle the images. You do not need a program to suit your particular camera or scanner in order to undertake image editing. The camera produces images in a standard format such as Jpeg, and virtually any photo-editing software can be used to process and print the images. The images can also be imported into word processors and desktop publishing programs.

Hardware and software computer standards have both been something of a joke since the early days of home computing. Often each company had its own idea of how a supposed standard should operate, and manufacturers often invented new standards rather than using existing ones. Possibly the constant stream of new standards was an attempt to avoid the copyright and patent problems associated with the existing ones. Anyway, rather than one universal graphics format, or even one format for photographic images, numerous image file formats have been produced over the years. Most of them have fallen into obsolescence, and the ones that remain are the ones that have achieved large scale use for one reason or another.

These are the image file formats you are most likely to encounter.

Jpeg or Jpg

Whether called Jpeg or Jpg, it is pronounced jay-peg. This is now the most common format used for bit maps such as photographic images. A bitmap is simply an image that is comprised of pixels, such as the output from a digital camera. Bitmap formats tend to produce very large files or relatively poor results when applied to line drawings such as charts and diagrams. This file format is mainly used with photographic images, or pseudo photographic images, where it enables good results to be obtained without resorting to large file sizes. The modest file sizes are achieved using compression. With some programs you can use varying degrees of compression and up to three different types. It is safest to stick with the standard variety, which should be compatible with any program that can handle Jpeg files.

As explained previously, the small file sizes obtained when using high degrees of compression are obtained at the expense of reduced picture quality. In Internet applications it is clearly helpful to have small files in order to keep download times to a minimum. On the other hand, there is no point in having an image that downloads quickly if no one can see what it is meant to be! The borderline between acceptable and unacceptable quality is a subjective matter, and can only be determined using the "suck it and see" approach. Particularly for web use, it is very useful to have a photo-editing program that permits varying degrees of Jpeg compression to be applied. Ideally there should be a preview facility that enables the effect of compression to be viewed prior to saving an image.

Figure 1.18 shows a photograph that has been saved in Jpeg format using minimal compression, and Figure 1.19 shows the same photograph with maximum compression. These produce file sizes of just over 900k and a little less than 100k respectively, and there is surprisingly little difference between them. However, with a colour image any artefacts added by the compression tend to be more noticeable, so this monochrome image is perhaps overstating the case for using large amounts of compression. However, it does demonstrate the fact that large amounts of compression do not necessarily produce very poor quality. Jpeg is a standard format for web use, and it is also compatible with practically any desktop publishing software, so it is a format that you are likely to use.

GIF

The full name for this format is CompuServe Graphics Interchange Format, and programs that use it have to be licensed by CompuServe. This is another popular format for web use. However, this format is generally preferred for line art such as graphs and most diagrams, or practically any non-photographic images. In fact the GIF image format is sometimes used for monochrome photographs, but these days Jpeg is the more popular choice for images of this type. Consequently, and despite its web compatibility, digital camera users are unlikely to have any need for the GIF format.

Png

This is a relatively new file format for images, and it is apparently pronounced pong, as in nasty smell or Ping-Pong. Png stands for Portable Network Graphic. It is designed to be a sort of universal licence-free image format that will eventually replace the GIF format. It combines small file sizes with the ability to use an unlimited colour range. Although relatively new, any reasonably modern browser should be able to handle Png images (Internet Explorer 4 or later for example). However, it is less universal than either the Jpg or GIF formats.

TIFF or TIF

TIFF (Tagged Image File Format) is one of the older image file formats, and it stores images as bitmaps. It is sometimes called TIF rather than TIFF, and files of this type usually have TIF as the extension to the filename. Although popular at one time, it has to some extent given way to Jpg files which offer smaller file sizes. It is still quite popular for use with desktop publishing programs though. There is also an Enhanced TIFF format that supports layers, but this might give compatibility problems with some programs.

EPS

Encapsulated Postscript is another format that is mainly used in desktop publishing, and it is compatible with many desktop publishing and graphics programs. However, it is primarily used for charts and diagrams rather than photographic images. It can handle bitmaps, but it seems to store them in non-compressed form, giving relatively large file sizes.

BMP

This is a simple bitmap format, and judging from the file sizes produced using this format, no compression is used. It is the standard Windows bitmap format, and should be supported by any Windows graphics program.

PDF

This is the Adobe portable document format, and it is a cross-platform format. PDF is actually a general-purpose file format that can handle text and any type of image. This book was sent to the printers in the form of a single PDF file for example. A high degree of compression is used, but results of excellent quality are produced. Adobe Acrobat reader is needed to view PDF files, but the reader program is free from the Adobe web site and is available for several types of computer and various operating systems. The popular web browsers link to the reader program so that they can effectively be used to display PDF documents. This format is a popular choice for complex and (or) large documents, but it can be used with single images.

PICT

Files that use this format normally have PIC as the extension. This is a Macintosh format that is mainly used in desktop publishing. Many Windows programs support this graphics format.

PCX

This is an early bitmap format that was very popular at one time. Not surprising really, since there was little serious competition in those days. It is not used very much now, and you are unlikely to encounter it unless you use old software or happen to have some old image files in this format.

RAW

Not exactly a file format in the conventional sense, it is more a means of importing and exporting images. It is used a great deal with the more upmarket digital cameras as a means of uploading images with the highest possible quality. In other words, the raw image data is exported with no compression or file conversion.

PSD

Photoshop is the most popular photo-editing program for professionals, and this is its native format. It is also used by Photoshop Elements and Photoshop LE. Photoshop and its variants can handle images in standard formats such as Jpeg, so why is its own format necessary? The popular formats such as Jpeg are perfectly adequate where only basic processing such as adjusting the brightness and contrast is required. In general, they do not permit more advanced forms of processing such as those that involve the use of layers. Layers are often likened to images that are comprised of several separate pictures on transparent film, laid one on top of the other. Elements on higher layers may obscure or partially obscure elements on lower layers. With the elements of a picture on separate layers it is possible to move and process one element without damaging or in any way altering the others.

Layers

Figures 1.18 and 1.19 show a simple demonstration of layers in action. In Figure 1.18 some text has been added to an image, and it has automatically been placed on a new layer by Photoshop Elements. It is on a layer above the main image, so the text is visible and partially obscures the image below. Because the text is on its own layer there is no problem if it is moved. Also, it is possible to edit the text, much like editing text in a word processor. In Figure 1.19 the text has been altered slightly and moved from the top to the bottom of the image. This has not left holes in the image where the text was originally positioned, because the lettering was not merged into the main image. It was kept as a separate entity that did not affect the underlying image.

The same would not be true if the text was added onto the image, replacing the material beneath it. Even minor repositioning or editing would then require the damaged part of the image to be repaired, which could be difficult and time consuming. The practical lesson to be learnt from this is that anything other than very basic editing might require the

Fig.1.18 The text is on a new layer that is above the image of the camera, and is effectively a separate image

image to be switched into the native format of the photo-editing software. In this example Photoshop and the PSD format were used, but many graphics programs have their own format that must be used when undertaking complex editing.

A slight problem with most of these formats, including PSD, is that they are not supported by many other programs. This makes it difficult to export images to other programs and they are not suitable for web use either. This is not a major drawback as it is usually possible to save the images in a common and more portable format such as Jpeg. Doing so will remove all the layer information and flatten the image into a simple bitmap, making further editing difficult. It is therefore a good idea to keep a copy of complex images in the native format of the image editing software so that further editing can be applied quite easily, should it be necessary at some later date. Flattened versions of the images in Jpeg format (or whatever) can then be made as and when required.

Fig.1.19 The text can be moved without harming the image beneath

Which format?

With so many different formats in use things can be a bit confusing for beginners. Probably the best advice is to keep things as simple as possible. If a camera produces images in Jpeg format, as many do, then it is probably best to stick with that format unless there is a compelling reason to do otherwise. Jpeg images can be used on the web, and there is no problem in producing prints from this format. There might be an enforced change to the native format of the photo-editing software if some fancy editing is required, but it should still be possible to produce Jpeg versions for web use.

Probably the only reason for going to another format such as EPS or TIFF is to obtain compatibility with a desktop publishing or word processor program. These days most programs that can import graphics can handle Jpeg files, so a change of format could still be unnecessary. In the early days of desktop publishing it was often necessary to try various graphics formats in the hope of finding one that would import properly. These days most of the problems have been ironed out and there should be no difficulty in importing bitmaps in any common format. Jpeg is such a popular format that any desktop publishing program should be able to import glitch free versions of images in this format.

I would definitely advise against storing your images in an obscure format used by a little known program. It is much better to use a common format that is widely used by other programs. If you move on to a different image editing program in the future there will then be no difficulty in loading your images into the new program. Over the years many computer users have found themselves with masses of data in an obsolete format. Even if the data can be converted to a common and more usable format it can take vast amounts of time to do it. By using a common format in the first place it is possible to avoid this type of problem.

Points to remember

Digital cameras come in a variety of shapes and sizes, just like film cameras. There are digital equivalents to most types of film camera from the smallest of compact cameras to professional SLRs. If you already use a film camera it should be possible to find a digital one that offers similar features.

A digital camera converts the image into electrical signals that are stored in memory. The memory can be in the form of plug-in cards, or built into the camera, or built-in with the option of using memory cards as well. The amount of memory required per picture depends on the resolution and amount of compression used. It can be anything from about 0.1 to 20 megabytes.

Digital images are comprised of thousands or even millions of tiny dots, or pixels as they are termed. The more pixels in the image, the larger it can be printed. A camera that produces images containing about 3.2 million pixels is about the minimum requirement for printing A4 size images. About one million or so is just about adequate for ordinary postcard size prints.

While using compression is definitely not going to improve the image quality, it does not necessarily produce a significant degradation either. Reducing the amount of data by a factor of around three or four is unlikely to produce any significant reduction in quality. In fact the quality is generally very good with compression ratios of up to about eight to one. Going beyond this is almost certain to produce an obvious reduction in image quality.

The software supplied with some cameras simply uploads the pictures to the computer's hard disc drive where it is stored in a common file format. Most cameras are supplied with TWAIN drivers, either instead of or in addition to simple uploading software. TWAIN drivers enable images to be uploaded from the camera straight into an image editing program. These days most image editing programs support the use of TWAIN drivers.

Hard disc drives can and do fail from time to time. It is best to make at least one backup copy of each image on something like a CD-R disc before erasing the memory in the camera. Data can sometimes be rescued from a hard disc drive, but there is no guarantee it will be possible and professional data recovery services are expensive.

There are numerous file formats for storing digital images. Jpeg is the one most commonly used for web images, and it is the nearest thing to a standard format for photographic images. Some types of image editing require the use of layers, which usually requires the native format of the image editing software. It should still be possible to produce Jpeg versions of the images so that they can be used on the Internet, etc.

Pros and cons

Advantages

Photography using film of one kind or another has served us well for more than 150 years, and until quite recently there was no viable alternative technology available. Digital cameras have been around for a number of years now, but the early examples were only capable of low resolution results. They were fine for producing images for use on the Internet, but were not much good if you required prints bigger than large postage stamps! The best of today's digital cameras genuinely rival good quality film cameras, but remain relatively expensive. The upmarket technology of today tends to become the "bog standard" technology of tomorrow, so top quality digital cameras at bargain prices are presumably not too far away. Indeed, unless you require prints significantly larger than A4 size they are already here.

Digital cameras are becoming more and more competitive with traditional film cameras, but do they have real advantages? Are these advantages great enough to warrant parting with what could be quite a few "hard and readies" in order to get into digital imaging. There are certainly a number of advantages, but the relative merits of the two technologies depend to some extent on the way in which they will be used. If you need images for use on web pages then it is clearly necessary to have digital images. It is possible to take photographs using a film camera and then use a scanner to produce digital images from the negatives, transparencies, or prints. This has to be regarded as doing things the hard way though, since even the cheapest of digital cameras can produce images of adequate quality for most web requirements.

A digital camera produces images in a form that can be loaded straight into a computer and used in web pages. It will often be necessary to do some processing of the image before it is used in a web site, such as adjusting its size or the colour balance, but this type of processing is easily and quickly accomplished using any photo-editing software. When using a film camera it is first necessary to have the film developed, and where appropriate, prints are then made. Either the film or the prints are then scanned to produce the digital images. This method involves the extra cost of the film and processing, plus the cost of a scanner or having the film scanned.

Most film processing companies now offer a scanning service, and for an additional fee will supply a CD-ROM containing a digital version of each photograph. Unfortunately, the resolutions are often a bit disappointing, making it impossible to produce large prints of good quality. However, if you would like to try digital photography at minimal cost and you have a 35mm film camera or some existing 35mm negatives, this probably represents the best option. Whether digital images come straight from a camera or from film via a scanner, once in digital form they can be manipulated in exactly the same ways.

Speed?

Speed is often quoted as an advantage of the digital approach, but some would dispute this. I seem to remember an article in a photographic magazine where they had a sort of photographic race. The idea was to take the same 36 photographs using a digital camera and a film type, and to then get 36 postcard size prints from each camera as quickly as possible. In the case of the film camera the prints were obtained by taking the film to a nearby one-hour processing shop, and the prints were duly obtained about one hour after taking the photographs. The prints from the digital camera were obtained by uploading the image files to a computer, making any necessary adjustments to the brightness, contrast, and colour, and then printing them via a typical colour inkjet printer. In other words, the digital images were handled in the way that a typical home user would deal with them.

Surprisingly perhaps, the film camera and the one-hour laboratory won the race. However, the general conclusion was that the digital approach was better. The first point to make is that this test was carried out a few years ago. Uploading 36 images to a computer was often quite time consuming back then, but many modern cameras would take no more than a couple of minutes or so to complete this task. Inkjet printers have also speeded up over the years, but they are still not particularly quick. The prints in the test were not very big at around 6 inches by 4 inches (152 x 102 millimetres), and there are plenty of modern inkjets that could produce 36 prints of this size in well under an hour. On the other hand, there are plenty of budget models that would probably take longer than this.

Convenience

The conclusion of the test was that traditional photography was faster under the test conditions, but that it was not necessarily better. Although this test was interesting, in many ways it missed the point. The test conditions were in some respects slanted in favour of film photography, and tended to ignore the way in which digital cameras are used. How often do you need exactly 36 6-inch by 4-inch photographs? Probably not very often, if ever. I often need four or five low resolution digital photographs for use on Internet auction sites. Using a digital camera I can take and process these in what is usually well under half an hour. In fact it usually takes about 15 minutes or so. If there is a problem with one or two or the photographs it takes only a few minutes more to redo them.

Using a film camera it would take about half an hour to take the photographs, unload the film, and take it to the nearest processing laboratory. 12-exposure films are manufactured, but most shops only sell the 24 and 36-exposure varieties, so a lot of film would be wasted. If some of the photographs were flawed it would be necessary to load another film into the camera and go through the whole process again. Having produced suitable prints it would still be necessary to scan and process them in order to produce the image files for web use.

Clearly this example is weighted in favour of digital photography, but it does demonstrate the point that the digital approach is more versatile and convenient. Digital photography was competitive in the test involving 36 smallish prints, even if it did not actually win. With modern equipment it probably would win this test. When only a few digital images are required it is definitely a case of "no contest". Unless something quite expensive was being sold in an Internet auction it would not be worth the time, effort, and money involved in producing the images via film.

Where it is necessary to take and print a large number of photographs it might still be better to use a film camera, especially when travelling. You take a few films with you on the photographic trip, drop them in at the processing shop when you get back, collect all the prints a couple of hours later, the next day, or whatever. The time and effort required is minimal. The amount of equipment and materials you need to take with you can also be kept to a minimum.

Taking large numbers of photographs using a digital camera can still be a bit awkward. The digital equivalent of film is memory that is either built into the camera, or (more usually) fitted into a slot in the side of the camera in the form of a small memory card. In order to take large numbers of photographs in one session it is necessary to take large amounts of memory along with you, or to keep downloading batches of photographs to a laptop computer so that the same memory can be reused. There is actually a third option in the form of minute hard disc drives, which are essentially scaled-down versions of the hard drives used in computers. These fit into the camera much like a memory card, and they have quite high storage capacities. One drive might not be sufficient when taking large numbers of high resolution pictures.

Printing out large numbers of photographs on an inkjet printer can be very time consuming. The time taken per print varies significantly from one printer to another, and the size of the print is also an important factor. In general, the larger the print the longer it will take to produce. It typically takes about 2 to 10 minutes per print, so 200 prints could take over 30 hours. You would not have to sit and watch the printer for all that time, but it would be necessary to check for problems and load fresh paper periodically. Of course, many photographic laboratories will now produce prints from digital images, so professional printing might be the best option.

Battery drain

Another slight shortcoming of digital cameras to bear in mind is that they run down batteries much faster than film cameras. There is substantially more electronics in a digital camera and most of them are fitted with a small liquid crystal monitor so that you can view and check the pictures that have been taken. With the early digital cameras it was not unusual for rechargeable batteries to need recharging after about 20 minutes of use, with the non-rechargeable type fairing little better than this. Although generally higher in specification, modern digital cameras still manage to give better battery lives. Even so, fresh batteries could still be required every hour or so with intermittent snapping, which compares with a battery change every few months with most film cameras.

In the real world

In the real world, probably few camera users only take small batches of photos for web use, or at the other extreme, vast numbers of photographs on location. Most users need to take the occasional batch of photographs and have prints made from them. We take photographs at family events, days out at the zoo, on holiday, and so on. The number of photographs taken could be five, 55 or anything in between. When using film you often end up with a half used film which has to wait for processing until you take some more photographs at the next family event. Alternatively, you can snap away at anything to finish the film, or simply have the unfinished film processed. In other words, you have to wait what could be weeks before you finally get the photographs, or waste some film and processing.

One of the main attractions of digital cameras is that they fit in well with the photographic habits of most users. If you take a few shots there is no need to worry about how long it will be before the film is finished. You simply upload the image files, do any necessary processing to get them just right, and print them out. Things are much the same if you take a lot of photographs. You can take as few or as many pictures as you like, upload them, and produce the prints.

Even those with the best photographic equipment and a lot of talent produce some pictures that are not very good. I would guess that most of us produce a fair proportion of shots that are not worth printing. In some cases there are technical problems such as poor focussing accuracy or gross underexposure. In other cases the composition is poor or you simply find that there are a lot of pictures that are practically the same. With digital photography there is no need to waste money printing photographs that for one reason or another are not "up to scratch". Conversely, images that are exceptionally good can be printed larger than the others.

Cost

The image files in the camera can be deleted once the files have been safely uploaded from the camera to a computer. The camera's memory is then free and more photographs can be taken. Prints are made from the image files, but it is advisable to store the image files in case you need to make more prints at some later time. The image files are the equivalent of negatives in film photography. It is possible to make more prints by copying the original prints, but this is unlikely to give anything like the quality of the original prints.

Fortunately, most computers are equipped with a CD-RW drive that can store masses of data on CD-R discs that cost a matter of pence each. Even when dealing with high resolution images it should be possible to get around 100 to 200 images on each disc. In other words, the cost of archiving images is only about 0.2 pence per picture at most. With lower resolution images it is probably more like 0.01 pence per image. It is a good idea to make a backup copy of each disc, but this still leaves the cost of archiving at a pretty insignificant level.

With no film processing costs and cheap long term storage, are the running costs of digital photography virtually nonexistent? They are, but only where images are required for web use, desktop publishing, or some other application where the images are only needed in electronic form. The situation is very different when prints are needed. If you ask an inkjet printer user about running costs they will probably go a funny colour and change the subject. The current low prices of inkjet printers are a bit misleading, and tend to suggest that the running costs are lower than they really are. Some of these printers are supplied with low capacity ink cartridges, but there have been instances where new printers complete with cartridges have been sold at less than the cost of replacement cartridges.

Overall cost

These are odd economics by any standards, but the printer manufacturers have adopted a policy of selling printers at very low prices and the ink cartridges at high prices. In some instances they would seem to be literally giving away the printers in the hope of making their profit by selling users replacement cartridges. The lesson to be learned here is that the price of replacement ink cartridges must be taken into account when buying an inkjet printer. A cheap printer that costs less than forty pounds is not cheap if it requires numerous replacement cartridges at about sixty pounds per set.

The cost per print can be quite high, but you have to keep things in perspective. To print out a full A4 photograph on good quality inkjet paper is unlikely to cost much less than about one pound. This compares to around 20 pence per print when a film is processed and a set of prints are produced. However, the A4 print is about four times the area of the prints normally supplied when a film is processed, so by printing four photographs on each sheet the actual cost is not much more than the commercially produced prints. Most modern inkjet printers produce pretty good results using budget inkjet photographic paper, and by shopping around for the consumables it is possible to cut costs still further.

Inkjet running costs are therefore quite competitive provided you are sensible about things. Many users tend to get carried away in a burst of initial enthusiasm, producing numerous large prints of every photograph they take. You can also find yourself doing several copies of each print in an attempt to get each one just right. This inevitably becomes quite expensive due to the size and quantity of prints produced.

A big advantage of the digital approach is that you do not have to print images that are clearly below par. Many film processors print every frame that is not a complete blank, which means that you are paying for a percentage of prints that are of little or no use. When making your own prints there is the option of not printing substandard pictures and printing the good ones at the maximum size the printer can handle, which usually means A4 size. This is more cost-effective than the traditional method of having everything printed small and then having the best photographs printed larger.

If at first...

I think that it is fair to say that early digital cameras were something less than smash hits. The low resolutions limited their range of practical applications, but they were ideal for the growing band of people producing their own Internet sites. Rightly or wrongly, the feature that is usually attributed with starting the upsurge in popularity is the built-in liquid crystal monitor. One role of this monitor is to show the picture that you are about to take. Virtually all digital cameras also have a conventional viewfinder, but these can suffer from parallax errors when shooting close-ups and most digital cameras can take pictures at almost point-blank range.

Of more importance to most users, the monitor can be used to view pictures stored in the camera, and for a few seconds it usually shows the picture that has just been taken. This enables the user to search the picture for problems. Do not expect to get full-size television quality from a liquid crystal display that measures a few centimetres across diagonally opposite corners. The built-in screens operate at quite low resolutions, and with modern cameras they certainly operate well below the camera's maximum resolution. The quality is usually good enough to spot any major problems though. Some shots are unrepeatable, but it is often possible to erase a faulty picture and try again.

This ability to preview pictures can help to rectify the odd disappointing picture in each batch, but it can also help to avoid major disasters. When auto-focus compact cameras first came along it should have been the end of blurred photographs. In fact the statistics from the film processors suggested that it made little difference. The problem with any auto-focus

Fig.2.1 This photograph is underexposed and lacks contrast, but it is not beyond redemption

system is that it does not know what you are trying to focus on. With a picture of two people standing side by side it is quite likely that the camera will focus on the area between them, which will usually be well into the background.

Another popular problem is photographs taken through windows from within cars and coaches. Some types of auto-focussing tend to focus on the window rather than the scene beyond. This has sometimes resulted in people putting one or two films through a camera, only to get packs of totally blurred photographs back from the processors. With a digital camera this type of thing will usually be spotted quite early in the proceedings, and steps can be taken to correct the problem. The trouble with film cameras is that you do not know that there is a problem until the faulty pictures come back from the processors. By then it is too late to do anything about it.

*Fig.2.2   The corrected version of Fig.2.1 has plenty of contrast
and detail*

Biggest advantage

Of all the advantages of digital cameras, there is no doubt in my mind as
to which is the most important. When using a film camera and commercial
processing the photographer is completely at the mercy of the person
(or machine) doing the processing. With some processing laboratories
the results are generally quite good, while others they are consistently
bad. In order to get each print individually assessed and printed it is
necessary to resort to upmarket processing packages at relatively high
prices. It is possible to undertake your own colour processing, but this
is certainly not for the faint hearted. Do-it-yourself colour printing can be
quite expensive.

By contrast, making your own prints from digital photographs gives
tremendous control over the final results. There are printers that can be
used to produce pictures direct from the memory cards of digital cameras.
This is a quick and convenient method, but the amount of control is

likely to be relatively limited. It is sometimes likened to a sandwich without any filling. Much greater control is available if the picture files are loaded into a computer, processed using photo-editing software, and then printed out once everything is exactly as required.

What type of processing can be undertaken, and why is it necessary? In an ideal world photographic prints would always accurately reflect the scenes that you remember, with perfect composition, colour balance, brightness, and contrast. Also, every shot would be "pin sharp" with no trace of blurring. In the real world we are not perfect photographers, and we do produce pictures with wonky horizons, trees appearing to grow out of peoples' heads, slightly "soft" focussing, and so on. It is not possible to cure all ills using digital photography, but a fair proportion of faulty images can be rescued.

In fairness to amateur snappers, it is not always the fault of the photographer when things do not go perfectly. It is not necessarily the fault of the camera either. Modern cameras are mostly quite sophisticated, but they can not mind-read. The camera does not know what part of the scene is the area of main interest, and it could still get the exposure wrong even if it did.

Some of the problems stem from innate inadequacies in the system. The difference in the light level at the darkest and brightest parts of a scene can be truly massive. A ratio of thousands to one would not be exceptional. The difference in the light levels coming from a high contrast print is very much less, and would be unlikely to be as high as 100 to 1. This means that it is usually necessary to condense the wide range of light levels in a scene into a much lower range that a print can handle. This often requires the brightness and contrast to be carefully manipulated in order to obtain realistic results. Fortunately, this is something that is quite easy using most photo-editing software. The photograph of Figure 2.1 looks pretty dire from the technical standpoint, but there is actually plenty of detail hidden away in the image. Some manipulation of the brightness and contrast produced the very reasonable result shown in Figure 2.2.

Camera never lies?

Of course, using digital photography it is possible to go beyond adjusting the brightness, contrast, and colour. If there is something in the photograph that you would like to remove, it is usually possible to "paint" over it. The popular problem of trees and other objects in the background

Fig.2.3 The original version of the photograph

seeming to grow out of peoples' heads can usually be solved with a bit
of retouching. Of course, this type of thing is possible with conventional
photography, but it is much easier using digital techniques. Also, the
final result is usually somewhat better using digital methods. With digital

*Fig.2.4 The boat in the background has been painted out and the ship
has been moved to the left*

retouching it is possible to "paint" onto the picture using complex patterns
and textures that cover the unwanted element very convincingly.

In Figure 2.3 the boat in the background on the left is not doing a great
deal for the composition of the picture. It is easy enough to paint over it

Fig.2.5 The "mirrored" version of Fig. 2.4

with material cloned from the sea and sky areas, and this has been done
in Figure 2.4. One of the ships in the background has also been moved
into a clear space to the left of its original position. In the version of
Figure 2.5 the whole image has been "mirrored" horizontally to see if

Fig.2.6 A simple sketch filter effect produced this version

this gives a more pleasing composition. Finally, in Figure 2.6 an effects filter was used to produce an artier image. While this process was not totally skill-free, it was much easier than using traditional methods of achieving the same thing. Also, it took a matter of minutes rather than hours.

Fig.2.7 The added dinghy was copied from another image

Things can be taken a stage further, and objects in an image can be duplicated or copied and used in another image. The image of Figure 2.5 has a large vacant area in the bottom right-hand section. In Figure 2.7 this area has been filled with a boat and a mooring buoy copied from another image using the normal Copy and Paste facilities. Some resizing

*Fig.2.8 Mind out below! The pigeon problem in central London
threatens to get out of hand*

was needed to get the scale about right, and the copied material also
had to be rotated slightly. The shadow was copied as well, and the
reflections were cloned from other parts of the image. For a few minutes
work the end result is reasonably plausible.

Probably the most popular trick of this type is to combine a picture of
yourself with someone famous such as a film star, so it looks as if they
posed for a picture with you. All sorts of spoofs can be engineered
using the same basic technique, including such things as flying saucers
landing in your back garden. Visual jokes that use unrealistic scaling
are also popular, such as giant cats roaming the city. London has a well
publicised pigeon problem, but Figure 2.8 clearly shows that the problem
is far bigger than most people thought.

Through the lens

35-millimetre cameras are broadly divided into two types, one of which is the compact variety that most people use. The main alternative is the SLR (single lens reflex) where the image in the viewfinder is obtained via the camera's lens. The advantage of this system is that the image obtained should be the same as what you saw in the viewfinder at the instant the picture was taken. In particular, with close-ups there should be no parallax errors. These occur with an ordinary viewfinder because it is slightly offset from the taking lens. This offset is too small to be of any consequence with most types of shot, but it becomes very significant when shooting at short distances.

The viewfinders of most cameras have lines to indicate the field of view when the camera is close to the subject, but these lines are at best an approximation. Most digital cameras permit the built-in monitor to be used as an extra viewfinder, and it provides a form of through-the-lens viewing. It therefore gives parallax-free viewing like an SLR camera, and should give accurate results even with extreme close-ups. It does pay to bear in mind that the monitor usually shows significantly less than the full image, so it is possible to frame pictures more tightly than the image on the monitor would suggest. Incidentally, most viewfinders show somewhat less than the full image.

Drawbacks

Digital photography has its advantages, but it inevitably has a few drawbacks. As already pointed out, digital cameras tend to run down batteries relatively fast, which can be more than a little awkward if you need to take large numbers of photographs in the middle of nowhere. Taking large numbers of high resolution photographs requires either large amounts of memory or a computer that can be used to store image files so that the same memory can be used over and over again. The memory option is the most convenient but it is unlikely to be cheap. Uploading batches of pictures to a computer is fine when taking pictures at home, but on location it requires a laptop or other form of portable PC, together with yet more batteries of course. With a 35-millimetre film camera a couple of sets of fresh batteries and 20 films are sufficient to take 720 high quality photographs.

Probably the biggest drawback is the cost of digital photography. As explained previously, the running costs are negligible if you only require image files for use on web sites or for desktop publishing. There is probably little to choose between film photography and the digital variety when producing prints. The problem with digital photography is "up front" costs incurred before you can start snapping away. With film photography there are plenty of quite good cameras in the sub-one hundred pound bracket and excellent second-hand cameras for less than this. A so-called "disposable" camera can be used if photography "on a shoestring" is required.

The initial cost of digital photography can be kept quite low if you only need low resolution images for use on web pages. There are cameras for less than one hundred pounds that can produce photographs of adequate quality for web use. In fact there are budget digital cameras at around half this price. Of course, if you need to take something like sport or wildlife photographs that involve the use of big telephoto lenses, some upmarket equipment will be needed even if only low resolution images are required. With anything like this the costs are likely to be relatively high whether film or digital imaging is used.

Producing your own prints from digital image files substantially increases the equipment costs. You need a camera that is up to the task, a computer, and a colour printer. The cost of the camera does not have to be very high if only small prints are required. By small I mean prints at up to about 200 millimetres or so wide. There are low-cost cameras having about 2.1 million pixel resolution, and these can handle prints of up to this size. For A4 size prints the cost escalates a little, since a minimum of about 3.2 million pixel resolution is required. Going above A4 size prints requires one of the more upmarket digital cameras and a substantial increase in cost.

As pointed out previously, there are printers that "cut out the middle man" and produce prints direct from certain cameras. This saves the cost of a computer and removes the need for any computer skills. Although these printers normally produce quite good results, much of the versatility of digital imaging is lost by using a system that does not include a computer. A computer, colour printer, and photo-editing software are needed in order to get the most from digital imaging.

Powerful computer?

Due to improvements in computer hardware it is no longer the case that the fastest possible PC is needed in order to undertake photo-editing. There might be some advantage in using the latest "turbo" PC, but a low cost PC and a reasonable 17-inch monitor are perfectly adequate for the task. A CD writer is needed for archiving images on CD-R discs, but a CD writer is fitted as standard on many PCs, and it is usually offered as a low cost extra on the rest. There are plenty of inexpensive colour inkjet printers on offer, and low cost photo-editing software as well. In fact suitable software might be supplied with the digital camera. A complete setup capable of producing A4 prints could probably be put together for under a thousand pounds, but this is clearly a substantial initial outlay.

Of course, many households are already equipped with a computer, and many of these computers are connected to a colour inkjet printer that is used for letters, personalised greetings cards, and so on. A system such as this should be well able to handle photo-editing. It is really people who already own a computer that are in the best position to switch to digital photography. They already have all or most of the computer hardware required, so the only cost involved is that of the camera outfit. Photo-editing software will also be needed if something suitable is not included with the camera, but this need not cost very much. Equally important, those already using computers will not need to spend time learning the basics of computing before they are in a position to start using the camera. They can buy the camera, load the software that came with it, and starting taking pictures straight away.

Is it worthwhile buying all the computer equipment and learning to use it in order to take up digital photography? It is probably not worthwhile in the case of someone wishing to take occasional snapshots. The time and money involved would both be out of proportion to the number of pictures taken. It is likely that more time would be expended learning to use the equipment than would actually be spent taking photographs.

The situation is different where someone wishes to take up photography as a serious hobby. Funds permitting, digital photography would seem to be a better bet. Apart from its advantages, digital imaging is a technology that is very much on the way up, whereas film photography would seem to be in decline. No doubt film cameras and films will be available for many years to come, but it would seem to make sense for someone starting from scratch to invest in an advancing rather than a declining technology. I suppose that another big plus point for digital imaging is that the computer would almost certainly find other uses. The range of practical applications for modern computers is vast, and in most households a new computer soon becomes an indispensable tool.

Incidentally, it is not necessary to be a computer expert in order to follow the examples or understand the basic concepts covered in this book. However, in some instances it is assumed that the reader has a basic knowledge of using a computer, and some familiarity with computers and software is needed to follow the examples. Anyone new to computing really needs to conquer the fundamentals of computing before trying to get deeply into photo-editing.

Developing technology

There is a down side to the fact that digital technology is still developing. Equipment that is at the forefront of digital imaging technology is unlikely to stay there very long. Expensive cameras, while not becoming worthless after a year or two, are quite likely to be worth only a fraction of their original cost. As the technology matures this becomes less of a problem, and the new wonder cameras will offer little more than the models they are replacing. This stage has not yet been reached though. There is no great problem if a budget or mid-range camera meets your requirements, since the costs involved are relatively low and there is little scope for massive price reductions. Buying an expensive digital camera is more risky. Unless it is genuinely a case of "money is no object" the best advice is probably to wait until the prices drop to more affordable levels.

Probably some prospective digital camera users are put off by the apparent complexity of it all. It would be misleading to say that digital photography is free from complexities and technicalities. On the other hand, there are plenty of digital cameras of the "point and shoot" variety and photo-editing programs that can be used effectively by non-technical users. It is possible to get started without getting too deeply into the technicalities. You can then delve deeper into this aspect of digital imaging, or not, as preferred. As with most creative pastimes, there are definite advantages in having plenty of background knowledge and expanding your range of skills. However, digital photography can be pursued enjoyably and effectively at a relatively low level if that is all you wish to do.

Quality

In the past it was certainly true that digital photography was very much the "poor relation" in terms of quality. Some upmarket digital cameras can now at least equal good quality 35-millimetre cameras in this respect. Cameras in more affordable price ranges probably fall some way short. Comparisons tend to be difficult because it is often the graininess of the film that limits the quality of photographs shot on film. In other words, plain areas on a big enlargement often have a texture that looks rather like grains of sand.

The grains are actually the crystals in the film's emulsion, and they are more obvious with some films than with others. Grain is also more obvious in some types of photograph than in others. In general, the grain is masked by contrast and fine detail, and exposed by low contrast and plain areas. With good quality 35-millimetre cameras it is possible to produce prints up to at least 18 by 12 inches (about 457 by 305 millimetres), but only if you are prepared to put up with what is normally fairly obvious grain in parts of the pictures.

There is no real equivalent of grain in digital photography. Some prints made from digital sources do show something that looks a bit like film grain, but this is the result of imperfections in the printing process and is not inherent in the underlying digital image. The quality available from digital images is governed by the number of pixels in the "raw" version of the image. The number of pixels can be artificially boosted to remove pixilation but detail can not be added. It is therefore a lack of detail and a perceived fuzziness that limits the maximum print size with digital imaging.

Provided you are happy with prints of up to about A4 size (297 x 210 millimetres), a camera having three to five million pixel output should be perfectly adequate. A camera producing at least six to seven million pixels is needed for good quality A3 prints, and these remain very expensive. A3 colour printers and their running costs are also relatively high. No doubt the technology will soon improve to the point where budget digital cameras can produce large prints, but at the moment the film option would seem to be best for those requiring anything much beyond A4 prints. A film camera and a negative scanner are worth considering. The cost need not be astronomic and the scanned images can be processed in exactly the same ways as images produced from a digital camera.

Longevity

I first purchased a colour inkjet printer about 20 years ago in the days when digital cameras were huge and mostly just manufacturer's prototypes that never went into production. The inkjet printers of that era had a very limited repertoire of colours and were mainly intended for things like business and financial charts. A few people used them with paint programs to print out digital works of art, but found a major flaw in the printouts. They looked good enough when freshly printed, but when left exposed to air and normal room lighting the image soon started to change. With my own printer the colours started to change noticeably within a week or so, and after a few months the image had virtually faded to nothing!

This lack of longevity dogged colour inkjet printers for many years. Framing the prints behind glass, as is the norm for conventional photographs, certainly helps to slow down the fading process. Storing prints in a box also helps to slow fading quite considerably. Neither guaranteed long life with prints from early inkjet printers. The inks and the printing papers have improved over the years though, and a modern inkjet printer used with good quality paper should produce prints that will look good for a large number of years. Even so, do not be surprised if a colour shift gradually develops with a print that is not framed behind glass. Regular doses of direct sunlight are more or less guaranteed to produce major colour changes or fading. However, a conventional photographic colour print is unlikely to fare much better under these conditions.

I think it is worth making the point that most people who try digital photography are pleased with the results, and this general way of doing things. Perhaps it is not well suited to everyone, but those finding it seriously lacking in some respect are very much in the minority. This is demonstrated by the huge popularity of digital photography, which is something that simply did not exist a few years ago.

Points to remember

If you need to take photographs for use on the Internet there is probably no point in considering anything other than using a digital camera. The film and scanner route will be much more costly, particularly in terms of running costs. The all digital method is very much quicker.

Most inkjet printers are not particularly fast and they are unlikely to produce good quality prints at a significantly lower cost than commercial machine-made prints of the same size. However, you need only print the pictures that you really like, and you are effectively getting handmade enlargements at machine print prices.

Probably the biggest advantage of digital imaging for most users is that you can adjust each picture to exactly meet your requirements. The colours, the contrast, and the brightness can all be set the way you think they should be, rather than the way the photographic labs automatic production line thinks they should be.

If you only need to take a few photographs, with digital imaging you simply take a few pictures, upload them to the computer, and print them. There is no need to wait until the film is finished or get the film processed right away and waste film. You take and process pictures as and when you need them.

If you need to take large numbers of photographs while on location in out of the way places you would probably be better off using film.

Getting really high quality results from a digital camera is certainly possible with the current technology, but it remains relatively expensive. For really large prints a film camera is probably the best option, but do you really need monster prints. Most people settle for about A4 size or smaller prints. Middle of the range digital cameras can easily handle prints up to A4 size.

Most inkjet printers are now capable of producing prints that will not seriously deteriorate for many years. However, this is conditional on good quality paper being used. It is also dependent on the prints being stored and (or) displayed under suitable conditions. Neither inkjet prints nor conventional photographs fair well under direct sunlight or in damp conditions.

Digital photography is most cost effective for those who already own a computer and a colour printer. All you need to get started is a digital camera and some photo-editing software, and suitable software is often supplied with digital cameras. Those who are already computer literate will also have less to learn.

3

The right equipment

Which computer?

Having decided to "take the plunge" into digital photography there is the all important matter of buying the right equipment. If you already have a personal computer of some kind, it will almost certainly be suitable for use with a digital camera and image editing software. There could be problems if the computer is bordering on antique status and has a small amount of memory. A computer having something like a 200MHz Pentium class processor and 32 megabytes of memory should be adequate, but it might not be capable of running some of the more complex photo-editing programs. A PC having an 800MHz or faster processor and 128 megabytes or more of memory should give good results and be capable of running any modern image editing software.

Some people seem to be under the impression that a Macintosh computer is required for photo-editing and that PCs are not up to the task. This probably stems from the fact that early PCs were not well suited to graphics applications. Consequently, most professional users opted for Macintosh computers, which were significantly faster but also more expensive. For professional users "time is money", and the extra expense was probably well justified. Some top quality graphics programs were produced for the early Macintosh computers, and in one form or another they are still around today.

Whether Macintosh computers still have any advantages in graphics applications is debatable. Enormous sums of money have been invested in the quest for faster PCs, and the PC I am using to produce this book is over a thousand times faster than my first PC. Screen speeds and resolutions have also been greatly improved over the years. There is no shortage of top quality graphics software for PCs, and most of the popular programs are available in both PC and Macintosh versions. For someone buying a computer for the first time a PC is a cheaper and safer option, that is well capable of handling demanding tasks such as image editing.

Storage

As pointed out in chapter 1, some means of storing image files is required. Modern PCs have high capacity hard disc drives, but even the biggest of drives will eventually begin to fill up with data. A more serious limitation of hard disc drives is that they are not totally reliable in the long term. The reliability of modern drives is very good, but they are not designed to last forever. It would be an exaggeration to say that the data stored on a hard disc drive will definitely be lost when the drive goes wrong. On the other hand, it could be. Also, in most cases where the data can be rescued, the only way of recovering it is to use a specialist data recovery service. This can be quite costly. Prevention is better than cure, and at least one backup copy of any important data should be made.

Due to the relatively large size of image files it is necessary to have some form of mass storage device to store your digital pictures. A variety of mass storage devices having interchangeable media are available, but there is little point in using anything other than a CD writer and ordinary CD-R discs. Most PCs have a CD writer as standard, and internal units can be purchased for about thirty to forty pounds. A box of 10 CD-R discs complete with jewel cases can be obtained for under five pounds and will provide about six or seven gigabytes (6000 to 7000 megabytes) of storage. The cost is so low that there is no problem in making a duplicate of each disc as a backup in case something goes wrong with the original or it is lost.

Most CD writers are quite fast, so even writing 100 megabytes or so to a CD-R disc should take no more than a minute or two. The software provided with the CD writer (or built into Windows XP) will provide multi-session operation, which means that you do not have to write all the images onto the disc in one go. New batches of images can be added as and when you take them. Using ordinary CD-R discs it is not possible to erase files and replace them with new ones. This is possible with CD-RW discs, which are somewhat more expensive. However, you will presumably require a permanent archive of the images, so ordinary CD-R discs would seem to be the better choice.

Printers

Contrary to popular belief, there are alternatives to colour inkjet printers. However, as far as I am aware, there are no printers currently using alternative technologies that are available for the low prices associated with inkjet printers. Dye sublimation and colour laser printers are highly desirable pieces of equipment, but they generally cost more than ten times as much as typical colour inkjet types. While this does not put the alternative technologies totally beyond budgets of all home users, there are relative few with the means or inclination to pay this sort of money for a printer. The quality available from modern inkjet printers is such that there is now relatively little to be gained by using a more expensive alternative. Here only colour inkjet printers will be considered.

In the past most printers had parallel interfaces, but relatively few currently have this type of interface. It might be worthwhile seeking out a printer that has a parallel interface if you are using an old PC that lacks USB ports. It is probably the only option in the case of a PC that is running Windows 95, which does not support USB ports. With a PC that is running a later version of Windows but lacks USB ports it might be better to add a USB card to the PC. This makes a far wider range of printers compatible with the PC, and also enables the PC to be used with other USB devices such as scanners and graphics tablets. Standard PC serial and parallel ports are due to be phased out in the next few years, so it would be prudent to buy a printer that is not dependent on a parallel interface that could soon be obsolete. Some printers have both types of port, which gives maximum flexibility.

Dots per inch

Printer specifications usually give the resolutions in dots per inch, but it is important to realise that dots per inch and pixels per inch are not necessarily the same thing. In fact, with printers they are hardly ever the same thing. This point was demonstrated to me a few years ago when I was shown two colour prints that used resolutions of about 200 and 1200 dots per inch. Results from the 200 dots per inch printer were clearly better than those from the one using the higher resolution.

The prints at the lower resolution were produced by a dye sublimation printer that operated on the basis of one dot per pixel. The 1200 dots per inch output came from an inkjet printer that used a process known as dithering. There is nothing intrinsically wrong with the use of dithering, but it relies on using a number of dots per pixel, giving an effective resolution that is much lower than the stated figure.

Fig.3.1 This greyscale image uses dithering to produce the shades of grey

Dithering in a greyscale image operates on the basis of having fewer dots in light areas and more in dark areas. Provided the dots are small enough, the individual dots will not be visible to the unaided eye. The dots effectively merge to form shades of grey. This process is demonstrated by Figure 3.1, which shows a greyscale image that uses dithering to give the shades of grey. It might not reproduce too well here, but the original gives quite convincing shades of grey, even though it is actually comprised of black dots on white paper. A highly zoomed view of the image in Photoshop (Figure 3.2) shows the patterns of dots that are used to produce the variations in tone.

Colour

A similar process is used with colour, but the three primary colours are used instead of black. The dots are too small to be seen individually, and instead merge together in the viewer's eye to produce what appears to be a full range of colours. This process is called optical mixing. It is not quite as simple as that, because lighter and darker shades require white and black respectively to be added to the primary colours. The

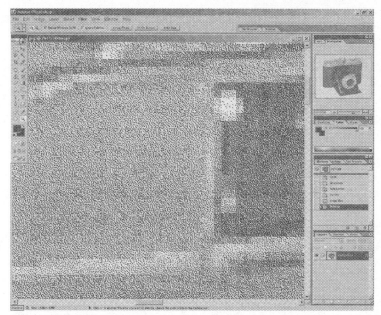

Fig.3.2 The dithering pattern can be seen in this zoomed view

white is usually provided by the paper, and fewer dots are used where light shades are required. The paper shows through between the dots and merges with them to produce what appear to be the lighter shades. Black dots are added to produce the darker colours. It is possible to see the individual dots if you look at colour photographs in magazines and newspapers using a suitably powerful magnifier. One giving a magnification of about ten times is adequate.

This method of printing is used in colour inkjet printers, and it is for this reason that they normally have four reservoirs of ink. These are usually in the form of a colour cartridge that has the three primary colours (cyan, magenta and yellow), and a black cartridge. It is possible to print in black and white if the colour cartridge is empty or absent, because only the black ink is used in this mode. Proper colour printing without the black cartridge is not possible though. The black dots needed for dark colours would be replaced by white paper, giving the opposite effect to the one required. Incidentally, this method of printing is termed CMYK (Cyan, Magenta, Yellow, and blacK) reproduction. Some inkjet printers actually have two extra reservoirs in the colour cartridge, but these are used for paler versions of the cyan and magenta inks. This is done in an attempt to obtain better pale colours.

Some inkjet printers use colour mixing on the paper to a certain degree, rather than relying solely on dithering. Although the resolutions may seem low when the specification sheet is viewed, the quality of the prints might actually be quite good in comparison to those produced by higher resolution printers. Also, the accuracy of placement is as important as the number of dots. In practice, the only way of comparing print quality is to subjectively assess prints produced by the printers you are interested in buying. Specifications are not a reliable guide in this respect. Some computer superstores and smaller computer shops have demonstration prints, and possibly even demonstration facilities that enable you to produce sample prints. Either way, you can check the quality of the output before parting with any hard earned cash.

Speed

Manufacturers' speed ratings have been notorious since the early days of computer printers. In general they are probably quite accurate but misleading. On reading the fine print the test conditions will probably be rather different to those found in everyday printing. The speed tests published in reviews in magazines and on the Internet give a better idea of how quickly (or otherwise) each print will be produced. In general, the bigger the print, the longer it will take for the printer to produce it. Simple text documents normally take far less time to print than complex colour prints. A printer that does five pages per minute when producing black and white text documents could operate at something more like one page per five minutes when producing full page colour prints.

The print speed is often to some extent dependent on the computer used. Many printers have relatively little built-in memory or processing power. Much of the data processing is done by the computer and its printer driver software. A fast computer with plenty of memory therefore produces quicker print times than an older computer having only a small amount of memory.

Do not assume that an expensive inkjet printer will produce better results than an inexpensive model. The main difference between the top and bottom models in a range of printers is often print speed rather than quality. Some of the more expensive printers will probably give better print quality than the low cost models, but there are plenty of low cost printers that can produce good quality colour prints if you are prepared to wait. A good budget printer should be perfectly adequate unless you will need to do large amounts of colour printing.

Some manufacturers produce printers that are specifically designed for producing photographic prints. Printers of this type will usually produce top quality results, but they usually have limited potential as general purpose printers. In fact some of these units have no significant potential for anything else. They are designed to produce (say) 6-inch by 4-inch borderless prints on special sheets of paper, and that is all they are capable of doing. Another printer is needed for anything else such a producing letters or larger prints. One of these printers is fine if you really only need to produce prints of the sizes that it can handle, but most users prefer something a bit more versatile.

Running costs

As pointed out in the previous chapter, the running costs for colour inkjet printers can be quite high. The cost of the consumables (ink cartridges and paper) can soon rise well beyond the initial cost of the printer, so it is a factor that is worthy of investigation before buying a printer. The manufacturer's data will usually give some indication of the cartridge life, but it is essential to read the fine print to determine the test conditions. Reviews in computer magazines and web sites often have some useful information on this aspect of things.

Bear in mind that the number of prints available per set of cartridges is inversely proportional to the area of the prints. If you get 600 6-inch by 4-inch prints per set of cartridges, only 300 8-inch by 6-inch prints can be produced. Print density is another important factor. Prints that are predominantly pale use less ink than prints that have large areas of strong dark colours. It is for this reason that it is not possible to give a definite number of prints per cartridge, even if a certain print size is specified. Dark prints can use more than twice as much ink as pale ones. However, manufacturers' data and information from reviews should give a good guesstimate of the likely running costs.

There are ways of reducing the running costs. Simply buying the cartridges from a specialist mail order or Internet supplier can give a significant reduction in cost compared to buying locally. With some printers, and especially the more popular types, it is possible to obtain cartridges from independent producers. These cartridges are usually very much cheaper than the "real thing". Many of them are recycled cartridges, and using them is therefore very "green". The printer manufacturers warn against using cartridges from third parties, and doing so could invalidate the guarantee. I have used them on a few occasions and have never experienced any problems, but you obviously do so at your own risk.

Another option is to refill the original cartridges, and refill kits are available for many printers. This can be a bit messy though, and getting accurate colours can be more difficult than when using new cartridges. Again, the printer's guarantee might be rendered void if the cartridges are refilled. In fact it is virtually certain that the guarantee would be invalidated by refilling the cartridges. The big attraction of this method, and the reason for its popularity, is that the running costs are minute compared to using new cartridges. My experiences with ink refill systems are mixed. It has always worked well with black cartridges, but was consistently problematic with the colour variety. It is certainly not something I could recommend.

It is perhaps worth mentioning that there are two distinctly different types of ink cartridge. The most common type simply has reservoirs of ink and plays no further role in the printing process. The other type has the print head built into the cartridge. The popular Hewlett Packard range of printers utilizes this second method. Having the print head in the cartridge tends to increase the cost slightly, but it means that the print head is replaced each time a new ink cartridge is fitted. This helps to give good print quality throughout the life of the printer. Also, if the print head should become damaged or blocked, simply fitting a new cartridge will cure the problem.

Paper

Early inkjet printers would only work properly with special coated papers that were relatively expensive. Modern inkjets will work with practically any paper, including "run of the mill" copier paper at about 0.5 pence per sheet. Working with and giving top quality results with are not necessarily the same though. Many inkjet printers will give quite nice looking prints using cheap copier paper, but the results are not really comparable to a photographic print. Also, prints made on cheap paper are unlikely to have good long term stability.

Special inkjet papers are produced for making colour prints, and these are available with a variety of finishes such as satin, gloss, and high gloss. Results using these papers and a modern inkjet printer are usually very good, and give normal photographic prints "a run for their money".

Most of them are designed to give long-lasting results. The only drawback of the papers is the relatively high cost, which usually works out at around 15 to 60 pence per sheet. If you require top quality results that will last, it is well worth paying the extra for good quality photographic inkjet paper. The cost is high in comparison to cheap copier paper, but the overall cost fares quite well against that of ordinary photographic prints. Try a selection of papers, and use the one or ones that give the best results at a good price.

These days there are other media that can be handled by inkjet printers, and most can print onto envelopes, labels, thin card, and transparency film. In a digital photography context it is more than a little useful if the printer can handle thin cards. Making personalised greetings cards is a popular application of digital photography, and there are greeting card kits available that make this task easier. Photographs printed onto transparency film can look quite impressive when placed in front of a light source, which need be nothing more than daylight coming through a window. Make sure that you obtain transparency film that is specifically intended for use with inkjet printers. The ink does not usually adhere to the surface properly when using ordinary transparency film for use with laser printer, copiers, etc.

The camera

No doubt many potential users of digital photography will already have a computer and a colour printer, and it is then just a matter of buying the camera itself. The range currently available is huge, and it also tends to change quite quickly as old models are deleted and new ones are introduced. Before going off to buy a camera it is definitely advisable to get a good idea of what is available by reading a couple of digital photography magazines and (or) looking at advertisements and reviews published on the Internet. This should help you to decide on the exact type of camera needed, and it will show the likely cost involved.

As pointed out in the previous chapter, there are digital equivalents for most types of film camera. Whether you require the most simple of "point and shoot" cameras, a professional SLR, or anything in between, there will probably be something suitable. Unless something out of the ordinary is required there will probably be a number of suitable cameras to choose from. The importance of adequate resolution has also been covered previously. Bear in mind that resolution is not the only feature that is of importance.

On the face of it, even the cheapest of digital cameras are suitable for taking pictures for web use, where resolution is not normally an issue. However, a digital camera at a "rock bottom" price will probably have a very basic specification in other respects. This is fine if you only need to take simple snapshots of people and places. The camera will not be up to the task if you need to take extreme close-ups, wide-angle panoramic shots, or anything other than very straightforward shots. It is important to consider both the types of photographs that will be taken and how they will be used.

Lens

One of the main parameters of a lens is its focal length, which is usually specified in millimetres. What this figure is really indicating is the angle of coverage. The longer the focal length of the lens, the narrower the camera's angle of coverage. With 35-millimetre cameras, and other film cameras, things are very straightforward. The focal length of a standard lens is equivalent to the distance between diagonally opposite corners on the negative, or about 43 millimetres or so for a 35-millimetre camera. Most standard lenses for 35-millimetre cameras actually have slightly longer focal lengths at about 45 to 50 millimetres, but the discrepancy is too small to be of any great significance.

The actual angle of coverage is roughly 45 degrees, and a standard lens is generally accepted as "seeing" things very much as a person sees them. Photographs taken using a standard lens therefore have a natural look with no odd perspective effects. A lens having a focal length greater than the standard focal length gives a narrower angle of view. In other words, it is what is generally known as a telephoto lens. Shorter focal lengths provide a wider angle of coverage.

The problem when comparing the focal lengths of digital camera lenses is that there is no standard size for the sensor. There are some at a comparable size to a 35-millimetre negative, but the vast majority are much smaller. Many of the sensors are only about 5 millimetres from corner to corner, and a standard lens would therefore have a focal length of about 5 millimetres rather than 50 millimetres. The larger sensors are often about 10 to 15 millimetres from corner to corner, which is still far smaller than a 35 millimetre negative. Because the sensors have different sizes, what constitutes a standard lens varies from one sensor to another.

One way around the problem would be to give an angle of coverage instead of or in addition to the focal length. Most manufacturers instead

Fig.3.3 The sort of view obtained with a standard lens

decided to give equivalent 35-millimetre focal lengths. This is fine if you are familiar with 35-millimetre cameras, but is otherwise of little help. This table should help to clarify matters if you are not familiar with 35-millimetre photography. It shows some popular focal lengths for 35-millimetre camera lenses and their type/main uses.

Focal length	Type of lens
20 and 24mm	Very wide angle/Interiors and landscapes
28 and 35mm	Wide angle/Landscapes and groups of people
40 to 50mm	Standard lens/General
70 to 135mm	Mild telephoto/Portraits and pets
200 to 500mm	Strong telephoto/sports and wildlife

Many digital cameras have zoom lenses that cover the equivalent of something like 35 to 70 or 35 to 105 millimetres. Ranges such as these

*Fig.3.4 The image obtained with the lens at its shortest focal length
clearly has much greater coverage*

are also fairly typical for compact 35 millimetre cameras. It would be
unrealistic to expect compact cameras for general use to cover the more
extreme focal lengths. If you require either very wide or very narrow
angles of view it is usually necessary to resort to an SLR having
interchangeable lenses. Unfortunately, digital SLRs that will take
interchangeable lenses are still quite expensive.

Figure 3.3 shows a photograph taken with a zoom lens set to give the
same sort of coverage as a typical standard lens. Figure 3.4 shows the
same scene with the lens at its widest angle of view and Figure 3.5 shows
the scene with the lens fully zoomed at the telephoto end of its coverage.
The equivalent range of this camera is from just under 35 millimetres to
about 100 millimetres or so, giving a 3:1 zoom range. The variation
available is generally more than one might expect from the specification
of the lens. Bear in mind that a doubling of the focal length gives half the
coverage horizontally and vertically. In other words, in terms of area
only one quarter of the coverage is provided. The lens used in this
example has a 3:1 zoom range, so Figure 3.4 provides about nine times
the coverage obtained in Figure 3.5.

Fig.3.5 Much narrower coverage is obtained with the lens at maximum telephoto setting

Zoom lenses greatly extend the usefulness of a camera, but they are not without drawbacks. One of these is simply that they add significantly to the cost of the camera. In my opinion it is money well spent, and there are some quite good budget zoom models available. The performance of a zoom lens is usually inferior to a non-zoom lens, or prime lens as they are usually called. Flare tends to be more problematic with zoom lenses. This usually manifests itself in the form of low contrast in the main subject when there is a bright background. It can also produce "ghost" images of bright objects.

Flare is caused by reflections from the individual glass elements that comprise the lens, and the dispersion of light within the glass. Modern optics have coatings to reduce the reflections and they are made from high quality glass. This does not completely cure the problem though, and the large number of elements used in zoom lenses makes them more vulnerable to flare. Another problem is that many zoom lenses produce distortions. In other words, straight lines can appear slightly curved in the image, especially if they are near its outer limits. Distortions are often unnoticeable unless there is a long straight line, such as the horizon in a seascape, close to an edge of the image.

F numbers

The second important parameter of a lens is its F number. This is the ratio of the focal length to the effective diameter of the lens, and its practical importance is that it indicates the light gathering power of the lens. The exposure can be varied via the shutter speed or via the F value. In dim conditions it is possible to get sufficient light onto the sensor by using a slow shutter speed, but this often gives poor results. What is termed "camera shake" becomes a problem when slow shutter speeds are used. Movement of the camera during an exposure tends to blur the image, often giving a double-image effect that is unpleasant to look at.

It becomes more difficult to avoid camera shake when using telephoto lenses, because magnifying the image also magnifies the effect of any camera shake. In 35-millimetre photography it is generally accepted that the slowest "safe" shutter speed for hand-held photography is the reciprocal of the lens's focal length. For example, with 50 millimetre standard lens, exposures of about $1/50^{th}$ of a second or less should give acceptable results. Of course, this assumes that the photographer is reasonably competent. Most modern cameras have a warning light or beeper that operates when there is a likelihood of camera shake occurring. Using a tripod should reduce camera shake to an insignificant level, but any slight subject movement during the exposure will still produce blurring on the image.

An iris mechanism within the lens permits the amount of light reaching the sensor to be varied, and it effectively varies the F value of the lens. Opening the iris to maximum gets as much light as possible onto the sensor, but in dim conditions it could still be necessary to use a long exposure. The greater the light gathering power of the lens, the better the chance of avoiding an overlong exposure. Note that the lower the F value, the greater the light gathering capability of the lens. One having a maximum F value of 2 is therefore better than one having a maximum value of 4. In fact an F2 lens has four times the light gathering power of an F4 lens.

In theory, the lower the F number of a lens, the greater its resolution. Real world lenses do not achieve theoretical perfection though, and the resolution can be slightly "soft" when a lens is used at maximum aperture. Any lack of resolution tends to be worse towards the edges of the image. Using a large aperture also tends to give limited depth of field. When the lens is focussed a certain distance in front of the camera, it is not only objects at precisely that distance that are acceptably sharp. There is a field of acceptable sharpness that extends in front of and behind the plane of perfect focus. This is the depth of field. A low F value gives limited depth of field, and a high F number brings much more into focus. The depth of field reduces as the lens is focussed closer.

Due to the small size of the sensors used in digital cameras, depth of field is unlikely to be a problem unless you do some extreme close-ups. It is still best to avoid using the lens at full aperture in the interest of optimum quality. Some compact cameras enable the user to select shutter speeds and aperture values, but most restrict the user to some form of programmed exposure.

The camera's electronics set a fast shutter speed and small aperture under very bright conditions. The exposure is progressively lengthened and the aperture is opened wider as the light level is reduced. Some cameras have program modes that are optimised for different types of photography. For example, there could be a sports photography mode that always uses the fastest usable shutter speed in an attempt to "freeze" the action.

With programmed exposure the only way of avoiding small F values is to make sure that there is adequate light available for a good exposure. This ensures that the lens is not used wide open and that a reasonably fast shutter speed is obtained. Of course, it will not always be possible to ensure that there is an adequate light level. Practically all modern cameras have a built-in electronic flashgun, and this will often solve problems with inadequate light. However, bear in mind that small integral flashguns are only effective at quite short ranges. You often see amateur photographers at outdoor events or in large halls taking flash photographs, but with most flashguns having a maximum operating range of only about 3 to 5 metres there is little chance of the flashes having the desired effect.

Speed rating

Films of various speeds are available for film cameras. So-called slow films are relatively insensitive and have ASA/ISO ratings of about 50 to 100. They are suitable for use when there is plenty of light. Fast films are more sensitive and have ASA/ISO ratings of about 400 to 1000. They provide reasonable shutter speed and aperture settings in relatively dim conditions. An 800 ASA film is eight times more sensitive than one having an ASA rating of 100, so it could be used with a shutter speed of $1/120^{th}$ of a second in conditions that would require a $1/15^{th}$ of a second exposure with a 100 ASA film. Unfortunately, the image quality provided by fast films is noticeably inferior to that of slower films, although it is still perfectly adequate for many purposes.

Some digital cameras have several speed settings, and the instruction manual usually quotes the effective ASA value of each setting. The sensitivity of the sensor does not actually change when the speed setting is altered. Higher sensitivity is obtained by amplifying the signal from the sensor, but any electrical noise produced by the sensor is also amplified and its effects become more obvious on images. Like using a fast film, some loss of image quality might be apparent. It is a system that works much better with some sensors than with others, but the image quality is usually acceptable when the sensitivity is increased. A facility to increase the sensitivity of the camera is a decided asset if you intend to take pictures in low light levels. It is also useful if you will often take pictures with a zoom lens at the telephoto end of its zoom range.

Flash modes

Most digital cameras have several flash modes, and there will usually be at least this basic set:

Automatic

Most cameras default to this setting. The flashgun fires when the light level is too low for a fast shutter speed to be obtained. When taking close-ups and most indoor shots this should ensure that there are no problems with camera shake. The duration of the flash is extremely short, giving an effective shutter speed that is usually about $1/1000^{th}$ of a second or less.

Always off

In this mode the flashgun never fires, no matter how dark the conditions. This mode is used when taking photographs in dark conditions where the flash is not adequate to aid the exposure. For example, the flashgun is of little use with night time scenes. Using the flashgun will tend to give a bright area near to the camera with everything else very or totally dark. Using no flash and a long shutter speed gives much better results, as in the photograph of Figures 3.6. Note that the shutter speeds will usually be so long (typically about one second) that a tripod is needed for this type of thing. Fortunately, with compact digital cameras you can often get away with using the smallest of miniature tripods. Of course, if you

Fig.3.6 The flashgun is normally switched off for scenic shots at night, but a slow exposure is needed

intend to take this type of photograph it will be necessary to have a camera that has slow shutter speeds as well as a flash cancelling facility.

Always fires

This is the opposite of the previous mode, and the flash always fires when this mode is selected. It is mainly used for fill-in flash with backlit subjects. The main problem with backlit subjects is that the bright background tends to "fool" the camera's exposure system into giving an inadequate exposure. A typical example of a backlit subject is where someone has their photograph taken indoors in front of a window. The light level inside is generally much lower than it is outside during daylight hours, especially on a sunny day. Most exposure systems are weighted so that the light level near the centre of the image is given greater importance than the light level near the edges. However, with light intensity near the edges many times greater than the intensity near the middle, the result can still be something close to a silhouette.

One way of combating backlight problems is to use exposure compensation. This is not a feature on all compact cameras, but it is

Fig.3.7 Backlighting often defeats auto-exposure systems

present on many compact digital models. It simply enables the exposure to be increased or decreased by a certain amount, and sometimes two or three levels of overexposure and underexposure are available. With a backlit subject it is increased exposure that is needed, so that the main subject is lightened. This method usually works well with something like a building that has bright sky in the background, but it is often inadequate to give good backlit interior shots.

The somewhat contrived example of Figures 3.7 and 3.8 demonstrates the problem. In Figure 3.7 the bright background has resulted in the Russian doll being reproduced as a silhouette. The maximum amount of positive exposure compensation has been used in Figure 3.8, and the background is even brighter, but the doll is still virtually a silhouette. It is possible to greatly improve problematic pictures such as these using practically any image editing software, and Figure 3.9 shows an enhanced version of the compensated photograph. There is some detail in the doll, and it is possible to see what it is, but the image lacks contrast and is rather grainy. Fill-in flash has been used in the version of Figure 3.10, and in this close-up shot the light from the flash has swamped the ambient

Fig.3.8 Exposure compensation has been inadequate in this case

Fig.3.9 It was possible to rescue some detail from the image

*Fig.3.10 Fill-in flash gives a bland effect but with plenty of detail in the
main subject*

light. Of more importance, there is plenty of contrast and detail in the
doll. Fill-in flash is extremely effective under the right conditions.

Macro

Strictly speaking, macro photography is where the image is equal in size
or larger than the subject. Here we are talking in terms of the image on
the film or sensor, and not the print size. A 35-millimetre negative
measures 36 by 24 millimetres, so true macro photography in this format
means extreme close-ups. The sensors in most digital cameras are much
smaller than a 35-millimetre negative, and true digital macro photography
would involve even closer close-ups. In practice the term macro tends
to be used to describe practically any close-up photography. The area
of coverage when using a macro facility will therefore vary substantially
from one digital camera to another.

In general, digital cameras have very good macro facilities that permit
good photographs of quite small objects to be taken. Figures 3.11 and
3.12 respectively show photographs taken at the minimum acceptable

*Fig.3.11 The macro mode of this SLR is not as good as some digital
cameras, but it still provides useful results*

distances when using an ageing digital SLR and a more modern compact
digital camera. The macro facility of the SLR is not particularly good, but
it still compares quite favourably with most 35mm SLRs when fitted with
a standard lens or a typical zoom lens. It is certainly adequate for most
purposes. The modern compact achieves something close to what would
be true macro photography with a 35-millimetre camera, and it is certainly
good enough for photographing stamps, jewellery, and most other small
objects.

Note that with zoom lens the maximum magnification is normally obtained
with the lens at its longest focal length (maximum telephoto setting). In
general, results are best if close-ups are taken with the lens at its longest
focal length. This avoids having the camera very close to the subject
and it usually gives a more natural perspective effect.

Remember that parallax problems are likely to occur if the viewfinder is
used when framing extreme close-ups. The viewfinder is offset slightly
from the lens, and at close range this can produce a big difference
between what you see down the viewfinder and what the camera "sees".

Fig.3.12 Many compact digital cameras can provide extreme close-ups in the macro mode

There are often marks in the viewfinder that indicate the field of view at short ranges, but these do not usually accommodate extreme close-ups and are only approximate anyway. It is best to use the built-in monitor and ignore the viewfinder when taking anything approximating to a macro shot. Bear in mind that the actual coverage is somewhat greater than the area shown by the monitor. Of course, parallax problems do not occur when using an SLR camera due to its through-the-lens viewing system.

The importance (or otherwise) of a good macro facility depends on the type of photography you intend to undertake. It is clearly of limited use to someone who is primarily interested in photographing people and places. On the other hand, it is a facility that most people use if it is there, and it might open up a new field of interest. Bear in mind that camera shake is a major problem with extreme close-up photography. Magnifying small objects to make them large does much the same to camera movement. In practice this means that the use of flash is usually mandatory.

Fig.3.13 Rechargeable batteries and a charger are essential for most
        digital cameras

Batteries

As already pointed out, digital cameras tend to run down batteries at a
much higher rate than conventional cameras. Modern digital cameras
are much better than those of a few years ago, and many are now capable
of taking large numbers of photographs per set of batteries provided
there is minimal use of the LCD monitor and the built-in flashgun.
Unfortunately, in normal operation there will often be considerable use
of both. Most digital cameras can use ordinary AA batteries or other
conventional batteries, but running costs tend to be quite high when
using this method.

Rechargeable batteries are something I regard as essential with digital
cameras. Fortunately, many digital cameras are supplied with a set of
rechargeable batteries and a matching charger (Figure 3.13). Note that

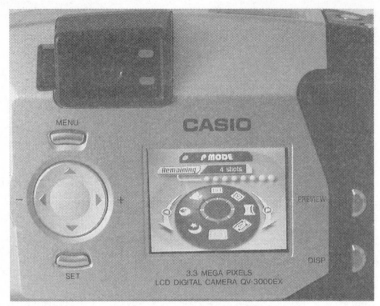

Fig.3.14 Integral monitors often perform several functions

standard nickel-cadmium (NiCad) cells have relatively low capacities, and only last about a third as long as good quality non-rechargeable batteries. This makes them far from ideal for use with most digital cameras. High capacity nickel-cadmium batteries or a more modern alternative such as nickel metal hydride batteries are a better choice. In addition to their higher capacity these higher specification batteries can be recharged relatively quickly.

Some digital cameras are supplied with a mains adapter, or it may be offered as a (usually) expensive extra. Even when shooting indoors it is very inconvenient to use mains power. A mains adapter is handy for emergency use, but my preference is an extra set of rechargeable batteries or even just some ordinary cells for emergencies.

Integral monitor

I suppose that a built-in monitor is not an essential feature for a digital camera, and conventional cameras have managed without this feature for 150 years or so. It is a feature of all but the cheapest of digital cameras though, and it is something that most users seem to regard as essential. As pointed out previously, the monitor can be used as an additional viewfinder, and it is extremely useful in this role when taking close-up shots. When a picture is taken it is displayed on the monitor for a few seconds so that you

Fig.3.15 Many digital cameras have a liquid crystal display

can assess the quality, framing, etc. The resolution of the monitor is often far lower than that of the pictures being taken, so a something less than detailed view is provided. Even so, any major problems with the focussing, exposure, etc., will often be apparent with careful scrutiny of the monitor.

The monitor is often used for other purposes. The ability to display the pictures stored in memory and delete any that you do not wish to preserve for posterity is a standard feature. In conjunction with some pushbutton switches it will often provide access to additional controls (Figure 3.14), allow certain default settings to be changed, and this type of thing.

LCD

There is a major problem with all the built-in monitors I have encountered, which is that the picture on the screen becomes almost impossible to see under bright conditions. This can be a severe drawback if you do a lot of shooting out of doors. Most digital cameras seem to sport an ordinary liquid crystal display (LCD), like the one in Figure 3.15. This shows things like the selected mode, approximate number of pictures that the memory can accommodate, and the amount of charge left in the batteries. The dependence on the monitor can be greatly reduced by an ordinary liquid crystal display, and this is a definite plus point for shooting outdoors.

Fig.3.16 Ulead's Photo Express 3.0 has a useful range of features

Software

A digital camera should be supplied with software that enables the pictures to be uploaded to a computer. Users of Macintosh computers must be careful to check for compatibility with their computer, because some digital cameras can only be used with PCs. The same is true if you are using a PC with an operating system other than Windows, or you are using an old version of Windows. Many cameras are only usable with a PC running a fairly up-to-date version of Windows such as Windows ME or XP.

Practically all digital cameras are supplied with some additional software, but the amount and quality varies considerably from one camera to another. As one would probably expect, the value of the bundled software tends to reflect the price of the camera. With an out-and-out budget camera there might be nothing more than a simple library program to help you store and retrieve images. At the other end of the price range the bundled software is likely to include a good image editing program such as a recent version of Paint Shop or one of the "light" versions of Photoshop.

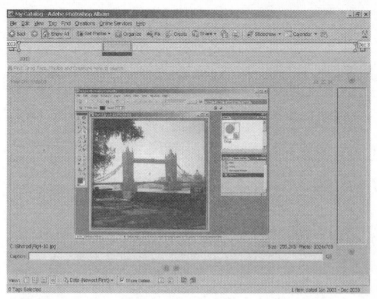

Fig.3.17 A picture displayed in Adobe's Photoshop Album 1.0

Ulead's Photo Express 3.0 SE (Figure 3.16) is typical of the software supplied with low cost cameras and scanners. It is designed as an easy means of acquiring images from a scanner or camera, storing and retrieving them, making any necessary adjustments, and printing them. It is designed for ease of use rather than as the ultimate in image editing programs. A program such as this is ideal if you are not interested in doing anything too clever and do not require the full range of manual controls. It is also a good starting point. Having gained some experience using a program such as this you are in a good position to move on to upmarket image editing programs.

There are plenty of combined album and image editing programs available if your camera is not supplied with something suitable, and they are mostly available at quite modest prices. Figure 3.17 shows Adobe's Photoshop Album in operation, and this has a similar range of facilities to Ulead's Photo Express 3.0. It is primarily for storing images in a sensible fashion so that it is easy to retrieve the required images. It also has a range of basic photo-editing functions (Figure 3.18), many of which are essentially the same as those found in the more upmarket versions of Photoshop. Again, if you only need to undertake basic editing

Fig.3.18 Photoshop Album has some useful editing facilities

such as cropping images, removing "red-eye", and adjusting the contrast, a program such as this should be adequate.

Image editing

Something a bit more potent is needed if you need more control or wish to become a bit more creative with your image editing. It is not necessary to spend large amounts in order to obtain an image editing program that has a full range of features. Jasc Paint Shop Pro 8.0 and Photoshop Elements 2.0 are both available at well under one hundred pounds and offer a huge range of facilities. A wizard style window appears when Photoshop Elements 2.0 is launched, but it is probably best to close that and get straight into its normal user interface. This has a fair range of menus, toolbars, etc., and it can look a bit daunting at first. However, programs such as Paint Shop Pro and Photoshop Elements are not difficult to use. The more you use them the easier they are to use, so it pays to put in some time trying the various facilities. This is quite good fun, so there is no great hardship in putting in an hour or two per day until you are reasonably fluent with the program.

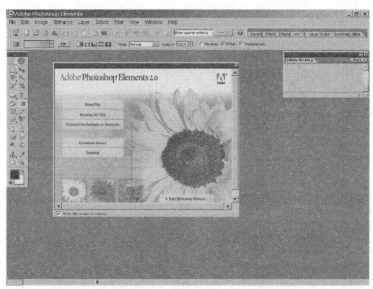

Fig.3.19 The opening screen of Photoshop Elements 2.0

Fig.3.20 Photoshop 7.0 is the standard choice for professionals

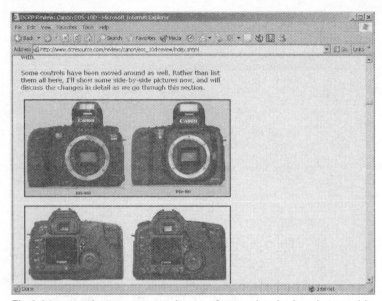

Fig.3.21 www.dcresource.com is one of several web sites that provide detailed reviews of digital cameras

For a few hundred pounds more you can have Photoshop 7.0 (Figure 3.20), which is the standard choice for professional use. Superficially it looks much the same as Photoshop Elements, but there are actually many more options available from the professional version. You often have several ways of achieving the same thing rather than just one. It also has a macro facility that enables a string of commands to be issued by operating one of the function keys. Whether all this is of much use to amateur users is debatable, but many seem to end up using the full version of Photoshop. Using Photoshop 7.0 is covered in "Using Photoshop 7.0 (BP536)".

Getting information

Getting information on digital cameras and related equipment is not exactly difficult, especially if you have access to the Internet. There are plenty of magazines that provide equipment reviews and other useful information about digital cameras, printers, and so on. The Internet is a better resource for this type of thing though, because most of the digital photography sites have built up a collection of reviews that cover most

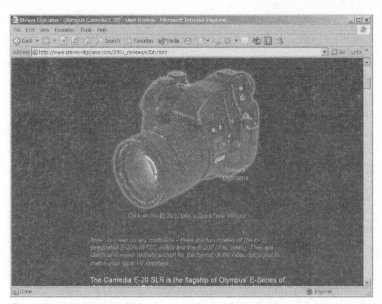

*Fig.3.22 www.steves-digicams.com is another site that provides
         detailed reviews*

of the cameras that are currently available. Some even retain reviews of
older models so that you can look up cameras you are thinking of buying
second-hand.

Many of the reviews are extremely detailed, showing numerous detailed
photographs of each camera. Each set of photographs is usually
accompanied by a full specification, details of the software provided with
the camera, an assessment of how well (or otherwise) the camera
performed, explanations of the various operating modes, etc. In fact
some of them effectively provide you with an operating manual for the
camera. The manufacturers' web sites also provide some useful
information, but are generally less detailed than the review sites. A few
sites provide a downloadable version of the instruction manuals, and
these should tell you everything you need to know about using each
model.

Many of the review sites and the manufacturers' sites include sample
photographs that can be viewed in a browser or downloaded. This is
more than a little useful, because you can see the picture quality available
from each model. If you have a colour printer it is possible to download

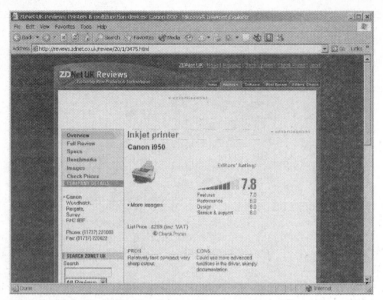

Fig.3.23 *The zdnet sites provide reviews for various pieces of hardware including digital cameras and printers*

a few sample images, load them into a photo-editing program, and then print them out. This way it is possible to ascertain beyond any doubt whether each camera is capable of producing results that meet your requirements. This can help you avoid spending money on a camera that can not meet you requirements, or spending an unnecessarily large amount on one that has a far higher resolution than you really need.

Putting a search string such as "digital camera review" into any good Internet search engine should produce plenty of links to useful sites. Three of the larger sites are at www.dcresource.com (Figure 3.21), www.dpreview.com, and www.steves-digicams.com (Figure 3.22). These sites have links to other sites of interest. The digital camera sites mostly have some printer reviews, but general computer hardware review sites are also worth investigating. Probably the biggest of these is www.zdnet.com/reviews, or you may prefer the UK version of their site at www.zdnet.co.uk/reviews (Figure 3.23). There are many others though, and any Internet search engine should soon track down a good selection of them. There should also be some digital camera reviews on these general hardware sites.

Bear in mind that the same camera can be sold under a different name or model number in different countries. This is quite common with Canon cameras for example, which often seem to have one name for the USA and another for the UK. This can be a bit confusing when looking at reviews on sites in the USA, but it is not usually too difficult to sort things out. Also bear in mind that the software and accessories supplied with a camera often varies from country to country. Always check the camera manufacturer's web site for your country for details of the bits and pieces supplied with the camera.

Points to remember

A modern and powerful computer may be desirable for image editing, but it is by no means essential. Older PCs are just about adequate for image editing, although some will lack the wherewithal to run the latest versions of the top end photo-editing programs. Image editing can take up large amounts of memory, so a memory upgrade to an older PC can improve its performance in this application, and many others come to that.

Most inkjet printers will produce quite good photographic prints of up to A4 size (297 by 210 millimetres), but most will not print right out to the edges. There are printers designed specifically for producing photographic prints, and the results are usually superb. However, the lower cost printers can only produce relatively small prints and the types than can do A4 prints are quite expensive. A good general-purpose inkjet printer is a more practical proposition for most users.

It is not possible to judge the output quality of a printer from its specification. Two printers having the same resolution can produce results of very different qualities. Reviews are helpful but it is better if you can see the results from prospective printers at your local computer store.

The angle of coverage for a lens is usually indicated via an equivalent focal length for a 35-millimetre camera. Around 45 to 50 millimetres is a standard lens. Telephoto lenses have greater focal lengths and wide-angle lenses have smaller focal lengths.

A lens having a small F-number has greater light gathering power than one having a higher F-number. This permits a faster shutter speed to be used, which gives reduced risk of camera shake.

A macro mode enables the camera to be used for extreme close-ups. The macro modes of most digital cameras are suitable for taking photographs of very small objects such as stamps and coins. Not an essential feature, but one that it is certainly worth having.

A simple photo-album program with a certain amount of image editing ability is all you need to get started. Software of this type is often provided with scanners and digital cameras. Before too long most people move on to a more potent image editing program, but a good budget program such as Photoshop Elements 2.0 or Paint Shop Pro 8.0 has a huge range of features and is adequate for most users. If you are lucky, a suitable program will be supplied with the camera.

There is a mass of information available on digital cameras and related equipment, both in magazines and on the Internet. Spend some time going through reviews and downloading sample images before parting with any money. With a little time and effort it should be possible to find at least one or two cameras at a reasonable price that meet your requirements.

Basic editing

Why process?

In an ideal world, having taken your photographs and uploaded them to a computer, the next step would be to print them out. You can in fact do things this way, but results would be far from ideal. Some processing using an image editing program will produce improved results with the vast majority of photographs. There are two general categories of processing that can be applied to digital images, which are correcting problems and creative processing. In this chapter we will only consider the first type, which is the type of thing that all digital camera users will need to do with most images.

Creative processing is optional, and includes such things as adding filter effects or combining elements from two or more images. The range of processing available from any good photo-editing program is vast. With Photoshop and Photoshop Elements for example, there are dozens of built-in filters and many more available as add-ons. Creative processing is not for everyone, but most digital camera users experiment with this type of thing from time to time. For others it is their main interest. Anyway, various aspects of creative processing are covered in later chapters.

For something other than creative processing to improve an image it is necessary for the original to be faulty, or at least less than perfect in some respect. Modern cameras mostly have quite sophisticated focussing and exposure systems, but it is impossible to get things absolutely spot-on every time. In some cases the correct exposure and ideal point of perfect focus is to some extent a subjective matter. The colour balance is something that is very subjective. It is a common ploy to slightly overdo colour casts to add atmosphere to an image. Snow scenes can be made bluer and "colder" and early morning scenes are often made a little redder and "warmer". A small amount of additional red can also be used to give more appealing skin tones.

The camera is more likely to do the opposite, and attempt to remove any colour cast. Even with all the "intelligence" built into many cameras, they do not have the ability to mind-read. Only you know how you would like the final image to appear. With the more simple cameras there could well be a fair number of faulty images where the camera's electronics is assuming every picture to conform to some sort of average conditions. In the real world relatively few images will meet these average conditions. Most images will then require some fine adjustment, and possibly some further changes to tailor them to your requirements.

Fortunately, good photo-editing programs are rich in features that enable problems with colour and exposure to be corrected, and they also have a host of other useful features for improving images. It is not possible to resurrect every faulty image. Realistically, there is little that can be done if you take a family group and frame the shot so that all the heads are "cut off"! However, apart from instances of serious "pilot error" with any half decent camera it should be possible to produce satisfactory results from most of the photographs you take.

Photoshop Elements

It is not practical to give precise instructions for using several different programs here, so one representative photo-editing program is used. This is Adobe's Photoshop Elements 2.0, which is a popular low cost image editing program. It actually has many features in common with Adobe's Photoshop 7 program, which is the standard image editing program for professionals. Although Photoshop Elements is several hundred pounds cheaper than the professional version, it has many of the features that are present in the more expensive program. It is aimed at the enthusiast, and has some features that are not present in Photoshop 7.

This program is certainly not in the so-called "crippled software" category, and it has more than enough features to satisfy most users. An advantage of Photoshop Elements is that having learned to use this program, it is easy to move on to the full Photoshop program should you wish to do so.

The general principles and methods described here still apply if you use a different image editing program, but each program has its own way of handling things. This will at the very least result in differences in points of detail. Also, bear in mind that all image editing programs have the same core functions, but they differ somewhat in the "extras" that are available. An alternative to Photoshop Elements will probably lack some of its features but have some that Photoshop Elements lacks. Some

*Fig.4.1 The main screen of Photoshop Elements 2. Much editing is
done using the Toolbox at the left edge of the screen*

digital cameras and scanners have the original version of Photoshop
Elements as part of the bundled software. This is largely the same as
version 2.0, but there are of course a few differences.

It will clearly be easier to try the editing techniques described in this
book if you use Photoshop Elements 2.0. Fortunately, a demonstration
version that is fully functional for 30 days is available from the Adobe
web site at www.adobe.com. It is certainly worthwhile downloading and
installing this in order to try out image editing for yourself and follow the
examples in this book. A few sample images are supplied with the
program, and there are plenty more available on the Internet, so you do
not need a scanner or digital camera to try out this software.
Unfortunately, it is a large download at over 100 megabytes, so it will be
a long download unless you have access to a broadband Internet
connection.

The program looks like Figure 4.1 when it is run and the wizard style
window is closed. Some aspects of the screen layout follow the normal
Windows scheme of things, with title and menu bars at the top and a
toolbar beneath the menu bar. There is also the usual status bar at the

bottom of the screen. The large blank area in the middle is where the image or images are displayed. Most programs permit several documents to be opened at once, but it pays to bear in mind that image files are often quite large. Having several images open simultaneously is fine, but only if your computer has sufficient memory to accommodate them all. Do not have several image files open unless it is really necessary to do so.

Screen layout

Although the program has something approximating to a conventional screen layout, it is rather more "busy" than most programs. This is a feature of practically all image editing software, and it is a consequence of the vast range of tools and facilities that they provide. The normal menus and toolbar permit a large number of features to be accessed, but the program has many more available. The small window near the right edge of the screen is called the Toolbox, and this provides a number of facilities for editing images.

These include various drawing tools including some for adding text, and there are tools for selecting parts of an image. The ability to select part of parts of an image and then apply processing to just those selections is one of the most useful features of digital imaging. There are also tools for zooming in on part of an image so that it can be viewed in detail. It is then possible to pan around the image so that any desired section can be viewed.

There is a second toolbar immediately beneath the main one, and in Photoshop terminology this is the Options bar. It is context sensitive and operates in conjunction with the Toolbox. In other words, the options it provides are different for each tool in the Toolbox. For example, when a text tool is selected the Options bar enables the text size to be changed, the font to be changed, and so on. When a paintbrush tool is selected, the size and style of the brush can be changed, the opacity of the brushstrokes can be altered, etc. The Options bar is an important aspect of the program as it enables the tools to be adjusted for exactly the desired effect.

Finally, the program includes palettes on the right side of the screen. More of these can be accessed via the tabs at the right end of the Options bar. A variety of facilities are available here, including the History palette. This enables up to the last 20 operations that affect the image to be undone and redone. A big advantage of digital photo-editing is the ease with which mistakes can be undone. If you make a mistake or change your mind it only takes one or two mouse clicks to go back to an earlier stage of the editing, and there is no residual damage to the image. The changes are completely reversed.

There is also a multilevel undo and redo facility available from the Edit menu, which a fairly standard Windows feature. In general though, a History facility is quicker and easier to use because it lists all the available states of the image. This makes it easy to jump backwards and forwards to the desired states.

Sizing up

Even with a perfect image it will be necessary to set the size before printing or exporting it to another program. It is important to realise that there are actually two sizes for a digital image. The first is its size in terms of the dimension in pixels, and the second is its physical size. An exception is where the image will be used on a web page. The image might still have a notional size stored in the image file, but it is almost certain to be ignored by the program used to make up the web page. You can then simply use the default physical size, as it is the size in pixels that determines how big the image will be displayed on the page.

The same is not true if you are producing prints. It is the specified physical size of the image that determines its size, and the number of pixels is ignored. The same is usually true when images are being exported to a desktop publishing program or a word processor. In most cases it is possible to resize images from within the word processor or desktop publishing program, but it is better to set a likely size for the image prior to exporting it. With luck, no resizing will be necessary. If any resizing is required, it should be minimal. Massive changes of image size within a word processor or desktop publishing program can sometimes produce odd looking results, and this type of thing is best avoided.

The terminology varies somewhat from one image editing program to another. The physical size of the image might be termed something like canvas size. Do not confuse canvas size (or the like) with paper size. The latter is the size of the paper used in the printer, such as A3 or A4. The canvas size is the physical size of the printed image, which is normally less than the paper size. Few printers can print right to the edges of the paper, so the image size normally has to be something like 10 or 15 millimetres smaller than the paper on both sides.

Setting the physical size of the image larger than the paper will result in some of the image being clipped. With most image editing software it is possible to print oversize images in two halves which are then joined together on a backing board. It is possible to produce some impressive images from suitably high resolution sources, but it is difficult to get really convincing results. I have seen few examples where "you can't see the join", and in most cases you can see it without having to look too hard.

Pixel count

Although it is the physical size that determines the dimensions of the printed image, the pixel count can not be ignored. The print quality will be very rough unless the image has a high enough pixel count relative to its physical size. As explained previously, anything much below 200 pixels to the inch (about 80 pixels per centimetre) produces a very noticeable lack of quality. If an image measures (say) 3000 by 2000 pixels, the maximum usable print size is about 15 by 10 inches, or 37.5 by 25 centimetres. The quality might be acceptable with a slightly larger print size, but anything much more than this is likely to give some rough looking results.

Most image editing software gives complete control over the physical size of an image and the number of pixels. The size in pixels is normally left unchanged when printing an image and it is only the physical size that is changed. When producing images for web use it is often necessary to reduce the size of the image in terms of the number of pixels. As explained previously, the physical size is usually of no importance and is left unaltered. The exact way of handling things varies somewhat from one program to another, but broadly the same set of basic features is available from all good image editing software.

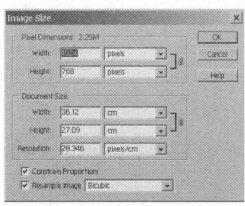

Fig.4.2 The physical size and size in pixels can both be changed

In Photoshop Elements the image size is altered by selecting Resize from the Image menu, followed by Image Size from the popup submenu. This produces the small dialogue box of Figure 4.2. The top section of the window shows the image size in pixels, and the middle section shows the physical size and the resolution in pixels per centimetre. The pop-down menus enable the sizes and resolution to be shown in inches rather than centimetres if preferred.

There are two checkboxes in the bottom section of the window, and one of these enables the proportions to be constrained. When this box is ticked it is impossible to alter the aspect ratio of the image, and any change to one dimension will then produce a proportional change in the other. In general it is best not to alter the aspect ratio of an image as it can produce odd perspective effects, or results that just look a bit odd.

The second checkbox determines how changes to the physical size and resolution settings will be applied to the image. Suppose that you are going to print an image, and the physical size must be changed without altering the number of pixels. Start by checking whether the Resample Image checkbox is ticked, and if necessary remove the tick. Any changes to the physical dimensions of the image will then have no affect on the number of pixels. The Constrain Proportions checkbox will automatically be ticked with the Resample Image option disabled, so changes made to one dimension will automatically make proportionate changes to the other one.

Resolution

When setting the size of an image it is essential to keep an eye on the resolution figure, and avoid printing the image at an excessive size. The minimum acceptable resolution is to some extent a subjective matter, so it is probably best to do some small test prints at various resolutions to determine the lowest figure that you deem acceptable. It is not usually necessary to reduce the resolution when making prints, since there is little likelihood of the resolution being grossly excessive. This could perhaps occur when making small prints, but the printer driver should be able to handle any excess resolution without producing any untoward effects.

It can be necessary to lower the resolution by reducing the number of pixels when exporting images to a desktop publishing program, because some commercial printing processes do not work well with high resolution images. The more normal reason for reducing the number of pixels is to make an image fit into its allotted space on a web page. In order to

Fig.4.3 The original version of the image

reduce the number of pixels the Resample Image checkbox must be ticked. It is then possible to restrain the proportions of the image or adjust the width and height independently, as preferred. However, as explained previously, it is best to retain the original proportions unless there is a good reason to do otherwise.

The number of pixels can be changed by altering the resolution or the physical size of the image, or by simply editing the pixel values. If an image for desktop publishing requires a maximum resolution of (say) 80 dots per centimetre, then the obvious way of handling things is to alter the value in the Resolution textbox to 80 dots per centimetre, having previously set the required physical size. In a web application you will presumably know the required width for the image in pixels, and it is then just a matter of typing the appropriate value in the Width textbox in the upper section of the window.

Image quality

There are a couple of important points to bear in mind when reducing the number of pixels in an image. The first and more obvious one is that the reduction in the number of pixels produces a reduction in the quality of the image. Whether this is of any practical importance depends on the nature of the image. In general, it is best to keep the subject very simple if the final resolution will be very low. This is particularly important with web images where the resolutions are often very low indeed.

A close-up of a face should be quite recognisable even if it is reduced to a low resolution image, but the same is unlikely to be true of a photograph showing a full-length view of 20 or 30 people. The group shot might still serve its purpose in low resolution form, but there is a risk that it will look like nothing much at all. It is unlikely that anyone in the image will be recognisable if each head is produced by a few pixels. The only way to find out if a low resolution image is adequate for your intended purpose is to try it and then make a subjective judgement. The chances of success will always be much better with simple subject matter.

The second point to bear in mind is that having reduced the size of an image, taking it back up to the original size will not restore the original image. Information is lost when the image is

Fig.4.4 The restored image lacks detail

reduced in size. Photoshop Elements and most other image editing software can be used to add pixels and take the image back up to the original number of pixels, but it can not put back the missing detail. This point is demonstrated by Figures 4.3 and 4.4. Figure 4.3 is the original image, which measures 400 by 300 pixels. Figure 4.4 is the result of reducing the image to 100 by 75 pixels and then restoring it to the original size. The loss of definition is very pronounced.

Consequently, it is important to use a copy of an image when the number of pixels in the image will be reduced. If you need a high resolution version of the image it is then just a matter of returning to the original image file. In fact it is a good idea to always work on a copy of an image when working with something like a picture from a digital camera, where

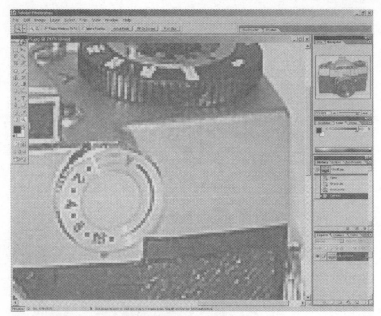

Fig.4.5 The pixels are clearly visible in this zoomed view

there is no way of obtaining the image again if the original is ruined. It is less important to work on a copy with something like a scanned photograph. If the worst came to the worst it would presumably take no more than a minute or two to rescan the photograph. Many digital camera users archive all images in their original state on some form of read-only media such as CD-R discs. The archive images can not be accidentally altered or overwritten, so you always have the option of going back to the original image if this should be necessary for some reason. I would certainly recommend doing things this way.

Pixel boost

Photoshop Elements can be used to artificially boost the number of pixels in an image, but again, adding pixels will not add detail to the image. It can still be useful to boost the number of pixels in an image, but you need to be aware of the limitations of doing this. The usual reason for increasing the number of pixels is that you have a low resolution image, perhaps from a low resolution digital camera or downloaded from a web

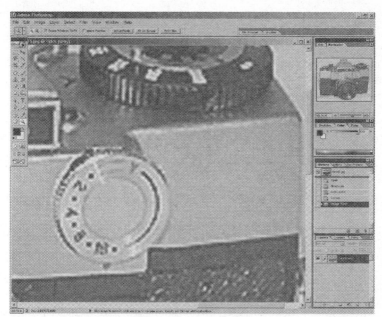

Fig.4.6 Increasing the pixel count makes the pixels less obvious, but does not add any detail

page. You would like to do a printout of the image, but at 200 dots per inch it is reproduced at little more than the size of a large postage stamp. Reducing the resolution to 75 or 100 dots per inch gives a more reasonable print size, but the pixels are large and obvious.

Keeping the resolution at 200 dots per inch but doubling or trebling the number of pixels in each axis should give much more convincing results. The image area is increased by a factor of four and nine respectively, but the pixel size remains the same. Although no detail has been added to the image, the pixels are kept small and unnoticeable. Simply scaling up an image tends to produce noticeable stepping on diagonal lines, but this is absent when the pixel count is increased as well.

Figure 4.5 shows a highly zoomed view of a photograph, and stepping is very noticeable in a number of places. It is particularly noticeable in the arc and numbers on the dial, and in several edges that are not precisely vertical or horizontal. Figure 4.6 shows the result of increasing the vertical resolution from 300 to 1500 pixels, with the horizontal resolution also being subjected to a fivefold increase.

There is clearly no more detail in the boosted version, and if anything, in a few places it looks a fraction "softer" than the original version. Where necessary, further processing can be used to sharpen an image that suffers from this problem. Although the sharpness may sometimes look fractionally worse, the stepping in the arc around the dial and the lettering is much less apparent in the version that has more pixels. The figure "2" on the dial does actually look much more like a figure "2" in the version that has more pixels. Stepping gives very rough looking results and it is important to avoid it if at all possible.

Glitches

It is only fair to point out that odd things can happen when an image is scaled up or down. There should be no major problem if the mathematics are simple, and the image has the number of pixels in each dimension doubled, trebled, halved, or whatever. In rare cases things can still go slightly awry though. Suppose there is a vertical line in an image that is one pixel wide. With the number of pixels halved in each dimension, leaving the line in the image effectively doubles its width. Simply removing it might result in an important element of the image being omitted. Including some pixels and omitting others would be unlikely to give convincing results either. Large reductions in the number of pixels will inevitably require some compromises in the fine detail.

If the number of pixels is boosted by an odd amount such as 1.57 times in each dimension, the mathematics are not straightforward and compromises have to be made. In the early days of image editing software, scaling images up or down more or less guaranteed some odd results. Photoshop Elements and most other modern image editing programs are very good at avoiding obvious problems, and they are good at maintaining detail when the number of pixels is reduced. However, there is no guarantee that the processed image will be entirely glitch free. Low resolution images are more prone to scaling problems than the high resolution variety.

Rotation

Some cameras have a built-in sensor that detects when the camera is held vertically to take portrait format shots. With this type of camera you should always find that the downloaded images are displayed the right way round on the monitor's screen. With most cameras though, it is necessary to rotate the images through 90 degrees in order to bring

them the right way round. Any
image editing program should be
able to rotate images in 90 degree
steps, and in Photoshop
Elements this feature is accessed
via the Rotate submenu of the
Image menu. There are options
to rotate the image 90 degrees left

*Fig.4.7 A precise amount of
rotation can be specified*

or right, which respectively mean 90 degrees counter-clockwise and
clockwise. There is also an option to rotate the image by 180 degrees.

There is a fourth option (Custom) that enables the image to be rotated
by an arbitrary amount. In other words, you can specify the degree of
rotation and the direction. The small window of Figure 4.7 appears when
the Custom option is selected. Note that you are not restricted to an
integer value, and rotation by (say) 2.5 degrees is permissible. It is

Fig.4.8 The leaning towers of London?

Fig.4.9 The towers are vertical, but the image still needs some work

therefore possible to rotate the image with a high degree of precision, provided it has suitably high resolution. Note that some image editing programs do not permit the same degree of precision as Photoshop Elements.

Arbitrary rotation can be used creatively, but its main use is to correct sloping horizons and similar faults such as people or buildings that seem to be keeling over. You can sometimes get away with a slightly sloping horizon if there are hills or trees hiding the true horizon. Even a slightly sloping horizon is pretty obvious in something like a seascape where the true horizon can be seen, especially where the horizon is very near the top of the picture. Sloping horizons and interiors that are keeling over apparently rank as two of the most common faults in photographs. Figure 4.8 shows this problem in its keeling over building guise. The two towers of Tower bridge are something less than vertical, and the image needs to be rotate to the right (clockwise) to correct matters.

Fig.4.10 A grid makes it easier to judge whether edges are horizontal or vertical

To correct this type of fault the appropriate radio button must be operated so that the image is rotated in the right direction, and you have to guess the correct amount of rotation. Initially there is a tendency to overestimate the amount of rotation required. In most cases only about one degree or so is needed, and in some cases less than one degree is sufficient. I tried 1.5 degrees initially, but had to reduce this to 1 degree to get more convincing results (Figure 4.9). It is usually necessary to undo the rotation and try again a few times using different amounts, but it should not take long to get it right.

Any image editing program should have a facility for placing a grid or guide lines on the screen, and either of these is helpful for judging accurate horizontal or vertical lines. In Photoshop Elements a grid can be placed over the image by selecting Grid from the View menu (Figure 4.10). Select this option again to switch off the grid, which is only displayed on the screen. Of course, the grid is not shown on printouts or included in saved images.

As can be seen from Figure 4.9, Photoshop automatically increases the size of the canvas so that it fully accommodates the rotated image. This

Fig.4.11 The area that will be cropped is darkened so that it is easy to see what the cropped picture will look like

leaves four blank areas that must be cropped or retouched. Cropping is quicker and easier, but some content near the edges of the frame will be lost. Retouching is reasonably quick and simple with some images, but it can border on the impossible with others. In this case cropping was used to produce the final version as there seemed to be no advantage in doing any retouching. Using the minimum amount of cropping that would do the job did not result in anything noteworthy being removed.

Crop tool

There is more than one way of cropping an image using Photoshop Elements, but the obvious one is to use the Crop tool in the Toolbox. This is the third button down in the right-hand column of buttons. Using this tool it is possible to drag a rectangle onto the image area. In other words, left-click the mouse in one corner of the required rectangle and then drag the pointer to the diagonally opposite corner while still holding down the mouse button. Then release the mouse button and the rectangle will be drawn on the screen (Figure 4.11).

Fig.4.12 The rotated and cropped version of the image

It is easy to see which parts of the picture will be cropped, as these are shown much darker than the rest of the picture. Eight handles (the small squares) appear on the outline of the cropped area, and these can be dragged to adjust the size of the selection. The selection can be dragged to a new position by using any part of it other than the handles. Press the Return key to actually go ahead and crop the picture (Figure 4.12), or right-clicking anywhere on the image and selecting Crop from the popup menu has the same effect. A third option is to select Crop from the Image menu. Right-click and select Cancel to remove the selection, or press the Escape key. I am not sure if the corrected version is absolutely spot-on, but it is possible to go back and try again as many times as it takes to get things to your satisfaction.

Fig.4.13 The full-frame version of the image

Cropping

Cropping is not only used after rotating an image. I would guess that cropping is the image editing function that I use most frequently, and it is certainly one that most users will resort to quite often. It can be used to slightly alter the composition of a picture by removing unwanted material near the edge. Group shots in public places for example, often have half a bystander encroaching at one side of the picture. Cropping the unwanted material and framing the main subject more tightly will often result in a vastly improved picture. Another common problem is a scan has gone slightly wrong, resulting in a blank strip along one or more edges of the picture where slightly too much has been scanned. A few seconds spent cropping the extraneous material produces a much better picture.

Many cameras give slightly more on the film than was included in the viewfinder. This "tunnel vision" is apparently used to compensate for the fact that machine prints cover slightly less than the full negative or transparency. However, most film scanners do cover the full frame, and therefore give more than was included in the viewfinder. Most digital

Fig.4.14 Cropping has effectively produced a new image

cameras also have less coverage in the viewfinder than appears in the image, but the reason for this is less than obvious. Anyway, an excess of coverage, for whatever reason, is easily corrected using image editing software such as Photoshop Elements.

It is possible to drastically alter the composition by massively cropping an image. With many photographs, but particularly with very wide-angle shots, there are often many good pictures within the overall scene. Many of the photographs used in magazines and newspapers have been cropped from much larger images. The image of Figure 4.13 is turned into a very different picture when cropped as in Figure 4.14, and it is different again with the very tight cropping of Figure 4.15. Bear in mind that the maximum usable print size is reduced proportionately if an image is cropped. The higher the quality of the original image, the greater the scope you have for using creative cropping.

With a top quality negative and a good film scanner it might be possible to obtain an image having 10 million or more pixels and the image quality to match. This might also be possible using a flatbed scanner and a top

Fig.4.15 Even tighter cropping provides another variation

quality print. Using a third of the image area it should still be possible to produce a reasonable A4 size print. A digital camera having 3 million or so pixels can just about produce an A4 print from the full-frame image, so cropping the image down to about 1 million pixels will limit the print to about postcard size. Creative cropping requires a very high quality source or you have to settle for small print sizes.

Marquee

The tool in the top left-hand corner of the Toolbox is called the Marquee tool, and it can be used to select a rectangular area for processing. Only the area within that rectangle will be subjected to any applied processing such as changes in brightness or contrast. There are actually two versions of the Marquee tool, which are the standard rectangular tool and an elliptical version. Right-clicking on the Marquee button in the Toolbox produces a popup menu (Figure 4.16), and the required version can then be selected. With the Marquee tool selected there are two buttons near the left end of the Options bar that also enable the desired version to be chosen (Figure 4.17). Most buttons in the Toolbox have more than one function and use these methods of selecting the required version.

When using the Marquee tools it is possible to constrain the shape to a square or circle by holding down the Shift key while dragging the shape onto the screen. Other fixed aspect ratios can be

Fig.4.16 Two versions of the Marquee tool are available

obtained by selecting Fixed Aspect Ratio from the Style menu. The desired aspect ratio is then entered into the Width and Height textboxes. The third option in the Style menu enables the size of the marquee (in pixels) to be specified via the Width and Height textboxes.

Incidentally, the Marquee name is derived from the fact that the outline of the selected area is indicated by a sort of moving broken line. This looks a bit like the moving light displays found on circus marquees. The

Fig.4.17 The Options bar with a Marquee tool selected

marquee is black on light areas and white on dark areas. This contrast, together with the moving light effect, makes it stand out quite clearly on practically any image content.

On the face of it, the image can be cropped to an elliptical shape by placing an elliptical marquee on the image and selecting Crop from the Image menu. In practice this method will not provide the desired result. An elliptical selection has been made in Figure 4.18 and then the Crop

Fig.4.18 Cropping an elliptical selection produces a rectangular image

function has been used. The picture is still rectangular, and it is just large enough to accommodate the selection. All the material outside the marquee has been left intact.

The problem is that the image must be rectangular as this is all that most image file formats support. The desired effect can still be obtained by first cropping the image, as before, to remove most of the unwanted material. Then select the Inverse option from the Select menu so that everything outside the ellipse is selected and everything within it is deselected. Pressing the Delete key then clears everything outside the ellipse, leaving what is effectively an elliptical picture. Figure 4.19 shows the end result, which will work just as well with much more elaborate shapes produced using the other selection tools.

Correcting perspective

The Crop tool can also be used to correct problems with perspective, such as converging verticals. This problem mainly occurs when buildings are photographed at relatively short range. The camera is usually aimed

Fig.4.19 Deleting everything outside the ellipse provides the desired effect

upwards slightly in order to get the top of the building into the photograph and avoid an excessive amount of empty foreground. Unfortunately, doing things this way results in the sides of the buildings leaning inwards towards the top. This is caused by a normal perspective effect, with the tops of the buildings looking smaller because they are further away. It is an effect that is mainly associated with wide-angle lenses. It tends to be more noticeable with wide-angle lenses as they give exaggerated perspective, but converging verticals are produced whenever the camera is used with a slight upward tilt.

While converging horizontals give an acceptable perspective effect, converging verticals tend to be perceived as the buildings being tilted away from the viewer and falling over. In other cases the photographs simply look a bit odd. Large format cameras have movements that can be used to avoid converging verticals, and there are expensive perspective control lenses available for some 35-millimetre and medium

Fig.4.20 Converging verticals can be dramatic, but are not always what you require

format cameras. Using digital photography it is not necessary to bother with any of this as you can take the photograph complete with converging verticals and correct it later. It is worth making the point that converging verticals can be used to make images look more dynamic, so in some cases their removal could be counterproductive. Only remove them if doing so will genuinely make the image look better.

Image editing programs often have more than one way of handling perspective corrections. Photoshop Elements is no exception, and one approach is to use the Distort function which is in the Transform submenu of the Image menu. The image used in this example (Figure 4.20) has the upper section of Big Ben in the background and an ornate streetlamp on Westminster Bridge in the foreground. The photograph was not taken using a wide-angle lens, but there

Fig.4.21 A new name can be added or the default can be accepted

is a big problem with converging verticals because the camera was aimed upwards at quite a steep angle. Some people might like it this way, but it was not the effect I was trying to achieve.

After selecting the Distort function an error message will probably appear on the screen stating that only layers can be distorted. Unlike Photoshop, Photoshop Elements does not automatically place everything on a layer, generating new layers as and when they are needed. This simplifies matters when undertaking the more basic types of processing, but it means that the main image has to be placed on a new layer before doing anything more complex. Operate the OK button to go ahead and

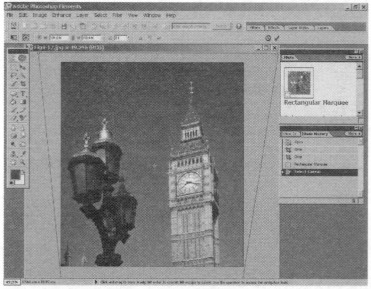

Fig.4.22 The image is adjusted via the handles

Fig.4.23 The straightened version of the image

generate a new layer. This produces the small dialogue box of Figure 4.21 where a name for the layer can be added if desired. Leave the other two settings unchanged and operate the OK button.

Eight handles should appear at the corners and edges of the image. It is advisable to display the image at a size that will comfortably fit onto the screen, and if necessary the Zoom Out option should be selected from the View menu. This gives plenty of room to manoeuvre when dragging the handles, at least some of which will have to be taken outside the image area. The corner handles can be moved freely, and when they are moved the image is distorted so that it fits exactly into the new shape. However, any part of the image that goes outside the canvas is clipped.

Fig.4.24 Distortions can be used to produce odd effects

To correct the perspective the top two corner handles are pulled outwards, just far enough to produce vertical verticals (Figure 4.22).

There can be a slight problem when a large amount of correction is used. In bringing the verticals properly upright the upper part of the image is widened slightly. This can produce a foreshortening effect, and in this case the clock face would appear to be slightly elliptical rather than circular. This can be corrected by pulling the top-centre handle upwards and (or) the bottom-centre handle downwards to make the image taller. Moving the side handles inwards to make the image narrower has essentially the same effect.

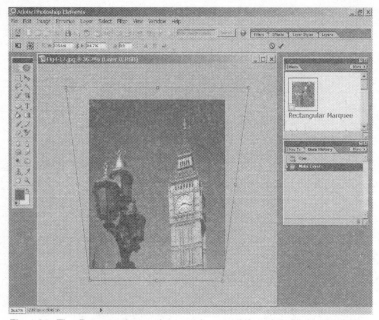

Fig.4.25 The Perspective option can be used if preferred, but it gives more restricted control

Stretching

When the image looks right, press the Return key to make the changes take effect. Operate the Escape key if you wish to abort the changes. Figure 4.23 shows the corrected version of the image. Of course, the Distort function is not restricted to correcting perspective problems, and it can be used to deliberately introduce wild distortions (Figure 4.24) if you like that type of thing. The Transform submenu has a Perspective command that operates in a similar fashion to the Distort type (Figure 4.25), but operating one of the corner handles results in equal and opposite movement in another handle. This is fine if symmetrical correction is required, but sometimes asymmetric correction looks better. It is a good idea to try both and use whichever one you find easier to work with.

Fig.4.26 The crop mask is rotated to match the rotation of the image

Alternatives

With image editing programs there is often more than one way of achieving the same or much the same result. It is definitely a good idea to read through the instruction manuals to determine the options that are available. Photoshop Elements is certainly not short of alternatives, and there is more than one way of rotating an image for example. The method described previously used the Rotate command to rotate the image followed by the Crop tool to tidy up the edges. However, it is actually possible to do the whole operation using the Crop command. Obviously this method is only applicable where the image is to be rotated and cropped, rather than rotated and then retouched so that no material is lost.

In order to rotate and crop an image, start by dragging a large rectangle onto the screen using the Crop tool. It is essential to leave some unselected areas around the selection so that you have room to manoeuvre. Then drag on the image but outside the selected area.

Fig.4.27 The image after combined rotation and cropping

This rotates the selection, and it must be carefully rotated so that the top edge is parallel to the horizon or the sides are parallel to the sloping vertical, as appropriate. Next, make any necessary adjustments to the selection by dragging the handles in the usual way.

This should produce something like Figure 4.26, and Figure 4.27 shows the cropped version of the image. As before, the sloping verticals have been straightened and a much more acceptable image has been produced. With an image that is seriously askew it is necessary to crop a significant amount of material from the edges of the picture. However, this method provides an almost instant fix where such cropping is acceptable.

Flipping

There are two options in the Rotate Image submenu that permit the image to be flipped horizontally or vertically. The Flip Horizontal option is mainly used where it is felt that a left-to-right reversal of the image gives a composition that fits better into a page layout. It works well with something like a still-life photograph where there is nothing to give away the fact that the image has been reversed. Figures 4.28 and 4.29 show "before" and "after" versions of a photograph that has been flipped horizontally.

It is essential to take due care when using the flip facility as it is easy to "drop a clanger". With most photographs it will be pretty obvious if they are flipped horizontally. Any text for example, will be converted into "mirror" writing in the flipped version of the image. Unusually, in Figure 4.29 this is not a problem because the sail of the dinghy has normal figures and "mirrored" figures showing through from the other side of the sail. It is unlikely that anyone would spot that the normal and "mirrored" figures had swapped places. In the vast majority of cases any "mirror" writing will be all too obvious.

With pictures of people, rings and watches appear on the wrong side, as do birthmarks, hair partings, etc. Over the years many magazines and newspapers have received complaints because they have flipped images of recognisable places. This type of inept manipulation of an image is usually pretty obvious. The flipped image of the Houses of Parliament shown in Figure 4.30 for example, clearly has Big Ben on the wrong end of the building. Always check a horizontally flipped image for any telltale signs that it has been altered. It tends to be of most use with a very basic and text-free composition such as the example used in chapter 2 (see Figures 2.4 and 2.5).

The Flip Canvas Vertical option produces an upside-down version of the image (Figure 4.31), but this is not the same as turning the picture upside-down using 180 degrees of rotation (Figure 4.32). The picture in Figure 4.31 is a "mirror" image of the original, which is demonstrated by the mirrored lettering, whereas the rotated image is not. With this book turned upside-down the nameplate in Figure 4.32 still says "Olympus", but this is clearly not the case with Figure 4.31. Rotation by 180 degrees must therefore be used if you wish to turn an upside-down image the right way up. The Flip Canvas Vertical function is mainly used for producing mirrored effects.

Hard copy

Image editing programs normally have the standard Print command, but there is often an additional feature that gives more options. In Photoshop Elements this is the Print Preview facility (Figure 4.33) and it

Fig.4.28 The original version of the image

is accessed via the File menu. Note that Figure 4.33 shows the Print
Preview window with the Show More Options checkbox ticked, so that
some additional options are provided in the lower section of the window.
By default the image is centred on the page, but the image in the preview
panel can be dragged to a new position if the tick is removed from the
Center Image checkbox. The position of the image on the page can
then be set by entering values into the Position textboxes if preferred.

The size of the image can be altered by entering a percentage into the
Scale textbox. Alternatively, a size can be entered into the Height and
Width textboxes, or the image can be resized by dragging the handles
on the preview image. In fact the image can be resized by dragging on
the edges of the preview image as well. If the dragging method is used

Fig.4.29 The horizontally flipped version of the picture

to reposition and (or) resize the image, the relevant textboxes will be automatically updated to reflect the changes.

Note that the four handles only appear on the preview image if the Show Bounding Box checkbox is ticked, and that the image can not be dragged to a new size unless this box is present. Also note that it is not possible to alter the aspect ratio of the image using the Print Preview facility. Make any changes of this type prior to the printing stage using the Image Size facility and (or) the Crop tool. Tick the Scale to Fit Media checkbox in order to print the image as large as possible without any cropping occurring.

There are various options available in the bottom section of the Print Preview window. Operating the Background button enables a

Fig.4.30 Flipping this image horizontally is less than convincing, with Big Ben at the wrong end of the Houses of Parliament!

background colour to be selected. In other words, the normally white area around the picture can be printed the selected colour. As most printers can not print right out to the edges of the paper, there will usually be a white border outside the background area. Operating the Border button produces a small dialogue box that enables the size of the border to be specified. A black border of this width is then added around the image.

Corner crop marks and a caption beneath the image can be added by ticking the appropriate checkboxes. The caption is not added via the Print Preview window though. It is added by going to the File menu and selecting the File Info option. This produces the dialogue box of Figure 4.34, which enables various types of information to be entered. Some file formats such as TIFF, Jpeg, and Photoshop's PSD format permit various types of information to be saved with images. In this case it is only the caption facility that is of interest, and the required caption is entered into the Caption textbox. With the Caption checkbox in the Print Preview window ticked, your text will be printed centrally and immediately

Fig.4.31 This image has been flipped vertically

Fig.4.32 This image has been rotated through 180 degrees

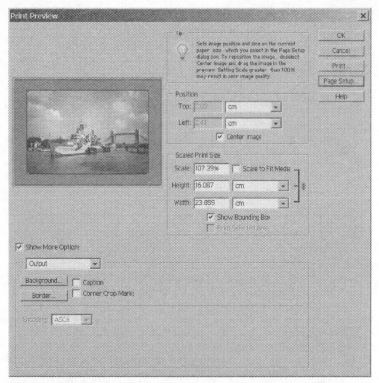

Fig.4.33 The Print Preview window has a useful range of options, including different background colours, resizing and positioning options, and a caption facility

below the image in black. Where more control of the captioning is required, the text must be added to the image using the text tools.

Operating the Page Setup button in the Print Preview window produces the control panel for the default printer. This permits things like paper size, orientation, and print quality to be altered. The options available depend on the printer in use, and this window is therefore different for each printer. The instruction manual for your printer should have detailed explanations of all the available options.

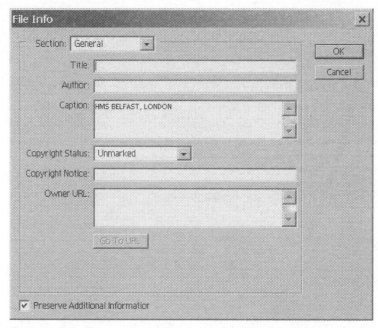

Fig.4.34 A caption can be added via the File Info dialogue box

Points to remember

In an ideal world it would not be necessary to edit photographs. In the real world most images can be improved by applying some simple processing such as cropping and rotation. On the other hand, it is a mistake to process every image regardless of its merits. Apply processing because an image needs improvement and not just for the sake of it.

An image has a physical size and a size in pixels. The latter is often called the canvas size or something similar. The physical size is often of no consequence with images that will be used in web pages. It is usually the size in pixels that has to be adjusted in order to make an image fit into the allotted space on a web page. For desktop publishing and making prints it is the physical size that is of importance.

The number of pixels often has to be reduced to make an image fit a web page. This inevitably results in a loss of detail, which has the potential to make the image unusable. Low resolution works best with images that have simple composition and do not contain masses of detail. The number of pixels can be increased when making relatively large prints. This keeps the pixels small but does not add detail and might not give good results.

It is often necessary to crop an image in order to remove irrelevant but distracting material near the edges. It can also be used to alter the composition and find images within the overall image. Bear in mind that cropping an image reduces the number of pixels and the maximum print size that will produce acceptable results..

Most image editing software enables images to be rotated by small amounts to correct problems with sloping horizons, etc. Rotation produces four blank triangular areas at the edges that must be cropped or retouched.

Converging verticals can be used to produce dynamic results, but they often just give the impression that buildings are falling over, or that room interiors were build by someone who was drunk at the time. Most image editing programs have at least one facility that can be used to correct converging verticals, or add them in order to produce zany effects.

Flipping a picture will sometimes produce a composition that fits into a web page better than the original, or you may simply prefer the image that way around. Due care needs to be taken though, and flipping does not usually work with pictures of recognisable places or where there is text in the image. It can give problems with other subject matter including pictures of people.

Colour mixing

Mixing it

There are three main aspects to optimising photographs, and one of these (cropping, rotation, etc.) was covered in the previous chapter. The second is retouching and similar manipulations, which are non-essential but open up a range of possibilities that can provide much improved images. Retouching and related processes are covered in a later chapter. The third aspect is getting the colour balance correct. In other words, getting rid of any colour bias in the photograph, or adding one to give the desired effect. Changes to the brightness and contrast are also included in the third category, since changing either of these has an effect on the colours.

With image editing programs there are two main aspects to colour, which are mixing a colour to use when drawing or painting on the screen, and adjusting the colour balance of the image. Adjusting the colour balance is much easier if you already understand colour mixing, so we will start with the mixing process. You may never need to mix a colour so that you can paint with for retouching purposes, as there are usually better ways of handling things. It is still necessary to mix colours for other purposes though, such as selecting the required text or background colour.

There is an obvious problem when discussing colour in a book that is printed in black and white. There is no way of showing colours or changes in colour. Even if this book was printed in colour, there is no guarantee that the colour reproduction would be accurate enough to illustrate the points properly. In order to follow the material in this chapter you really need to have Photoshop Elements up and running on your PC so that you can try things for yourself and see the results of adjusting the colour controls. It is a good idea to do things this way with all the subjects covered in this book, but it is especially important when dealing with colour. Remember that the free demonstration version of Photoshop Elements has a full range of features, and is all you need in order to try any aspect of the program for yourself.

Colour models

There are several ways of handling colour when using photo-editing software, but you are only likely to encounter these three:

RGB (red, green, blue)

HSB (hue, saturation, brightness)

CMYK (cyan, magenta, yellow, black)

Photoshop Elements only uses the first two for colour mixing, but for the sake of completeness all three will be considered here. The normal way of mixing or picking colours with Photoshop Elements is to use the Color Picker (Figure 5.1). The Color Picker can be launched by left-clicking on the foreground or background squares (the coloured squares) near the bottom of the Toolbox. It is then used to choose a new foreground or background colour, depending on which button was operated.

When the pointer is outside the Color Picker window it changes to the pointer for the Eyedropper tool. The purpose of the eyedropper tool is to permit a colour within an image to be selected. Simply left-click with the tip of the pointer on the desired colour and it will be set as the current foreground or background colour, as appropriate. It can be difficult to select the required colour in areas where there are fine textures, but the easy way around this is to zoom in on the area of interest.

Select the Zoom tool from the Toolbox and then drag a rectangle around the part of the image that is of interest. This area will then be expanded to fill the image window. It will probably be possible to see the individual pixels, making it easy to select the desired colour. Select Fit on Screen from the View menu to return the full image to the screen at something close to the largest size that will fit into the available space. The basic colour in the Color Picker can also be changed by moving the slider on either side of the bar down the middle of the window.

RGB

RGB is the system used to produce the colours on televisions and computer monitors. In theory at any rate, a full range of colours can be produced by mixing these three primary colours at the right intensities. Photoshop Elements uses 24-bit RGB colour, with eight bits being used

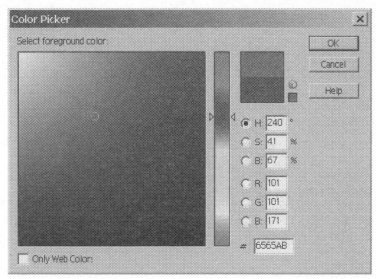

Fig.5.1 The standard version of the Color Picker

for each primary colour. For each primary colour this gives 256 different intensities from 0 (off) to 255 (maximum). The total number of colours available is 256 x 256 x 256, which works out nearly 16.8 million different colours. Estimates of the number of colours that can be perceived by average human vision vary somewhat. Most seem to put the figure at considerably less than 16.8 million.

Using the same intensity for each colour provides a greyscale that has 254 shades of grey plus black and white. This is more than adequate to produce good black and white images, or greyscale images as they are more accurately called. You can demonstrate that identical values produce greys by typing the same value for R, G, and B into the appropriate textboxes of the Color Picker. The circle in the large panel in the left-hand section of the Color Picker shows the currently selected colour, and will instantly respond to changes in these values. The two rectangles near the top of the colour bar show the newly selected colour (top) and the colour that was already in use (bottom). The upper rectangle responds to changes in the colour values so that you can clearly see newly selected colours. Left-click the lower rectangle if you change your mind and wish to return to the original colour selection.

By using different intensities for the primary colours it is possible to produce a wide range of colours. In theory a full range of colours can be produced, but it pays to bear in mind that real-world monitors and printing systems have some limitations. A huge range of colours can still be produced though, giving convincing results with practically any image. In general with the RGB system, the higher the values used, the lighter the colour that is produced.

Some image editing software has slider controls that can be used to vary the red, green, and blue levels, which in theory makes it easy to mix any colour. In practice it can be very tricky to precisely mix the required colour using this method. With Photoshop Elements it is possible to operate the R, G, or B radio button in the Color Picker and then use the slider control on the colour bar to vary the intensity of the selected primary colour. You can therefore mix a colour by adjusting the intensities of the primary colours if you prefer to do things this way. It is likely that it will prove to be much more difficult than you expected, and it is definitely a good idea to try the HSB method. After a little acclimatisation, most people find the HSB system the easier one to work with.

CMYK

Before going on to the HSB system it is perhaps as well to consider the CMYK colour model. If you learned to mix colours in art classes at school you are probably puzzled by the primary colours being red, green, and blue. When mixing paints the primary colours are red, blue and yellow, except red and blue are not really true primary colours. In order to get accurate colours it is necessary to respectively use cyan and magenta instead of blue and red.

The primary colours for projected light (as in a monitor) and reflected light (as in painting and hard copy from colour printers) are different. If you did physics at school, you no doubt did projected light experiments where the primary colours suddenly (and confusingly) became different to the ones used in the art classes. This is because projected light is additive, and mixing the primary colours therefore produces white, as in the well known physics experiment. Reflected light is subtractive, and mixing the primary colours produces a dark grey colour.

By mixing cyan, magenta, and yellow inks or paints it is possible to produce a wide range of colours, but only in middle tones. Some artists obtain lighter tones by mixing white with the basic colour. Watercolourists mostly rely on using white paper with the paint applied thinly so that the paper shows through. Colour printers such as inkjet units use the watercolourist method of producing pale colours and, of course, white. Thus, using coloured paper in an inkjet printer produces some odd results.

Dark colours are produced by mixing black with the three primary colours. Four inks (cyan, magenta, yellow, and black) are therefore used in inkjet printers. I assume that K rather than B is used for black in CMYK because B is already used for blue in RGB. Note that some inkjet printers use more than four inks in an attempt to obtain better colour accuracy, but they still use what is essentially the CMYK system. The additional inks are usually lighter versions of cyan and magenta.

Most image editing software operates in the RGB colour mode, as used for computer monitors. This does not mean that these programs can not be used with a CMYK device such as an inkjet printer. The program and the printer driver software will convert the RGB colour values into CMYK equivalents and should produce reasonably accurate results. Real-world monitors and printers have their limitations, and some compromises usually have to be made during the conversion process, but results should be as accurate as the hardware permits. Even where a photo-editing program does have a CMYK colour mode, there is usually no point in switching to it when producing hard copy on a non-professional CMYK device such as an ordinary inkjet printer.

HSB

HSB is similar to the CMYK method, but it uses a range of preset colours, or hues. Although it can handle the RGB method, the Photoshop Elements Color Picker seems to be primarily aimed at this method of colour selection. The hues are the colours in the colour bar, and the full rainbow spectrum of colours is included here. The colour value runs from 0 to 359 degrees, and it is based on the positions of colours on a conventional artist's colour wheel. One of the basic colours can be modified by changing its saturation and brightness. Saturation is the purity of the colour, and it is a pure red, blue, or whatever with 100 percent saturation. Lower saturations are produced by mixing neutral grey with the selected colour. This gives a less strong colour, with neutral grey being produced at zero percent saturation.

Note that mixing grey into a colour reduces the strength of the colour, but not its brightness. The latter is controlled via the third setting, and this runs from zero with no brightness (black) to 100 at maximum brightness. Although zero brightness always produces black, maximum brightness does not necessarily produce pure white. If the saturation value is more than 0, some colour will be added to the white. The left-hand panel of the Color Picker shows all the variations for a given hue value. Colours higher up the panel have greater brightness than those further down. The further to the right, the stronger the colour saturation.

This gives black along the bottom of the panel and a greyscale up the left-hand side. Anywhere else there is a true variation on the selected hue. Bright colours with strong saturation are found towards the top right-hand corner, and dark colours with strong saturation are available in the bottom right-hand corner. Colours in the top left-hand corner have weak colour but high brightness, while those in the bottom left-hand corner have low brightness and weak colour content.

This system can be a bit confusing at first, but it is actually very easy to use. Suppose you require a dark but strong blue colour. The saturation must be high to give the strong colour but the brightness must be fairly low in order to produce a suitably dark shade of blue. The likely location of the required colour is therefore about half way up the main panel (about half brightness) and well over to the right (strong colour saturation).

To find the required colour it is a matter of setting the pointers on the colour bar to the middle of the range of blue colours, and then looking at the appropriate area of the main panel. If a suitable colour can not be seen, moving the pointers up and down slightly should produce something suitable. When a suitable colour is found, left-click on it and look at the appropriate rectangle to the right of the panel, where the selected colour will be displayed. Remember that the upper rectangle shows the currently selected colour, and the lower rectangle shows the colour that was in use previously. Try left-clicking around the initial point to see if a better result can be obtained.

If you find a colour that is close to the one you require, but you would like to experiment further, make a note of the RGB values. You can then go back to that colour at a later time, should you wish to do so. An alternative ploy is to select it by operating the OK button and then go back into the Color Picker. The colour selected previously will then be shown in the lower rectangle to the right of the main colour panel, which is handy for comparison purposes. In order to revert to the previous colour selection, either left-click on the lower rectangle and operate the OK button, or just operate the Cancel button.

As a simple example of colour selection I tried to match the deep red colour of a pen in the collection of oddments on my computer desk, and

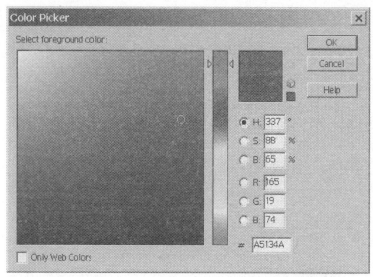

*Fig.5.2 More or less the expected settings produced the required
colour*

Figure 5.2 shows the result. As expected, the required colour was about
one third or so down the main panel and well over to the right. Even if
the correct colour was somewhere else on the panel, it would soon be
spotted. Once you have a basic understanding of the Color Picker it can
be used to quickly produce any required colour.

Greyscale

Greyscale images can be handled by the RGB colour mode, but there is
a Grayscale mode available in the Mode submenu of the Image menu. It
is better to use this mode for greyscale images as it gives smaller file
sizes. Only one byte per pixel is required for greyscale images as
opposed to three bytes per pixel for colour images. Greyscale images
loaded into Photoshop Elements, and most other image editing programs,
will use greyscale operation by default.

A colour image can be converted to a greyscale type by selecting the
Grayscale mode. Answer OK when a warning message asks if you wish
to discard the colour information. While the image is still loaded it is
possible to go back to the original version by selecting the Revert option

Fig.5.3 This dithered image is just about recognisable

from the File menu. However, the colour information is lost for ever once the image is saved. It is advisable to make copies of the original colour versions so that you can go back to these if it should prove necessary to do so at a later date.

Selecting the Color Picker in the greyscale mode does actually produce the standard version of the Color Picker, and the colour bar is still present down the middle Color Picker window. However, using the controls to select a colour actually results in what the program deems to be an equivalent shade of grey being selected. When using the Color Picker in the Grayscale mode it is only the shades of grey down the right-hand side of the main colour panel that are of interest.

Fig.5.4 Dithering has worked a bit better with this image

Bitmap

The term bitmap tends to be used for any image that is made up of pixels. In the early days of computing, bitmap images were true bitmaps that used one bit per pixel. The problem in using just one bit of information for each pixel is that it limits each pixel to two states. In other words, each pixel is either black or white, with no shades of grey available. Bitmap images do not necessarily appear to be strictly black and white though.

It is possible to produce a pseudo greyscale from black and white dots using a process known as dithering, but this only works if the dots are small enough to "fool" the eye. The basic technique is to use several dots per pixel. By using a lot of black dots per pixel, what appears to be a dark pixel is produced. Using a few dots per pixel gives what appears to be a light pixel. Dithering works well with something like a monochrome laser printer where the individual dots are so small that they can not be seen by the human eye.

The Bitmap mode of Photoshop Elements can use a form of dithering to produce a pseudo greyscale, but with one dot per pixel it is inevitable that images become greatly simplified when converted to this mode. Figure 5.3 shows the improved version of the Big Ben photograph, but it has been converted to a greyscale image and then to a bitmap. Note that it is not possible to convert direct from a colour image to a bitmap type. Clearly a great deal of information has been lost in the conversion, and the converted image is barely recognisable. Simple bitmaps work better with some pictures than with others, and it is rather more convincing when applied to the photograph of a fake Leica camera (Figure 5.4).

Better results can be obtained by boosting the number of pixels during the conversion. The small dialogue box of Figure 5.5 appears when the Bitmap option is selected. Various types of dithering are available from the Method menu near the bottom of the window. The upper section shows the input and output resolution of the image. The input resolution is the resolution used in the non-converted image, and by default the output figure is exactly the same. For this example the output resolution was

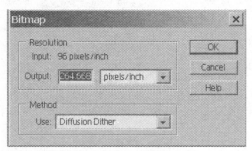

Fig.5.5 The Bitmap dialogue box

increased from about 264 dots per inch to 600 dots per inch. The converted image therefore has about 5 dots for each pixel in the original image, giving much more scope for producing a pseudo greyscale using dithering. Figure 5.6 shows the converted image, which clearly has much more detail than the original version of Figure 5.3.

In practice it is unlikely that it would be necessary to resort to the Bitmap mode and dithering where good quality is required. Greyscale operation would give better results. The Bitmap mode is normally used to deliberately introduce graininess as a special effect. It is not essential to use any form of dithering in the bitmap mode. Figure 5.7 shows the Big Ben photograph converted to Bitmap mode, but using the 50% Threshold option of the Model menu. This model operates on the simple system of setting a pixel to black or white depending on whether its brightness is above or below 50 percent brightness. The result can be quite dramatic, as in this case, but it can go seriously wrong. There can be large areas

Fig.5.6 Increasing the number of dots gives better results

of black and white and the picture might look like nothing much at all. It works best with simple compositions that have good contrast.

When saving a bitmap image you might find that it can not be saved using the original file format. This is simply because some formats do not support something as basic as a true black and white bitmap. One solution is to save the image in a format that does support this type of image, such as TIFF or Photoshop's own PSD format. If you need the image in a format that does not support basic bitmaps, such as Jpeg, the image can be converted back to a greyscale type again. Only two grey levels (black and white) will be used in the converted image though,

Fig.5.7 This image is strictly black and white with no dithering

so it will still look the same as the true bitmap. This is demonstrated by Figure 5.8, which is the Jpeg version of the PSD image shown in Figure 5.7.

Indexed Color

There is a fourth mode available in Photoshop Elements, and it is called Indexed Color. This mode is used when the final output will be to a device that supports a relatively limited range of colours. These days most monitors and printers support a huge colour range, making the Indexed Color mode of relatively little use. Its main application is probably

Fig.5.8 The Jpeg version of Fig.5.7 looks much the same

in the production of images for web pages. The problem in mixing web colours on one computer is that they may be somewhat different when displayed on another computer. One reason for this is simply that different monitors produce different colours from the same colour values. In actual fact, the same monitor will produce different colours depending on how it is set up.

A second problem is that not all computers have the same colour capabilities. The main problem here is differences between Macintosh computers and PCs. There can be differences between computers of the same general type, and some PCs have simple graphics cards offering relatively few colours, while others have graphics systems that can handle

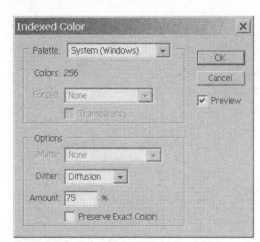

Fig.5.9 The Indexed Color dialogue box

millions of different colours. However, this is not a major problem these days as even budget PCs and most laptops tend to have good graphics capabilities.

It is the Macintosh and PC differences that are of prime concern to most web designers. There is no point in them worrying about poorly adjusted monitors, since there is nothing web designers can do about it. The Macintosh/PC problem is different. There is a set of so-called "browser safe" or "web safe" colours that can be reproduced by the popular Microsoft and Netscape browsers in both their Windows and Macintosh versions. Using these 200 or so colours does not guarantee that precisely the specified colour will be produced on every computer, but it does at least keep the inevitable divergences to a minimum.

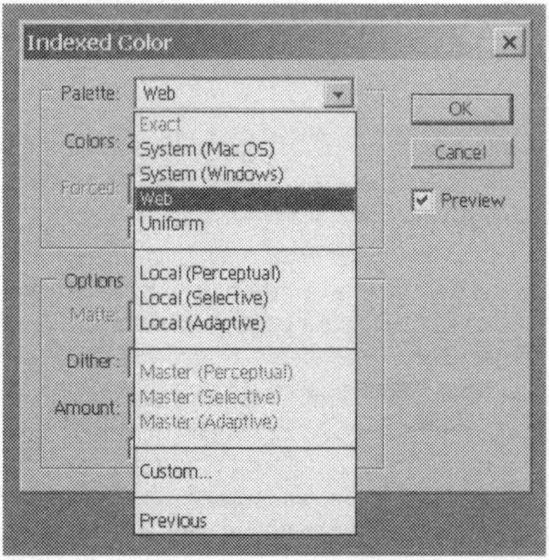

A small dialogue box like the one in Figure 5.9 appears when the Indexed Color mode is selected. In this example Photoshop Elements is running on a PC, so it is the

Fig.5.10 The Web option gives the 216 "web safe" colours

Fig.5.11 The normal version of the rose photograph

Windows system colours that are offered by default. Various options are available from the Palette menu though (Figure 5.10), and it is the Web option that provides the web safe colours. If you try converting a colour photograph to this mode it will probably not look much different after the conversion. This is perhaps a little surprising when one considers that the maximum number of colours on the screen has been probably been reduced from millions to just 216.

The reason for the lack of change is that Photoshop uses dithering in an attempt minimise any change in appearance. Zooming in will often reveal the dithering, with the smooth changes in colour being replaced by a noticeable pattern. Figures 5.11 and 5.12 respectively show close-up "before" and "after" views of a photograph of a rose. Although the dithering is obvious on close inspection, it is usually something less than obvious with the image viewed at normal size, which is really all you need to be concerned about with web images. When using the Indexed

Fig.5.12 The "web safe" version has a grainier appearance

Color mode with web safe colours, the Color Picker will not automatically limit the selection to web safe colours (Figure 5.13). However, it will do so if the Only Web Colors checkbox near the bottom left-hand corner of the window is ticked.

Whether it is worth bothering with web safe colours when producing photographic images is debatable. Slightly improved colour accuracy may well be obtained, but only at the expense of somewhat grainier images. This is a subjective matter that you have to judge for yourself. I prefer not to bother with web safe colours for images that will be used on the Internet.

Greyscale to colour

It is worth noting that it is possible to convert a greyscale image to a colour type such as RGB. This might seem pointless, since the converted

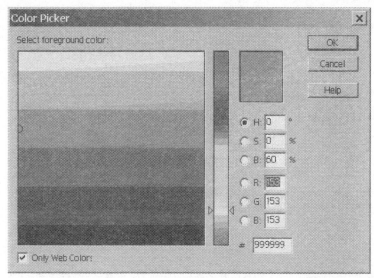

Fig.5.13 The Color Picker with the Only Web Color option selected

image will still be a black and white type, and colours will not miraculously appear after the conversion. However, once the image is a colour type it is possible to add coloured text, adjust the colour balance to produce a sepia effect like the one used for old photographic prints, add colour to parts of the image to make them stand out, and so on. You can even try colouring the image to make it look like a genuine colour image.

Swatches

Operating the Swatches tab towards the right end of the Options bar produces a colour swatch (Figure 5.14), and this

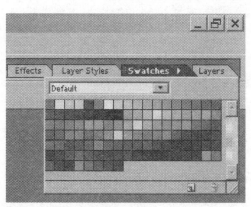

Fig.5.14 The Swatches palette

is a common feature in photo-editing programs. The menu at the top of the palette enables a range of swatches to be accessed, including one that contains all 216 "web safe" colours. The preset swatches are a useful feature, but the swatches are even more useful if you add your own custom colours. This gives almost instant access to any colours that you use regularly.

To add a colour, first set it as the current foreground colour, either by mixing it using the Color Picker, or by selecting it from an image using the Eyedropper tool. Next place the pointer in the vacant area near the bottom of the swatches palette that you wish to augment. The pointer will turn into the paint bucket icon when it is over a suitable section of the

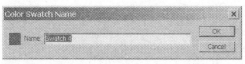

palette. Left-click the mouse and a small dialogue box like the one of Figure 5.15 will appear. Change the default name of the colour if you wish, and then operate the OK

Fig.5.15 The new swatch can be renamed

button. The new swatch should then appear at the bottom of the Swatches palette, and it can be used in the same way as the other colours. Just left-click on a colour and it will be set as the current foreground colour. A swatch can be removed by dragging it to the Trashcan button in the bottom right-hand corner of the Swatches palette.

There are a couple of arrows in the Toolbox close to the foreground and background colour buttons, and operating this button results in the foreground and background colours being swapped. This is useful if you wish to paint with the background colour. Just operate the button, complete the painting operation, and then operate the button again to return things to normal. Operating the other small button near the bottom of the Toolbox sets the foreground and background colours back to the default settings, which are black and white respectively.

Wrong colour

Sometimes when using the Eyedropper tool to pick a colour from an image the colour obtained does looks very different to the area of colour that you selected. Making several attempts to select the colour can produce a series of totally different results! The reason for these discrepancies is that an area that appears to be filled with more of less the same colour actually contains a complex pattern of colours. In some

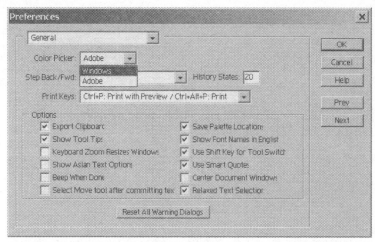

Fig.5.16 An alternative version of the Color Picker can be selected

cases the pattern of colours is real, but you do not normally look close enough to notice it. Often the problem is caused by an image that has been scanned from a newspaper or magazine, and the multi-coloured dots are simply part of the printing process. Many colour printing processes use dithering plus a few colours to give the illusion of a full colour range.

With the default setting the Eyedropper tool samples a single pixel at the point on the screen that was left-clicked. Results are often better if it is set to sample either a 3 by 3 or 5 by 5 block of pixels. When sampling a block of pixels the colour produced is the average of all the pixels sampled. The sample setting can be altered by right-clicking somewhere on the image with the Eyedropper tool selected. Then select the required option from the popup menu. Rather than repeatedly left-clicking when searching for the right colour, try dragging the Eyedropper tool while looking at the foreground colour in the Toolbox. The colour of this rectangle will change as the Eyedropper tool is dragged around the image, making it easier to find the required colour.

Alternative picker

An alternative version of the Color Picker can be selected by going to the Edit menu and selecting Preferences and then General from the submenu that appears. This produces the dialogue box of Figure 5.16

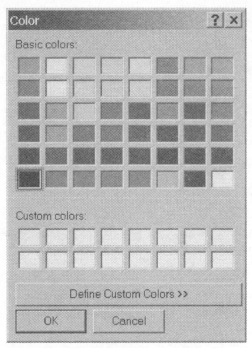

Fig.5.17 The alternative colour window

where Windows can be selected from the Color Picker menu. Activating the Color Picker then produces the window of Figure 5.17, which is really just a collection of colour swatches rather than a colour mixer. However, operating the Define Custom Color button creates the enlarged version of the window shown in Figure 5.18.

The right-hand section of the window looks similar to the standard Color Picker, but there are some major differences. The basic set of colours appears across the top of the main panel, and less saturated versions of these colours are provided below. The colours become less and less saturated towards the bottom of the panel, producing neutral grey along the bottom. A full range of colours is provided on the main panel, but only at middle brightness. However, the slider control to the right of the main colour panel enables the selected colour to be lightened or darkened.

Colour selection is therefore a matter of first selecting the nearest colour on the main panel, and then adjusting the slider control for the correct brightness. Alternatively, set a brightness level and then drag the pointer around the main panel until the required colour is obtained. The rectangle below the main panel shows the currently selected colour. Simply operate the OK button to exit the Color Picker and set the new colour as the new foreground or background colour. In order to add the new colour to the custom swatches in the left-hand section of the window, left-click on one of the swatches to select it. Then left-click the Add to Custom Color button, and the new colour will be added to the selected custom swatch.

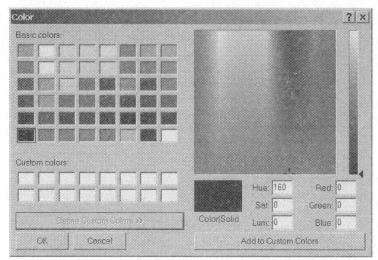

Fig.5.18 Here the window has expanded to provide the alternative version of the Color Picker

Once you get used to it, the Adobe version of the Color Picker is probably the easier to use. However, the Windows version is more typical of the way other programs handle colour selection. It might be preferable to use the Windows method if that is one you already use with other programs, or if you simply find that method works best for you.

Points to remember

The primary colours for reflected light, as in painting and printing, are cyan, magenta, and yellow. Inkjet printers produce the basic colours from inks of these three colours. Black ink is added to produce darker colours, and less ink plus the whiteness of the paper is used to produce the lighter colours. This system is known as the CMYK colour model. Expect some odd results if you use coloured paper with an inkjet printer.

The primary colours for projected light are different to those for reflected light. They are red, green, and blue, and these are the primary colours used by colour monitors and television sets. This is known as the RGB system. Most image editing programs use the RGB system to handle colour, but there is often the option of using another system or systems. There is no need to switch to CMYK operation when producing hard copy on an inkjet printer. The applications and driver software should make an accurate conversion from one system to the other.

It is difficult to mix accurate colours using the RGB system, so many image editing programs offer an alternative. This is usually in the form of HSB (hue, saturation, and brightness) system, or a slight variation on it. The hue controls gives access to a range of basic colours. The saturation control governs the strength of the selected colour, and the brightness control is just an ordinary brightness type.

Dithering uses small dots to give what looks like a greyscale image even though it only uses only black dots on white paper. A similar system can be used with cyan, magenta, yellow, and black dots to produce colour images. Most colour printers use this system with its optical mixing rather than genuinely mixing the ink to produce a range of colours.

A true bitmap mode gives only black and white images, but a pseudo greyscale can be produced using dithering. The main use of bitmaps is as a special effect to produce images that are strictly black and white with no attempt at a pseudo greyscale being made. This type of thing generally works best with images that are simple but bold compositions.

There are 216 so-called "web safe" colours that should be produced accurately on properly adjusted Macintosh and Windows computers. Whether it is worth limiting photographic images to this limited colour set is debatable. The advantages could be outweighed by the drawbacks.

Colour and contrast

In control

For many users the biggest advantage of the digital approach to photography is the tremendous control that can be exercised over the colour balance of an image. A similar degree of control is probably available using conventional photographic printing techniques, but few photographers do their own colour processing. For those that do, getting things just right can be a slow, difficult, and expensive business.

Most amateur photographers rely on commercial processing, and you are then at the mercy of the processing laboratory. Machine printing inevitably gets it wrong in a significant percentage of cases, resulting in washed out sunsets, unrealistic skin tones, interior shots with strong orange colour casts, and so on. Getting handmade enlargements produced is an expensive business with no guarantee that the end result will match your requirements.

The situation is very different with shots taken using a digital camera, or digital scans taken from photographic prints, negatives, or transparencies. Using an image editing program it is easy to remove even quite strong colour casts, sunsets can be as subtle or gaudy as you like, and skin tones can be perfect every time. Using the selection tools it is also possible to process certain parts of the image while leaving others unaltered. Problems such as "red-eye" can usually be corrected in a matter of seconds. In fact you have complete control over the colour balance of digital images.

Of course, you do not have to stick with the original colours at all. There is plenty of scope for being creative with colour. The same techniques that permit "red-eye" to be corrected also enable any object to be given a new colour. If you require an image that has blue roses and red bananas it is quite possible to do this using most image editing programs. In fact any object in an image can be selected and turned to any desired colour.

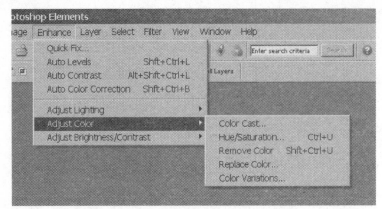

Fig.6.1 The Enhance menu provides access to a range of facilities for adjusting colour balance, brightness, and contrast

Enhance menu

In Photoshop Elements most of the facilities required for adjusting colour, contrast, and brightness are to be found in the Enhance menu and its submenus (Figure 6.1). Some of the facilities require little explanation, such as the brightness and contrast controls, but others are a little more involved. Although most images can benefit from the facilities available in this menu, it is not a good idea to start altering things like colour balance and contrast just because the facilities are there. You should resort to the Enhance menu because there is something wrong with the image that you wish to correct, or there is an enhancement you would like to make. Fiddling with the settings for the sake of it is likely to make images worse rather than better.

Variations

Correcting colour imbalances by adjusting the relative strengths of primary colours is the obvious way of handling things, but this method is a skilled task. Most image editing programs provide at least one more simple method, and Photoshop Elements is no exception. The easiest method I have encountered is to have thumbnail versions of the image with a different type of correction applied to each one (lighter, darker, redder, etc.). In Photoshop Elements this facility is provided via the Color Variations option. Figure 6.2 shows the Color Variations window, which is launched by selecting the Color Variations option from the Adjust Color

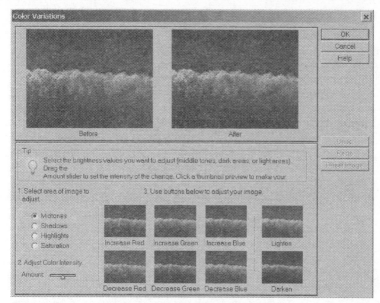

Fig.6.2 The normal version of the Variations window

submenu. The top section of the window shows "Before" and "After" versions of the image, but these will obviously be the same initially.

The lower section of the window shows six variations that have extra red, green, and blue, and reduced amounts of these colours. It is possible but unlikely that one of these variations will be exactly what is required. In that event, it is just a matter of left-clicking on the appropriate version, and the modified image will then adjust to match it. Operate the OK button to return to the image and make the changes take effect.

In most cases some extra processing will be required. The basic colour casts are reasonably strong, but by double-clicking on one of the tinted images two or three times it is possible to obtain even stronger effects. You can also double-click on different images to combine two tints. Double-clicking on the lighter and darker images in the right-hand section of the window respectively lightens or darkens the modified image by a small amount. Again, double-clicking two or three times gives a stronger effect. In this way it is possible to gradually "fine tune" the image until it is exactly as required.

Simply left-click the unmodified image or operate the Reset Image button to remove all the processing and start again. The OK button is operated

Fig.6.3 The original version of the image

when the desired effect is obtained, or the Cancel button is operated if you change your mind and wish to abandon the processing. The Undo button can be used to step back through the changes made, which is useful if things go slightly awry but you do not wish to go right back to the beginning. The Redo button can be used to reinstate changes.

Near the bottom left-hand corner of the window there is a small slider control that can be used to increase or reduce the amount of change per mouse click. The eight thumbnail views that show the variations will respond to this slider and shown the amount of change each mouse click will produce. It can be useful to move this control a little to the left

Fig.6.4 In this version the contrast has been reduced

in order to correct minor colour casts, of for "fine tuning" larger changes. The changes tend to become quite large if it is moved to the right, but this can be useful for combating strong colour casts or adding special effects.

Shadows and highlights

The four radio buttons above the slider control provide individual adjustment of the highlights, mid tones, shadows, and colour saturation. The mid tone option is used by default, and you might find that the desired

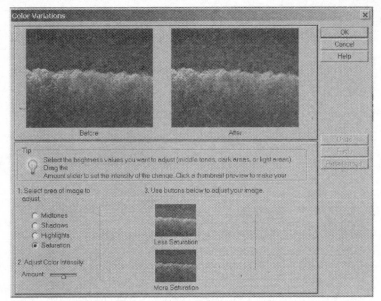

*Fig.6.5 The version of the Variations window for altering colour
        saturation*

correction can be obtained using this option. For best results the
processing should be applied separately to the shadows, mid tones,
and highlights. It is not possible to show the results of colour changes
here, but Figure 6.3 shows the original image while Figure 6.4 shows
one that has had the highlights darkened, and the shadows lightened.
This has reduced the contrast of the image, which shows that the Color
Variations screen provides contrast control, even if it is via a slightly
roundabout method.

Saturation

The fourth radio button permits the colour saturation to be controlled,
and the Color Variations window changes when this option is selected.
The simplified layout of Figure 6.5 is provided, and this still has the original
and current versions of the picture at the top. There are only two versions
of the image in the lower part of the window though. These show a less
saturated version of the image and a more saturated version. It is
important not to confuse brightness and saturation. The overall brightness

Fig.6.6 A high level of saturation can produce some odd effects

of a more saturated image is likely to be a little higher than that of a less saturated version, but this is not the main change.

Increasing the saturation produces stronger and purer colours. Reducing saturation gives weaker colours. In fact a greyscale image will be obtained if the saturation is reduced too far. In theory it is possible to make weak colours as strong as required by increasing the saturation, but with real-world images there can be problems. The usual problem is graininess or patterns appearing in what should be plain areas of the image. Figure 6.6 shows the type of thing that happens, but it is somewhat watered down by the conversion to black and white. While high saturation levels can produce some interesting and atmospheric effects, most of the time this will probably not be what you are trying to achieve.

Changes in the colour saturation are not only used to correct a saturation problem in the original image. Increasing the overall brightness of a picture tends to give weaker colours, and increasing the saturation slightly should cure the problem. Similarly, reducing the overall brightness might give excessively strong colours. This should be corrected by a slight reduction in the colour saturation.

Clipping

When adjusting colour, contrast, or brightness, it is important to be aware of a potential problem called clipping. Clipping is where one or more of the primary colours would be pushed beyond their maximum or minimum values by the processing. Of course, the values would not actually be taken beyond the normal limits. They would be set at the maximum or minimum figures, as appropriate. The problem with clipping is that very light and dark areas tend to become enlarged, with no detail at all in those areas. This will not necessarily matter, but in some instances it will result in the loss of important details. Where only one or two of the primary colours are clipped there will be a change in the colour balance of the affected areas.

Facilities such as the Color Variations feature of Photoshop Elements are generally designed to minimise this problem, but they are unlikely to avoid it altogether. Whatever method is used to adjust the colour balance, brightness, or contrast, always check the light and dark parts of the image to check for an unacceptable loss of detail. With careful adjustment it will usually be possible to obtain the required level of contrast and overall brightness without losing fine details due to clipping, but with awkward images it might be necessary to accept a compromise.

Histogram

Although the Variations facility can handle the vast majority of colour correction tasks, and it can also produce some special effects, many

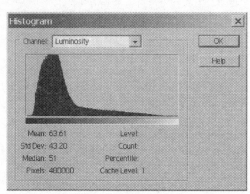

users eventually move on to the more direct forms of control. Once you gain some experience, the more direct methods are generally quicker and more accurate. Also, they are perhaps more suitable for images that need large amounts of correction or where special effects are

Fig.6.7 A histogram produced by a predominantly dark image

involved. It is only fair to point out that a picture having very serious colour or exposure problems is unlikely to produce top quality results however expertly it is processed. Using a good image editing program such as Photoshop Elements it is possible to make the most of the information in the image file, but it will not "make a silk purse out of a sow's ear".

The Histogram function in the Image menu is useful for showing the contrast and colour balance of an image. It only provides information about an image, and it is not possible to make changes via this function. Figure 6.7 shows the histogram produced for one of the sample images provided with Photoshop Elements. The bar immediately below the histogram shows a greyscale that goes from black on the left to white on the right. The height of the graph above each tone indicates the number of pixels that have that level of luminosity.

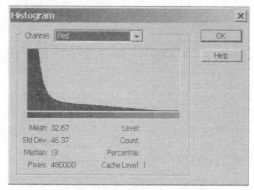

Fig.6.8 *The Red channel histogram for a largely blue image*

A well exposed picture would normally have a fair number of pixels from black right through to white. In this example a wide range or luminosity values are covered, but there are significantly more pixels at the dark end of the graph. The image is perhaps slightly on the dark side, but there is clearly plenty of

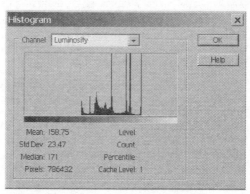

Fig.6.9 *This type of histogram normally indicates a major problem*

Fig.6.10 The original picture of the fox lacks contrast

information available. The image is predominantly dark blue, and actually looks quite good. This demonstrates the point that not all images conform to some form of average or standard set of figures. The Histogram feature is useful, but you also have to use your eyes and judge images subjectively. An image can have low contrast and be predominantly one colour and still be perfectly all right. In the real world not everything has high contrast and a wide range of colours.

Using the channel menu it is possible to show histograms for each of the (RGB) primary colours. Figure 6.8 shows the red channel histogram for the sample image. It is worth looking at these individual histograms when a print has a very strong colour cast. If the mean value indicated in the statistics is very low or high for one of the colours it might not be possible to correct the colour imbalance convincingly. Always keep the nature of the picture in mind when looking at these histograms. Clearly a picture such as a close-up of a bright red flower will not have a nicely balanced colour content, and adjusting the image for such a balance will not give good results. In this example the image is predominantly blue, and should be, so the lack of red content is not surprising.

Fig.6.11 The Auto Contrast feature has produced the desired effect

Figure 6.9 is a good example of the type of thing that you do not normally wish to see for either the luminosity or individual colours. This was produced from a scan of a rather pale print that lacked contrast. Although the print is seriously overexposed, there are no true whites or even anything approaching a true white. Things are even worse at the dark end of the range. With pictures of this type it is possible to boost the contrast so that it covers the full range, and the resultant picture might look quite good superficially. There is usually an obvious lack of detail though, and a massive increase in contrast tends to produce rather grainy looking results. It is often better to settle for a limited boost in contrast with pictures that are well out of kilter. As always, it is ultimately the look of the image that counts and not its statistics.

Auto Contrast

Photo-editing software often provides the option of a quick fix for those that do not wish to get deeply embroiled in manual settings. Most of these quick and easy solutions work well enough with a typical

Fig.6.12 This picture of a buttercup is seriously underexposed

photograph, but how many photographs are typical? Some types of subject matter are quite popular, but they probably represent only a small minority of all the photographs taken. Inevitably, most instant solutions fail to some extent when applied to the majority of photographs. The Auto Contrast feature of Photoshop Elements is one of the better quick fix facilities, and it is certainly worth using with most photographs. The Auto Contrast option provides an instant means of adjusting an image for a full range of tones.

Figure 6.10 shows a photograph of a fox in some long grass, and there is a noticeable lack of contrast. The white fur and other highlights are far from white, and the dark areas fall some way short of being black. An image such as this will usually look at its best with 100 percent contrast, making it a good candidate for automatic adjustment. The effect of the Auto Contrast function can be seen from Figure 6.11. If necessary the Auto Contrast function can be followed by some manual adjustment of the brightness and contrast, and only some slight adjustment will usually be needed. This method certainly represents the quickest and easiest approach where a full range of tones is required, or something close to a full range.

Fig.6.13 The Auto Levels feature has produced a reasonable result

There is also an Auto Color Correction option available for colour images. This is not something that could be regarded as one of most useful features of Photoshop Elements. There is no harm in trying this feature, since it can be undone using the History palette or the Undo facility. Photoshop does not know whether the image is a seascape or a bunch of flowers, so an automatic colour balance facility inevitably involves some technical guesswork. Sometimes it will be right or quite close, but often the results will be a long way out.

Auto Levels

The Auto Levels option in the Adjustments submenu provides the quickest of fixes for problems with colour balance, brightness, and contrast. Photoshop examines the data in the image file and adjusts it to produce 100 percent contrast and what it "thinks" will be the best colour balance. In other words, it is a combination of the Auto Contrast and Auto Color Correction features. This instant fix often works well when applied to images that are only fractionally below par, but it tends to be less successful with images that have serious faults.

It can be useful to try the Auto Levels function with images that are obviously lacking in contrast, are overexposed, or are underexposed. The results might be good, or sufficiently good that only a small amount of manual adjustment is needed in order to get the pictures just right. It only takes a click of the mouse to undo the processing in cases where it has totally missed the mark. Even if you do not use the settings it produces, Auto Levels enables you to see the effect of pushing the image to 100 percent contrast. If the boost in contrast produces obvious problems, then you know that a more restrained approach is needed.

Note that not all images are at their best with 100 percent contrast. With some images of flowers for example, there can be large colour contrasts but relatively little contrast in terms of luminosity. Pushing the contrast to its limits can produce odd effects with images of this type, such as flowers or other objects that seem to glow from within. Patterns and textures can become grossly exaggerated. On the other hand, it can sometimes work quite well with images that look beyond redemption. You have to be prepared to experiment a little in order to get the best results from technically inadequate images.

The close-up shot of a buttercup shown in Figure 6.12 is not just lacking in contrast, but is also seriously underexposed. Using the Auto Levels command has substantially brightened the flower while leaving the background virtually black (Figure 6.13). This is not really true to the original scene, where there was plenty of detail visible in the green foliage in the background. In its way the image is quite effective though, and it is unlikely that expert manual adjustment could make much more of this image. Sometimes you have to settle for the best image that can be produced, even if it is not a true reflection of the original subject.

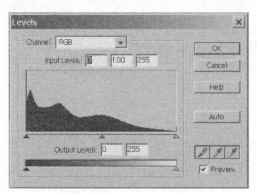

Fig.6.14   The Levels window includes a histogram

Levels

The Auto facilities are fine for many pictures, but with some images the automatic methods lack the subtlety required and

Fig.6.15 This image is too dark and lacks contrast

some careful manual adjustment is required. The Levels facility of Photoshop Elements gives excellent manual control over the contrast and brightness of an image. It is accessed by selecting Adjust Brightness/ Contrast from the Enhance menu, followed by Levels from the popup submenu. As can be seen from Figure 6.14, selecting the Levels produces a window that includes a histogram. However, in this case the window is a dialogue box that does include controls that permit the contrast and brightness of the image to be altered.

There are two sets of slider controls, and the lower set controls the maximum and minimum luminosity. Dark grey can be set as the minimum level instead of black by moving the left-hand slider to the right. Similarly, light grey rather than white can be set as the maximum level by moving the right-hand slider to the left. Reductions in contrast of this type are not often needed, but some subjects can benefit from this treatment. Some printing processes require a reduction in contrast of this type to prevent large dark areas from printing as solid areas of black.

The upper set of sliders is of greater use to most users. If the slider at the white end is moved inwards, areas that were previously light grey become white, and the lower levels of luminosity are shuffled upwards. Adjusting the slider at the other end produces a similar effect with dark greys becoming black and higher levels of luminosity being shuffled downwards. Neither type of adjustment is normally applied to a picture that already has a full range of tones. Doing so would result in clipping. The idea is to move the sliders inwards so that they match the lightest and darkest tones present in the image, as indicated by the histogram. This gives the full contrast range from the image.

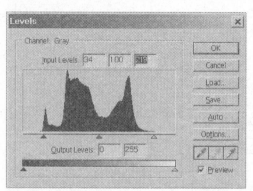

Fig.6.16 Setting the slider controls for a full contrast range

Figure 6.15 shows a photograph of a beach scene on a sunny but windy day, with waves that are backlit by the sun. It is somewhat lacking in sparkle, and the histogram shows a lack of highlights plus dark tones that are something less than black. Moving the two sliders inward to match up with the lightest and darkest tones present in the image (Figure 6.16) has given much better contrast without producing any clipping (Figure 6.17). Note that it is best to have the Preview checkbox ticked so that the effect of changes to the controls can be seen on the image. The effect on contrast is much the same as when using Auto Levels function, but when the levels are adjusted manually it is possible to set less than the full contrast range.

Fig.6.17 The image now has more contrast but it is still too dark

The upper set of slider controls includes an additional control in the middle. This is a very useful tool that should not be overlooked. A fair percentage of images will not look right unless this control is adjusted. It can be used to bring out details that are tending to disappear in dark areas of the image. I often photograph small objects that are being sold on Internet auction sites, and a lack of detail in dark areas is a common problem with this type of thing. It can happen with any type of photograph

Fig.6.18 Adjusting the middle slider gives greatly improved results

though, and it has happened with the image of Figure 6.17. The dark tones are suitably dark and the light tones are very light, and there is good overall contrast, but the general brightness is quite low. It is a bright scene in strong sunlight, but it looks almost like a night-time scene in the moonlight.

This demonstrates the point that a full range of tones does not guarantee that the overall brightness will be correct. In this case the likely cause of the problem is the very bright highlights "fooling" the camera's exposure system, resulting in some underexposure. A general increase in brightness would lighten the scene, but light areas of the picture would be clipped and detail would be lost. Simply increasing the brightness often produces rather "soft" looking results.

Better results are obtained by moving the middle slider control to the left. The tone selected using this control becomes the new mid-tone. The lightest and darkest tones remain unaltered, but the others are shuffled upward to accommodate this change. This brightens the darker areas of the picture (Figure 6.18), but it does not cause significant clipping. The middle slider control can be used to combat the opposite problem where a picture that has the full contrast range is too bright. Moving the middle control to the right produces a general downward shift in the brightness of the picture, but with minimal clipping.

Brightness/Contrast

Photoshop Elements provides conventional contrast and brightness controls as an alternative to the Level facility Figure 6.19, and any photo-editing program should have a similar feature. These two controls are much like those fitted to television sets and computer monitors. While they clearly represent the easiest way of adjusting the brightness and (or) contrast of an image, they also provide a relatively limited amount of control. I do not mean limited in the sense that only a small range of brightness and contrast levels are available. In this sense there

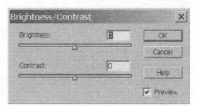

*Fig.6.19 The Brightness and
Contrast window*

is a massive amount of control available. It is subtlety that is lacking with this method of control. One of the other methods is needed if you find yourself moving the controls this way and that, unable to find satisfactory settings.

The brightness control simply moves all the colour values up or down by a certain amount. The contrast control produces a wider spread of values. In both cases severe clipping will occur if the controls are not adjusted with due care. In Figure 6.20 the photograph of the beach scene has been adjusted using the Brightness and Contrast controls, and plenty of detail can be seen in the previously dark areas of the foreground and middle section of the photograph. First the brightness was increased in

Fig.6.20 Adjusting the brightness and contrast has not been totally successful

order to lighten the overly dark areas. Then the contrast was boosted in order to counteract the perceived loss of contrast produced by increasing the brightness, and to correct the lack of contrast in the original image.

This processing has brought out the details in much of the photograph, but much of the sky has changed from shades of grey to pure white due to the clipping that has occurred. The highlights in the waves have suffered a similar fate. The image is not too bad, but it is still slightly lacking in "punch". However, setting the contrast any higher will increase the clipping problem. Using reduced brightness improves the sky but takes the image back to its virtual night-time appearance.

The Brightness and Contrast controls are the obvious tools for adjusting their respective aspects of an image, but in practice they are unlikely to provide the best results. Setting a good contrast range and then adjusting the mid tones using the Levels facility gives much better results with awkward images. Where there is a more sophisticated means of adjusting the contrast and brightness available, such as the Levels facility, it is a good idea to use it and largely ignore the standard controls. In some cases it is necessary to opt for selective processing in order to get the best results. With an image such as this for example, the sky can be processed separately from the rest of the picture. The sky can then be darkened without having to compromise on the settings for the rest of the image. However, in most cases quite good results can be obtained without resorting to selective processing.

Hue/Saturation

The Color Variations facility is normally used when the colour balance must be altered, but Photoshop Elements has an alternative method in the form of the Hue/Saturation facility. Its primary purpose is not for subtle changes in the colour balance, and the results it produces tend to be far from subtle. The name of this option suggests that there are two controls, but the Hue/ Saturation window actually has three slider controls (Figure 6.21). In addition to controls for hue and colour there is also a Lightness control. The Edit menu near

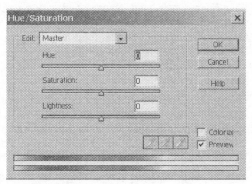

Fig.6.21 The Hue/Saturation window

the top of the window enables the individual colours to be processed, or the full range via the default Master option. Use the Master setting when making initial experiments with the Hue/Saturation facility. As with the other colour/brightness adjustment windows, the Preview checkbox should be ticked so that changes can be viewed on the image.

I think it is fair to say that the Hue control is a bit confusing. If you try experimenting with various settings it will probably appear to be producing random colour changes. The two colour bars at the bottom of the window were not placed there to make it look pretty, and if you move the Hue control to the right the lower colour bar will shift to the left. Although it is only a greyscale image, the shift can be seen in Figure 6.22 (compare this to Figure 6.21). Move the Hue control to the left, and the lower colour bar moves to the right.

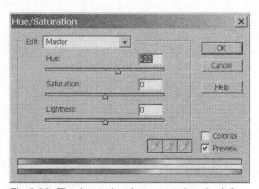

Fig.6.22 The lower bar has moved to the left

What the two colour bars are showing are the input and output colours. With the Hue control at a central setting the two bars are aligned and the input colour is always the same as the output colour. Move the control slightly to the left and yellow on the top bar (the input colour) is vertically aligned with orange on the lower bar (the output colour). There is a similar shift right across the spectrum. Move the Hue control slightly to the right and things are reversed, with orange being replaced with yellow, etc.

These small adjustments give what artists term warmer colours if the Hue control is moved to the left or colder colours if it is moved to the right. In other words, more red and more blue respectively. I find this is useful for adjusting skin tones. Skin tones that are too red giving a "lobster" effect can be corrected by moving the Hue control to the right. Slightly green and unnatural skin tones can usually be corrected by moving the Hue control fractionally to the left. More than slight changes produce massive colour shifts, and you are then into the realm of special effects.

So far it has been assumed that colour and brightness changes will be applied to the entire image. As already pointed out, any good image editing program should have various means of selecting an area or even

Fig.6.23 The Options bar with the Red Eye Brush Tool selected

several areas within an image. Processing such as colour and contrast changes can then be applied to the selected area or areas. Selecting parts of an image is covered in a later chapter. The Hue control works particularly well with single objects or small groups. Flowers, cars, boats and other objects can be changed from any colour to any other colour.

"Red-eye" removal

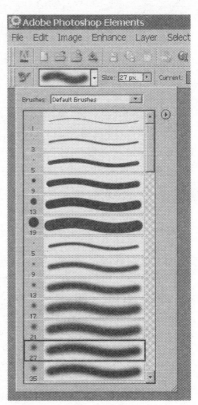

An obvious application for this type of editing is the removal of the dreaded "red-eye" problem, which often occurs when photographing people or pets using a flashgun built into or fitted on the camera. Selective processing plus the Hue control can certainly cure this problem, but most photo-editing software includes a facility specifically for combating "red-eye". Photoshop Elements has the Red Eye Brush tool, which is the seventh button down on the right in the Toolbox.

The brush tools of image editing programs are used to paint onto the image, and an ordinary brush tool simply paints with the current foreground colour. There are other types of brush tool that apply an effect of some kind rather than painting in the conventional sense. The Red Eye Brush tool paints with a colour that is selected via the Replacement button in the

Fig.6.24 The Brush menu

Fig.6.25 The original (red) rosebud

Options bar (Figure 6.23). Operating this button produces the Color Picker, and the required colour is mixed in the usual way. This tool does not simply paint with the selected colour though. It searches for the colour shown in the Current button on the Options bar, and replaces it with the colour shown on the Replacement button. However, it retains the luminosity value currently in the image. The idea is to produce a change in colour without losing texture and detail in the image.

Before using any brush tool it is necessary to select a brush having an appropriate size. The Brush menu on the Options bar offers a wide range of brush sizes and types (Figure 6.24). For most photographic work either an ordinary round brush or a round one having a fuzzy edge will suffice. There are plenty of preset sizes to choose from, or a size (in pixels) can be typed into the Size textbox. The brush size can also be adjusted by left-clicking on the arrow to the right of this textbox and using the popup slider control.

Suppose that a picture of someone having blue eyes has a severe red-eye problem. The first task is to operate the Replacement button and then choose a suitable blue using the Color Picker. Remember that there is no need to worry about the brightness or saturation of the blue, as the current values in the image will be used. It is just a matter of selecting a suitable hue. The Current colour is whatever colour is currently under the brush, so the next step is to move the brush over an offending red area of the image. Then operate the left mouse button and drag the brush over the red area of the eye. It is not necessary to be very accurate because this tool only changes areas that are the correct colour, or something quite close to it. Repeat the process for the other eye, and the red eyes should have been replaced with blue ones.

If it does not look quite right it is just a matter of using the Undo facility and trying again using a slightly different colour. Of course, this tool is not restricted to correcting red-eye problems. It provides a quick and easy means of replacing any colour with any other colour. A red rose can be changed to a blue rose, and green car can be

Fig.6.26 *The change in its colour has left the rosebud looking much the same in greyscale, with no loss of detail*

changed to a yellow one, and so on. There is no loss of detail as only the colour is changed. This is demonstrated by Figures 6.25 and 6.26 which show a red rosebud that has been changed to a blue rosebud. There is no difference in the detail and no change in the brightness levels, and in greyscale the two images are therefore the same.

Normally the colour that is replaced is the one that the Red Eye Brush tool is first clicked on when starting to paint, but a colour of your choice can be used instead. To use this method select the Current Color option from the Sampling menu. The Tolerance setting determines how close to the Current colour a pixel has to be in order to be changed by the Red Eye Brush tool. Using a high value risks altering areas you wish to leave unchanged. A low value avoids this, but might render the tool only partially effective. The Tolerance setting is not usually too critical, and in most cases it is quite easy to find a good compromise setting.

Saturation

Returning to the topic of the Hue/Saturation facility, it can do more than provide overall colour shifts. The Saturation control gives reduced colour saturation if it is moved to the left, and will leave a greyscale image if it is taken right to the end of the control range. Reducing saturation is helpful with an image that has excessively vivid colours, or it can be used to produce weak colours for special effect. Moving the saturation control to the right gives stronger colours, and weak colours can be corrected in this way. Many older scanners produce slightly weak colours and will benefit from a small boost in saturation. Resist the temptation to overdo the saturation and produce images that have so-called "Mickey Mouse" colours.

The Lightness control is a standard brightness type that requires no further explanation. Incidentally, the lower colour bar changes in response to adjustments of the Saturation and Lightness controls, and not just the Hue type. You can therefore see the full range of colours available for the current lightness and saturation settings. This is clearly useful, but it is better to judge the effect by the image rather than the colours in the lower colour bar.

Single colour

Selecting a single colour from the Edit menu changes the Hue/Saturation window slightly (Figure 6.27). Sliders appear on the colour bars to indicate the colour range that will be altered by the Hue, Saturation, and Colour controls. There are two sets of sliders, with the inner pair indicating the range of colours that will be fully altered by adjustments to the controls. The outer pair indicates the colours that will be affected to a lesser extent.

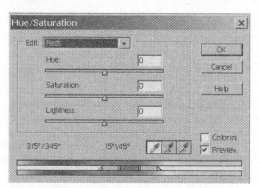

Fig.6.27 The Hue/Saturation window with single colour operation

With something like the rosebud photograph it is possible to alter the colour of the bud by adjusting the sliders to match the colours in the petals. Operating the Hue control then provides the colour shift. This type of thing does not work well with all photographs, since there will sometimes be other objects of a similar colour in the image. Where applicable, this method is usually much quicker and easier than using normal selection methods. Of course, where necessary it can be combined with normal selection methods. Remember that it is not just selective colour changes that can be implemented in this way. The lightness and saturation can also be limited to a particular colour range.

Fill Flash

There are a couple of useful options in the Adjust Lighting submenu of the Enhance menu, and one of these is the Fill Flash function. As explained previously, fill-in flash is often used for portraits and other shots that are backlit and have a bright background. Normally the main subject tends to be underexposed due to the bright background "fooling" the exposure system. Even if the correct exposure is used, results are often relatively poor with an over-bright and washed-out background. The light from the flashgun lightens the otherwise dark main subject, but in most cases it does so without making the background any lighter.

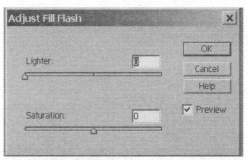

Indeed, if the light from the flashgun is strong enough and the background is a fair distance away, the background might be reduced in brightness. This is

Fig.6.28 The Fill-Flash adjustment window

due to the increased light falling on the main subject causing the camera to reduce the exposure. The reduced exposure often gives a better balance between the background and the main subject, although it can sometimes result in the background becoming too dark.

The Fill Flash facility is intended for use with photographs where fill-in flash should have been used but was not. It can also be used with

Fig.6.29 The original image shows no detail in the blackbird

images that would have benefited from fill-in flash, but where its use would have been impractical. For example, fill-in flash is of no use with landscapes that have an excessively bright sky, because the flashgun is not powerful enough to have a significant effect on the lighting. Using the Fill Flash facility lightens dark areas of the image but leaves the light areas largely unchanged. This avoids having already light areas bleached out completely.

Figure 6.28 shows the small window that appears when the Fill Flash option is selected. The Lighting control is moved to the right to make the image lighter, but the dark tones are affected far more than the light ones. Bright backgrounds are left relatively unchanged while the dark subject matter has its brightness boosted more significantly. The best setting is a subjective matter, but it is generally better not to get carried away with this type of thing. Using the Lightness control tends to reduce the contrast, so advancing it well to the right could give rather "flat" looking results.

Lightening the image but leaving the colour saturation unaltered can give some odd effects. Brightly coloured objects can look rather unnatural

Fig.6.30 The Fill Flash processing has brought out the available detail

and might exhibit a sort of glowing effect. Problems of this type can be corrected by moving the Saturation control to the left in order to reduce the colour saturation slightly. A little juggling with the two controls should soon produce some good results. Figure 6.29 and 6.30 show "before" and "after" versions of a photograph of a blackbird. Getting good results with a dark subject such as this is always awkward, and it is virtually impossible with such a bright background. However, the small amount of lightening in Figure 6.30 is sufficient to at least remove the silhouette effect and give the bird a bit more shape.

The Fill Flash facility is useful with scenes where a bright sky has rendered the foreground more or less black, as in the example of Figure 6.31. In the slightly lightened version of Figure 6.32 a small amount of foreground detail and interest has been added. If parts of an image have been so underexposed that no detail has been recorded it is not possible for this facility to work effectively. Lightening the dark areas simply gives a paler silhouette. Any artefacts in the dark areas will be made more obvious, and there is some evidence of that occurring in Figure 6.32.

Fig.6.31 No detail is visible in the bottom half of the original image

Fig.6.32 The Fill Flash processing has again managed to produce a
certain amount of detail in the dark areas

Adjust Backlighting

Adjust Backlighting is the other option in the Adjust Lighting submenu. This is intended for use where the dark areas of the image have been exposed correctly and show plenty of detail, but the lighter areas are overexposed. This problem usually manifests itself in the form of dramatic skies that are decidedly underwhelming due to a lack of variation in tone. The Adjust Backlighting window only has one control (Figure 6.33), and moving this to the right darkens the light areas of the image. Some odd effects can be produced if this facility is used on

Fig.6.33 The Adjust Backlighting window

an entire image. Try it first on the whole image, but operate the Cancel button if the preview of the image does not look right. Then select the part of the image that you wish to darken and then try again.

Figures 6.34 and 6.35 show "before" and "after" images for an image where the sky area is somewhat overexposed. In Figure 6.35 the whole image has been processed, and it has produced some unwanted side effects. These are more obvious in the original colour version where a bright yellow field has been darkened to a sort of yellow ochre colour. There are one or two other noticeable colour shifts in the processed image. In Figure 6.36 the sky area was selected and processed in isolation using the Adjust Backlighting facility, leaving the rest of the picture unchanged. This method has produced much better results. There is no saturation control in the Adjust Backlighting window, but where necessary a slight increase in saturation can be provided via the Hue/Saturation facility.

Alternatives

Most photo-editing programs provide alternative ways of doing things, and Photoshop Elements certainly has plenty of options. The Color Cast option in the Adjust Colors submenu provides a simple and almost instant way of removing colour casts. The window of Figure 6.37 appears when this option is selected, and it is noticeably lacking in controls. This is because no adjustments are needed in order to remove a colour cast. The basic idea is to find a point on the image that should be black, white,

Fig.6.34 The original version of the photograph

Fig.6.35 The processing has darkened more than the sky

Fig.6.36 Selective processing has produced the desired result

or a neutral grey. The program then adjusts the colour balance to actually make that area black, white, or neutral grey, and changes the rest of the image using the same degree of colour correction.

This is certainly the quickest and easiest way of removing a colour cast, but it has the obvious limitation that it will only work if you can find an area of the image that should have a suitably neutral colour. It may not always be possible to do so, but there is no harm in trying. Simply hit the Cancel button if it proves to be impossible to obtain satisfactory results. You can have as many attempts as necessary, but operate the Reset button after each unsuccessful attempt so that the image is taken back to its original state before a fresh attempt is made. This type of facility is probably best when initially dealing with strong colour casts. With the cast largely removed it is quite easy to "fine tune" the colour balance using the Color Variations facility.

Replace Color

This is another option in the Adjust Colors submenu, and as its name implies, it can be used to replace one colour with another. The window

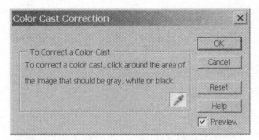

Fig.6.37 The Color Cast Correction window

of Figure 6.38 appears when this option is selected. The preview window in the Replace Color window can be used to show the image, but it is normally used to show the selection. In other words, it shows the areas that will be affected by the colour replacement. The selected areas are shown in white, the non-selected areas are shown black, and areas that will be partially affected are reproduced in grey. An area is selected by left-clicking on it using the pointer, which will change to the eyedropper type.

The Fuzziness control determines the range of colours that will be replaced. A low setting makes this facility very colour conscious, with a sharp division between the areas that are selected and those that are

Fig.6.38 The preview window can be used to show the selected areas

not. A high setting results in a wider range of colours being selected, with a broad surrounding area that is partially selected. The colour that will be used as a replacement is mixed using the Hue, Saturation, and Brightness controls.

The Remove Color option turns the image into a greyscale type, but it does not put the image in Grayscale mode. It remains an RGB colour type so that it is possible to add colour to the image.

Points to remember

The easiest way of correcting colour casts is to use something like the Variations feature of Photoshop Elements. Several thumbnail views of the image are shown, with a different type of correction applied to each one, and it is just a matter of selecting the one that looks best. Where necessary, two or more types of correction can be combined.

A histogram is useful for showing how well (or otherwise) a picture has been exposed. The information it provides can be useful when deciding on the corrective measures required. However, bear in mind that an odd looking histogram can be caused by unusual subject matter. Adjustments should be designed to make the image look right, not the histogram.

Most image editing programs have conventional brightness and contrast controls, but they will not always provide sufficient flexibility to provide really good results. More sophisticated control is provided by the Levels facility of Photoshop Elements. This makes it easy to set a full tonal range, but also permits repositioning of the luminance levels between the extremes.

Try to avoid clipping, which will occur if due care is not taken when adjusting the contrast and brightness. Clipping is produced when light areas are made white and (or) the dark areas are made black, losing detail in the affected areas. Setting the required contrast range and then using the Levels control to adjust the brightness should avoid serious amounts of clipping.

Automatic colour, contrast, and brightness facilities are useful, but can not be guaranteed to give perfect results every time. Automatic contrast controls provide a quick and easy means of setting a full range of tones, but a small percentage of pictures do not give best results with 100 percent contrast. Results using automatic colour correction are inevitably a bit more hit and miss.

It is possible to select a colour range and then change any part of the image that falls within that range to a new colour. A facility of this type can be used for "red-eye" reduction, or creatively to alter colours within an image. These days most image editing programs have at least one tool specifically designed for countering "red-eye" problems.

Many image editing programs have a facility that automatically sets the colour balance if the user clicks the mouse on an area that should be black, pure white, or a neutral grey. This method provides an instant fix, but only works properly if you can find an area that should genuinely be black, white, or a neutral grey.

Making selections

Getting choosy

In most cases it is possible to get good results from images by applying changes to the entire image, but it can sometimes be better to apply changes selectively. This was the case when darkening the sky in one of the examples in the previous chapter. If part of the image needs adjustment but the rest is perfect, it makes sense to alter only the part that needs adjustment. There will otherwise have to be a compromise to ensure that the correct part of the image is not spoiled while improving the faulty part. Selective processing avoids such compromises and should give perfect results. In practice a certain amount of care has to be exercised so that the image does not look as though it has been tampered with, and it is best not to get carried away with the freedom afforded by selective processing.

Selective processing can actually be taken beyond simple processing such as changes to colour and contrast. Using selections it is possible to make radical changes to an image or even take pieces from several different images to produce a totally new composite image. This type of thing is much used in the production of joke pictures containing objects that are out of proportion, upside-down, and so on. Selective processing can also be used to exchange an unattractive background for a prettier one. This is perhaps the most common application for this type of processing.

Suppose that you have an image of an object such as a watch or a piece of jewellery, and it is on a rather uninspiring background. You might decide to paint in a simple graduated background instead of the original. Alternatively, a plain white background can be used to make objects really stand out, as there will be nothing to act as a distraction. Both methods are much used in advertising, where the main subject is made to look more dynamic and stand out better by replacing the natural background. It can be used to good effect if you produce photographs for online auctions or something of this type.

Having to carefully paint around a complex object is very time consuming. It would clearly be much easier if there was a way of selecting the outline of the main subject and setting everything within it as a no-go area. It would then be easy to paint on the background using the brush tools or using flood fills, as there would be no danger of altering the main subject. Indeed, even if you tried to paint over the main subject it would not be possible to do so.

With the more simple image editing software there is often little in the way of features for selective processing. There might be a few brush tools that permit changes in contrast, brightness, etc., to be "painted" onto the image, but nothing beyond that. The more capable programs have the brush tools and various ways of designating areas that can be processed using the normal controls for colour balance, contrast, and so on. Photoshop Elements has quite an impressive range of brush tools and various means of selecting areas that can be exclusively processed or set as "no-go" areas.

Difficulty factor

It is only fair to point out that selecting precisely the right part of an image can be quite easy or very difficult depending on the nature of the image. Something that has "hard" edges that contrast well with the background is likely to be easier than something that has "soft" edges with a tendency to blend into the background. Photoshop Elements has tools and functions that help to deal with awkward parts of an image, but there is no guarantee of perfect results every time. This is true of the selection tools of any current image editing program. With uncooperative images it is necessary to draw at least part of the selection outline by hand rather than using automated help from the computer.

In order to increase the chances of selecting exactly the required areas, Photoshop Elements has several selection tools that operate in different ways. The Marquee tools are the most basic, and these were described previously. It is likely that you will use the basic Marquee tools a fair amount, but they are inadequate for selecting complex shapes. They are more versatile than it might at first appear, because it is possible to combine selections in various ways in order to produce more complex shapes. These methods can be used with the more complex marquee tools, and in most cases it is essential to do so in order to get things just right. There are a few other ploys that can be used to help "fine tune" results.

The pointer changes to an arrowhead when it is placed within any marquee, and this indicates that the marquee can be dragged to a different position. As you will soon notice when using Photoshop Elements, the pointer changes to suit the particular tool in use. The arrowhead is the pointer for the Move tool, and Photoshop is indicating an automatic change to this tool when the pointer is within a marquee. If the Control key is operated while dragging a selection, the contents of the marquee are dragged with it. In effect, a cut and paste operation is performed. Note that dragging the marquee thereafter results in the contents moving with it, and there is no need to hold down the Control after the first time.

Another useful ploy is to operate the Spacebar while dragging a marquee onto the screen. This

Fig.7.1 Selections can be added together

results in the marquee being moved rather than changed in size. Releasing the Spacebar takes things back to the normal sizing mode. It can be difficult to get it right the first time when using the Marquee tool, but the selection is easily "fine tuned" by switching between the sizing and moving modes via the Spacebar.

Multiple selections

Making a new selection while an existing selection is present normally results in the original one being deleted. However, it is possible to have multiple selections. Simply hold down the shift key while making a selection and any existing selection or selections will be left on the screen. Figure 7.1 shows a marquee produced from two rectangular selections

Fig.7.2 The Options bar for the Marquee tool

and one elliptical type. One slight snag with this method is that it is not possible to use the Shift key to constrain the Marquee to a square or circle, since it is being used to indicate that a multiple selection is required. With a Marquee tool selected there is a group of four buttons near the left end of the Options bar and some menus to the right (Figure 7.2). As will be explained shortly, one of the menus provides a solution to the problem.

By default the first button (working from left to right) is active, and this sets the selection process to the mode where a new selection replaces any existing ones. Using the next button along sets the mode where multiple selections are possible. With this mode in use it is possible to place several Marquees on the image and still use the Shift key to produce a square or circular selection. Note that in the multiple mode any overlapping selections are merged into a single selection. This is essentially the same as holding down the Shift key in order to produce multiple selections, and operating the Shift key temporarily places the Marquee tool in the multiple mode. If necessary,

Fig.7.3 It is possible to have several separate selections

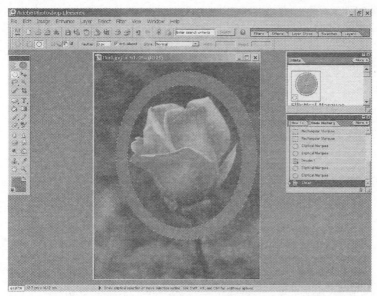

Fig.7.4 The Subtraction mode was used to produce this selection

quite complex shapes can be built up in this way. Multiple selections do not have to be merged and Photoshop Elements supports discrete multiple selections (Figure 7.3). Note that far from all image editing programs support this feature.

The third button puts the Marquee tool into Subtraction mode, which enables a "hole" or "knockout" to be placed within an existing selection. In Figure 7.4 an initial large ellipse has been placed around the rosebud. With the Subtraction mode selected, a smaller ellipse has then been placed within the original ellipse. The Delete key was then operated so that the selected area was erased. This clearly shows how the area within the smaller ellipse has been removed from the selection, since this area has not been erased.

Dragging marquees outside an existing selection is pointless in the Subtraction mode, since there is no selection to subtract from. Accordingly, Photoshop will ignore any attempts to do this. Where the new selection partially overlaps the existing one, the overlapping area will be removed from the existing selection. This can be useful since it enables an oversize selection to be nibbled down to exactly the required

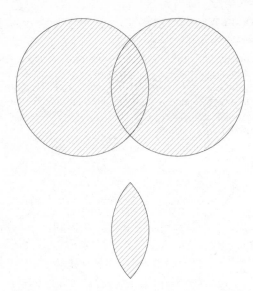

Fig.7.5 The two selections at the top combine to produce the one below when using the Intersect mode

size and shape. With some of the automatic selection methods there is a tendency to produce small unwanted selection areas, and these are easily removed using the normal Marquee tool and the subtraction mode.

The final button is the Intersect with Selection button. Normally two overlapping selections are merged to make one large selection. In the Intersect mode things operate in the opposite manner, with only the overlapping sections being used in the combined selection. The two selections of in the upper section of Figure 7.5 would therefore combine to produce the much reduced selection in the lower section. This method can be used to produce selections having shapes that are not otherwise possible using the basic Marquee tools.

Style

Three options are available from the Style menu on the Options bar (Figure 7.6). By default the Normal style is selected, and the Marquee tools then work in the standard fashion described previously. As one would expect, using the Fixed Aspect Ratio mode results in rectangular and elliptical selections having a fixed aspect ratio. This is rather like holding down the Shift key to force a square or circular selection, but other aspect ratios are possible.

The Width and Height textboxes just to the right of the menu become active when this mode is selected. The default aspect ratio is 1 to 1, but any desired ratio can be entered in the textboxes. Multiple selections are still possible when using a fixed aspect ratio, and the Spacebar can be used to move a selection while it is being created. This mode overcomes the problem mentioned earlier, where the Spacebar can not be used to constrain the selection to a square or circle, and provide multiple selections. Simply select the Fixed Aspect Ratio

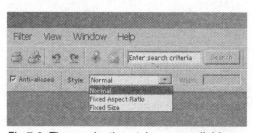

Fig.7.6 Three selection styles are available

mode and make the first selection. Then hold down the Shift key and make further selections. This method is more versatile as aspect ratios other that 1 to 1 are available. Note that it is possible to make a selection, change the aspect ratio, make a further selection, change the ratio again, add another selection, and so on.

The third option is for a marquee of a fixed size, and the two textboxes are again active when this option is selected. They are used to set the width and height of the marquee in pixels. In this mode the marquee is produced by left-clicking the mouse. Dragging the marquee obviously has no effect on its size, but instead moves it around the screen. Consequently, there is no need to hold down the Spacebar in order to move the marquee. Once in position it can be moved in the normal way, and multiple selections are still possible.

Deselection

Do not press the Delete key in order to clear marquees from the screen. As explained previously, this will delete the selected material, leaving the marquee in place. One or more marquees can be deselected by left-clicking anywhere on the image provided Normal mode is selected and the New Selection button is active. This effectively replaces the current selection with a new one having zero pixels. In the New Selection and

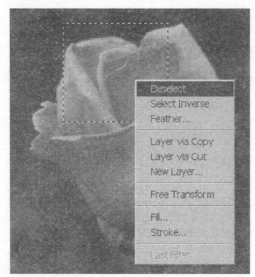

Intersect modes it is possible to remove the current selection or selections by left-clicking within one of the selections.

Another method is to right-click on a selection and select Deselect from the popup menu (Figure 7.7). Note that this clears away all the selections it there is more than one, and not just the selection that was right-clicked. The Deselect option is also available from the Select menu on the menu bar.

Fig.7.7 Right-clicking on a selection produces this menu

Remember that it is only possible to edit material within a selection when one or more selections are present. In order to edit other areas it is necessary to add another selection to cover the relevant area or delete the existing selections so that the entire image is available for editing.

Alternatively, select Inverse from the Select menu so that the selected and non-selected areas are swapped. Use the Inverse option again in order to restore the selections once you have finished editing outside them. Where it is necessary to process everything but a small part of the image, the easiest method of selection is usually to select the small "no-go" area and then use the Inverse option. In fact this will often be the only practical approach in these circumstances.

Lasso tool

The Marquee tools are adequate for many selection tasks, but they make heavy work of selecting complex shapes. It can be done, but a lot of merging and nibbling is needed to get things right. The Lasso tool is better for selecting awkward shapes since it enables you to draw around the required area. This is the second tool down in the left-hand column of the Toolbox. Most image editing programs have a selection tool of

Fig.7.8 This selection was made using the Lasso tool

this type. Although the Lasso tool is easy to use in theory, in practice it is difficult to use this tool with adequate accuracy. Even an experienced and skilled user is unlike to get it right first time. At first it is often a struggle to get anything approximating to the required selection.

A digitising tablet and a stylus is certainly much better than a mouse for this type of thing, and an inexpensive digitising tablet is certainly a worthwhile investment for anyone who does more than occasional photo-editing. The merge and subtraction methods work using the Lasso tool, so it is possible to "fine tune" the selection if you do not get it right first time. It is easier to get good accuracy using a zoomed view, so make good use of the pan and zoom facilities when making fine adjustments. Most people find that reducing the sensitivity of the mouse or tablet makes it easier to obtain good accuracy. By reducing sensitivity I mean that the pointing device should be set so that more physical movement is required for a given amount of movement on the screen.

To use the Lasso tool you simply drag a line around the area that you wish to select. There is no need to accurately match the start and finish points of the line. Photoshop will automatically connect the start and

Fig.7.9 The darker background makes the rosebud more promonent

finish points. On the other hand, leaving a large gap is unlikely to give adequate accuracy. With practice and the inevitable fine adjustments to the marquee it will usually be possible to obtain the desired result.

In the example of Figure 7.8 the aim was to darken the background while leaving the rosebud unaltered, to make the rosebud stand out more from the background. After a few adjustments the marquee accurately followed the outline of the rosebud, as can just about be seen in Figure 7.8. In Figure 7.9 the selection was inverted and the background was then darkened. Additionally, the selection was inverted again after which the rosebud was lightened slightly and given a small boost in contrast.

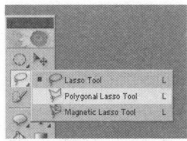

Fig.7.10 Selecting the Polygonal Lasso tool

Polygonal Lasso tool

There are two alternative versions of the Lasso tool available, and the first of them is the Polygonal Lasso tool. To access this control, right-click on the Lasso button in the Toolbox to produce the popup menu of Figure 7.10 and select the appropriate option. This tool is used to draw irregular

Fig.7.11 The sail panel were selected using the Polygonal Lasso tool

polygons, and on the face of it the regular Lasso tool is the more useful. The polygonal version draws straight lines between points drawn on the screen, which means that true curves can not be produced. There is no such limitation with the normal Lasso tool, where freehand drawing can be used to produce any shape, curved or otherwise.

However, as already explained, accurate drawing using the normal Lasso tool is very difficult. Even after you have gained some experience it can be very difficult to get really good accuracy without resorting to a great deal of "fine tuning". Drawing complex shapes by picking points on the outline is very much easier. Although it is not possible to draw true curves, a good approximation can be produced using several short lines. In practice, selections made using the Polygonal Lasso tool are often sufficiently accurate without the need for fine adjustments, which is rarely if ever true when using the normal Lasso tool.

In Figure 7.11 the sail panels have been selected using the Polygonal Lasso tool, and no "fine tuning" has been applied to the initial selection. Even so, they have been selected quite accurately. The Polygonal Lasso tool is good for this type of thing where the outlines consist mainly of

Fig.7.12 The previously dull sail panels have been lightened

straight lines. The curves are quite gentle, and it does not require many straight lines in order to track them reasonably accurately. In the original scene the light was shining through the sails, which helped to make the scene look more attractive. Unfortunately, in the image the sails are underexposed and look quite dull, rather spoiling the effect. Selecting the panels and boosting both the contrast and brightness should improve matters, giving an image that provides a better representation of the original scene.

The lightening and boosted contrast has been applied to the image in Figure 7.12. It has worked very well despite the lack of any fine adjustments to the selections. In fact there are no obvious errors in the processed areas of the image. It is unlikely that an equal degree of precision could be achieved using the standard version of the Lasso tool without making some adjustments to the initial selection. As always with this type of thing, it is a matter of using whichever tool you find to be the best for the job. In most cases it will almost certainly be the Polygonal Lasso tool rather than the standard version.

Using the Polygonal Lasso tool is very straightforward. Start by left-clicking to place the first point on the outline. The program then draws a line from this first point to the current position of the pointer, making it easy to position the next point on the outline. The next point is produced by left-clicking again, and the "rubber band" line then appears from the second point to the current position of the pointer. Add all the points needed to complete the outline and then left-click again on the first point

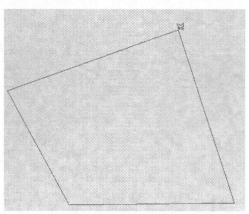

Fig.7.13 A circle appears on the pointer when the selection can be closed

to close the outline. The final point must be placed quite accurately, and a small circle appears on the pointer when it is close enough to close the shape (Figure 7.13).

An alternative method of closing the shape is to double-click on the final point. Photoshop Elements will then automatically place the line from there to the starting point. When using the double-click method you might sometimes find that the selection disappears! The final point was too close to the first point if the selection does this disappearing act. The two clicks close and then deselect the selection. Going back one stage using the Undo facility or the History palette will restore the selection.

If, having just placed a point you decide that it is not positioned accurately, operate the Delete key to erase it so that another attempt can be made. In fact the Delete key can be used repeatedly to go on deleting points right back to the first one. This ability to change your mind and retrace your steps is a huge advantage over the standard Lasso tool, where once you have started you have to go on until you have finished. Of course, using the Delete key once the shape has been closed will erase

Fig.7.14 The Magnetic Lasso tool has provided quite accurate results

everything within the selection, as normal, rather than deleting the last point. Any changes to the last few points must therefore be made before the selection is closed. Provided the shape has not been closed, operating the Escape key will completely remove all the lines.

Magnetic Lasso tool

Most of the more sophisticated image editing programs have selection methods that operate automatically or in a semiautomatic fashion. Photoshop Elements has both automatic and semiautomatic selection tools. The Magnetic Lasso tool is a sort of semiautomatic version of the standard Lasso tool, and it is typical of the semiautomatic approach. As already pointed out, getting accurate results using the normal Lasso tool is quite tricky. Photoshop will faithfully reproduce every little error in your rendering of the outline, and some editing will usually be required once the outline has been completed.

The Magnetic Lasso tool makes life much easier by looking for an outline to follow rather than simply following the exact path of the pointer. How well or otherwise this works depends on how well an object's outline is

Fig.7.15 With the processing added the picture looks as it should

defined. It should work very well if there is plenty of contrast in shade or colour. If there is no outline to follow, the Magnetic Lasso is not the tool for the job. It is probably not the best tool for the job if there is only an indistinct or intermittent outline to follow, or if the outline is very jagged with lots of sharp points.

In Figure 7.14 I have undone the original processing on the sails of the boat and used the Magnetic Lasso tool to select the sail panels again. The outlines were drawn using a mouse and I was not especially careful when following any of the outlines. Nevertheless, the Magnetic Lasso tool has done quite a good job of following the outlines of most of the sail panels. It has not gone right into the very sharp corners, but in other respects it has performed very well.

The only obvious flaw is that it has jumped to the wrong edge of the mast in one place, but this was due to "driver error" and could have been corrected by a second attempt. Less obviously, it has latched onto the lettering on the sail where it is very close to one edge of a panel. In Figure 7.15 the increase in brightness has been added, and despite one or two minor errors in the selections it actually looks quite passable. There are still no major problems in evidence and this method of selection has proved to be quick and accurate on this occasion. With more extreme processing any minor errors would be more likely to show up, and the selections would then have needed some minor corrections prior to adding the processing.

Options

There are some parameters in the Options bar that enable the Magnetic Lasso tool to be optimised for a given situation. The Width (detection width) setting controls how close the pointer has to be to an edge for the Magnetic Lasso tool to latch onto it. The larger this figure the less accurately you have to follow the outline. Do not be tempted to use a large figure for this setting though. The line might tend to jump off its intended path and onto another outline, particularly if the pointer is allowed to stray well away from the correct path. The Width setting is in pixels incidentally.

The Edge Contrast figure determines the difference in brightness value required for an outline to be recognised. Using a low value enables the outline to be followed even when there is relatively little contrast between the object and the background. Unfortunately, it also increases the likelihood of the line jumping over to a different outline or jumping to any small areas of slight contrast. A small Edge Contrast value normally has to be accompanied by a small Width value and careful drawing of the selection outline. This type of selection tool works best with well defined objects and a reasonably high Edge Contrast value.

The Frequency setting controls the number of anchor points that will be added as the outline is drawn. These anchor points are shown as tiny squares on the line while it is being drawn. The higher the number, the more anchor points that are used and the more accurately intricate outlines can be tracked. In the sail example used previously, the outline did not go right into the sharp corners. A high value gives better accuracy with this type of thing, but note that the maximum permissible value is 100. On the down side, a high value might have a tendency to produce rough edges, particularly when used with a low Edge Contrast value.

Using the Magnetic Lasso tool is again very straightforward. Drag the line making sure that the pointer is kept quite close to the outline you are trying to follow. Release the left mouse button when the pointer is back at the starting point. Alternatively, double-click the mouse with the pointer close to the starting point. Photoshop Elements will then draw a line from between the final and starting points, tracking what it considers to be the correct path.

If things go badly wrong, operate the Escape key to completely remove the line so that you can start from scratch. The last anchor point added can be removed by operating the delete key, and this key can be operated repeatedly to remove further anchor points back down the line. Keep the pointer still while deleting anchor points so that no new ones are added while you are trying to remove some of the existing points. This tool often gives better results with the pointer kept just to one side of the required path rather than trying to track the pointer right over the path. As is the case with most of the image editing tools, the more you use it the easier it is to get good results.

Magic Wand tool

With the Magic Wand tool is the Photoshop Elements version of a fully automatic selection tool. There is no need to draw around the object you wish to select. You just left-click at a suitable point on the image and Photoshop Elements automatically selects the right area. Of course, in reality it is not quite as simple as that, and Photoshop might not get it right. The Magic Wand tool tries to find an outline based on the colour values of the pixels. If there is good colour contrast between the object you are trying to select and the background it is likely that the Magic Wand tool will do a good job. Results are less sure if the object blends into the background at some points.

Figure 7.16 shows the original version of the boat photograph, but this time with the sail panels selected using the Magic Wand tool. In this case it is clearly not going to provide a one-click solution, since there are several separate areas to be selected. It was not even a matter of one click per panel, because there are significant variations in colour within most of the panels. Most of the selections therefore had to be built up using several clicks on different areas of colour within each panel. The outlines of the panels are quite well defined, so there were no major problems with areas outside the panels being selected. It took numerous mouse clicks to select all the desired areas, but it was a very quick and easy way of selecting the required areas. In terms of accuracy it was

Fig.7.16 The sail panels selected using the Magic Wand tool

actually better than the other methods, and results were close to perfection without any fine adjustments being made.

There is an apparent flaw, in that the lettering within the sail panels has been outlined as well. When the Magic Wand tool produces islands such as these, even though they are totally within the main selection, they do not form part of the selection. The lettering is therefore not selected, and it will not be processed along with the rest of each sail panel. This is not really a major problem, as where necessary it is quite easy to use the additive mode to select any islands. In some cases the production of these islands will be exactly what is needed. In this case it probably makes little difference whether or not the lettering is selected, but results might be a little better with these areas not included in the selections.

If things do go slightly awry when using the Magic Wand tool it is possible to undo the last selection and try again. Where necessary, areas that evade the Magic Wand tool can be added to the selection using any of the selection tools in the Add to Selection mode. Using this method it is possible to add areas outside the selection or remove islands within it. Remember that areas or parts of them can be removed using the subtract

*Fig.7.17 Once again, the selection was accurate enough for the
processing to be applied successfully*

mode. The four mode buttons are available with all selection tools, and
permit these tools and modes to be freely mixed. Figure 7.17 shows the
finished version of the image, and in this case the more or less "raw"
selections have provided excellent results.

It is only fair to point out that the Magic Wand tool does not always work
this well. Matters were simplified in this instance because the outlines of
the panels were quite well defined in terms of colour contrast. Without
the boundaries well defined in this way the Magic Wand tool may seem
to make rather random selections, and one of the other methods might
then be a better choice. An automatic selection tool such as the Magic
Wand type is generally the best choice in situations where it does work
reasonably well.

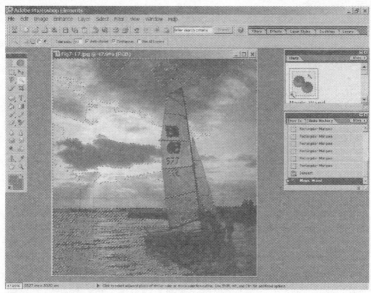

Fig.7.18 A high tolerance has resulted in a massive selection

Settings

There are a few Magic Wand settings available from the Options bar. The tolerance setting is important, and it is unlikely that good results will be obtained unless this is adjusted to suit each task. It controls the amount of colour contrast that is needed for Photoshop Elements to perceive the change as an edge. In Figure 7.18 a very high setting of 90 has been used. Left-clicking on one of the sail panels has produced a large and complex selection. In fact it is difficult to see what is and what is not selected. Operating the Delete key to delete the selection (Figure 7.19) reveals that most of the image was selected!

A much lower setting of 5 has been used in Figure 7.20, and only one very small area has been selected. Areas of the panel at virtually the same colour as the click point have not been selected. Unless the tolerance value is in the right "ball park" there is no chance of the Magic Wand tool finding the right outline in its entirety. Be prepared to experiment with various values in an attempt to find one that accurately locates the outline. Alternative, use a low Tolerance value together with the additive mode and build up selections piece by piece. The second method is the one that is most likely to succeed with awkward selections.

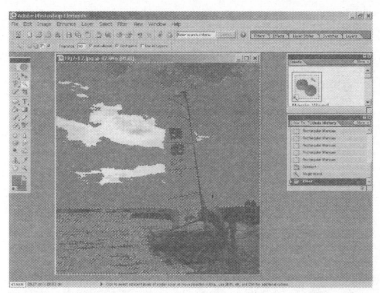

Fig.7.19 Deleting the selection reveals how much was selected

Fig.7.20 Very little is selected using a low tolerance value

Fig.7.21 The Contiguous mode seeks pixels of a suitable colour

It is also worth trying various points near and on the outline when left-clicking the Magic Wand tool. Bear in mind that the Magic Wand tool is colour conscious, and it is an outline of a certain colour that it seeks, not simply a path of about the same brightness. It therefore works best with objects that are predominantly the same colour, such as a patch of blue sky.

Contiguous

By default the Contiguous checkbox is ticked, which means that a continuous path of pixels is sought by the program, which tries to find a single outline. It will also find any "islands" within the outline and automatically subtract them from the selection. The Magic Wand tool simply selects any pixels at colours within its tolerance setting when this checkbox is not ticked. In other words, it tries to find any pixels of the right colour range, anywhere on the image, and it does not try to find outlines.

This is demonstrated in Figure 7.21, where the Magic Wand has been left-clicked on one of the dark shadow areas of the image. Anything

*Fig.7.22 Deleting the selection shows that all the dark pixels were
selected, wherever they were on the image*

black, anywhere on the image, has been selected. This is made clearer
in Figure 7.22, where the selection has been deleted. All the dark areas
including parts of the sea have been selected and erased. The non-
contiguous mode will often select far too much. However, if it accurately
finds the area you wish to select, it could still be a good choice.
Remember that the subtraction mode can be used to remove the
unwanted selections. The unwanted selections can soon be mopped
up with the Rectangular Marquee or Lasso tool.

Anti-aliased

Anti-aliased is a term that often crops up when dealing with digital images.
The Anti-aliased checkbox is ticked by default. It is also available and
used by default with the Lasso tools. Anti-aliasing smoothes the edges
of the selection or selections, which often gives better results than having
it faithfully follow every nook and cranny in an outline. On the other
hand, anti-aliasing will probably give less satisfactory results if the required
selection genuinely has rough edges. The smoothing will cause parts of
the required area to be omitted and (or) material outside the required

Fig.7.23 The selection menu

area to be included, giving entirely the wrong effect. With an area that has a smooth and well defined outline it is unlikely to make much difference one way or the other. Once again, it is a matter of experimenting to find the mode that gives the best results.

Selection menu

Do not overlook the facilities available from the Selection menu (Figure 7.23). A similar menu is also available by right-clicking within a selection. A Feather option is available when some selection tools are selected, and it also appears in the Options bar when appropriate. It is primarily intended for use with cut/copy and paste

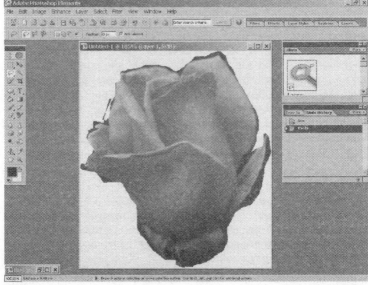

Fig.7.24 The rosebud has been copied in a very approximate fashion

Fig.7.25 Feathering can give a smooth but approximate outline

operations. There can be problems with objects that are pasted into an image having a two dimensional cardboard cut-out appearance.

Feathering offers one approach to integrating a pasted object into an image without getting the cardboard cut-out effect. It gives a blurred edge that blends into the new image more realistically, and the width of the feathering (in pixels) can be specified on the Options bar prior to selection. A small dialogue box appears when Feathering is chosen from the Select menu, and this is used to specify a value for the pixel width. This method can be used to add feathering to an existing selection.

Figure 7.24 shows the rosebud copied from the original image and pasted onto a plain background. The outline has not been traced very accurately, and the image is therefore a bit rough at the edges. Figure 7.25 shows the original image with the Feather setting at 80 pixels, and the outline has become very approximate. The setting has been deliberately set high so that the effect of feathering is shown very clearly.

In Figure 7.26 the rosebud has again been copied and then pasted onto a plain background, but the effect is now very different. What was previously a clearly defined edge has become extremely blurred. The

Fig.7.26 A large amount of feathering produces a soft focus effect

central part of the image is sharp, as in the original pasted version. Moving out towards the edge, the image is a combination of the pasted material and the background. The pasted image becomes progressively weaker towards the outer limit. Feathering helps to smooth edges and give more natural looking results when used in small amounts. When used more heavily it can give quite a good soft focus effect, as in this example.

There are four options available in the Modify submenu. The border option produces a small dialogue box that requests a pixel value to be entered. Instead of selecting the area within an outline, a band of pixels centred on the outline is selected. The value entered controls the width

Fig.7.27 The Lasso tool has been used to select the petals

of the band. The Smooth option does precisely that, and it will smooth out jagged edges in the marquee. The Expand and Contract options simply enlarge or shrink the selection by the specified number of pixels.

One application of the last two options is to take slightly more of an image than is really required for a copy and paste operation. The pasted background is then painted over using the existing background of the destination image. This is not a quick way of doing things, but it ensures that all the required source material is copied with no little bits missing, and the pasted image should integrate quite well with the rest of the destination image. You may find that some selection methods tend to outline slightly too much or too little material. The Expand and Contract options provide quick and easy solutions to these problems.

Grow

The Grow option in the main Select menu should not be confused with the Expand option in the Modify submenu. Grow does not expand the border of the selection by a certain number of pixels. Instead, it looks for

*Fig.7.28 Using the Grow facility has produced a more accurate
         selection*

pixels of a similar colour around the border, and the selection then grows
into these. In Figure 7.27 the Lasso tool has been used to roughly select
the petals of the rosebud, and I have deliberately kept well within the
true outline of the petals.

Using the Grow facility has enlarged the selection slightly (Figure 7.28),
engulfing a number of pixels that were previously left unselected. The
selection is not perfect, but in most places it has grown right out to the
edges of the petals. The selection is remarkably accurate considering
the very "rough and ready" initial selection. It is possible to use the grow
facility repeatedly in an attempt to encompass every last pixel, but doing
so is likely to enlarge the selection too far in some areas. It is generally
better to manually select any awkward pixels. Where a selection process
has missed some pixels at the edges, the Grow facility will usually give
more accurate results than the Expand facility.

Similar

The Similar function in the Select menu looks for pixels of similar colour
to the existing selection and adds them to the selection. Note that pixels

Fig.7.29 The Similar function selects any pixels of a similar colour

anywhere on the image will be included if they provide a suitable colour match. This is demonstrated by Figure 7.29 where a small black area on one of the sails was selected initially. With the aid of the Similar function, all the black pixels were then selected. This facility is similar to using the Magic Wand tool with the Contiguous option switched off. In both cases any pixels of a suitable colour will be selected.

Inverse

The Inverse option simply deselects everything that is currently selected, and selects everything that was not previously selected. In Figure 7.30 the selection of Figure 7.29 has been used again, but it has then been reversed using the Inverse option. The Delete button was then operated so that the original selection has been left and everything else has been erased. This gives a similar effect to converting the image to a true black and white bitmap, but it is far more versatile. When it is necessary to select a large percentage of an image it is often easier to select the other bits and then use the Inverse option.

*Fig.7.30 The Inverse facility was used to select everything but the dark
pixels, and then the selection was deleted*

The inverting and deleting technique is used a great deal to remove the
existing background from an object so that a new one can be added. In
Figure 7.31 the camera has been selected, the Inverse command has
been used, and the area outside the camera has been deleted.
Sometimes this is all that is needed, but in most cases a new background
is added. With a complex background the object can be copied and
pasted onto the background image. With a simple coloured or graduated
background it is just a matter of "pouring" it into place using the Paint
Bucket or Gradient tool. The Inverse selection must be left in place so
that the new background flows around the object.

In Figure 7.32 the Gradient tool has been used to provide the new
background. This is a rather spectacular blue that loses something in
the translation to a greyscale, but it gives an idea of the type of thing that

Fig.7.31 The Inverse facility was used to help delete the background

Fig.7.32 A graduated background was then added

Fig.7.33 The pelican on the left, together with its reflection, have been selected

can be achieved. There will usually be one or two rough edges on the object, but normal retouching techniques can be used to smooth these out and give a better appearance. It is worth trying this technique with the few images even if you have no immediate need for it. Any errors in the selection show up like the proverbial sore thumb once the background is removed, so it is a good way of perfecting your selection skills.

Masks and selections

Here we have been talking in terms of selections, but you will probably encounter the alternative term "mask". In a way there is no difference between the two. Suppose that you wish to select everything except a flower in an image so that you can alter the background without the risk of damaging the flower. You would select the flower using the normal selection methods and then use the Inverse command so that everything but the flower was selected. The selection process is being used to mask the flower so that it can not be accidentally altered, so this is an example of a mask.

Fig.7.34 The pelican has been moved, leaving a hole in the image

If the same selection process was used without the inversion at the end, so that the flower could be darkened perhaps, this would be considered a selection rather than a mask. However, the background is being masked so that changes will affect only the flower. In other words, the areas of the image that can be processed make up a selection, and the areas that can not represent a mask. In producing one you always produce the other.

Getting creative

You are not limited to using selections for selective processing. Selections can be used more creatively, are they are often used to make radical changes to a photograph or even to put together a new image from two or more images. In the example of Figure 6.33 the pelican on the left will be moved into the large vacant area in the left half of the image. The pelican has been selected using the methods described previously, as has its reflection in the lake. It is often easier if reflections and shadows are copied with the main subject, but each case has to be taken on its own merits. In certain circumstances it could be easier to (say) add a shadow after the move using the Burn tool. In this case, copying the

Fig.7.35 The blank areas of the image have been retouched

reflection with the bird certainly seems to be the easier way of doing things.

To move the selection to a new position it is just a matter of choosing the Move tool from the Toolbox and then using it to drag the selection to its new location. Alternatively, hold down the Control key while dragging the selection to a new position. After deselecting the pelican the job is only half done, because there is white space where the selection used to be (Figure 7.34). It is then a matter of using normal retouching techniques to fill in the gaps, as in Figure 7.35.

In Figure 7.36 things have been taken a stage further and the pelican on the right has been moved down slightly so that it is clear of the pipes for the fountain in the background. This is a bit more difficult because there is an overlap between the original material and the repositioned material. In this situation it can be helpful to copy more material than would normally be the case, and then use retouching techniques to repair the "holes" and to blend the moved selection into the rest of the image. Another technique, and the one used here, was to save the modified image under a new name and then load the original image. Material was then copied from the original image to the new one in order to fill in the gaps and make the reflections look plausible.

Fig.7.36 Further changes have been made. Compare this to Fig.7.33

One slight problem with this version of the image is that the pelican on the right looks slightly too small. It is the same size as in the original picture, but it has been moved forward so that it is nearer the viewer. The rules of perspective dictate that it should therefore be somewhat larger than it was originally. Scaling a selection up or down is very straightforward, and it is just a matter of selecting the Transform from the Image menu followed by Free Transform from the submenu that appears. The Skew, Distort, and Perspective functions in the submenu can also be used with selections. Use the handles on the selection box to provide the scaling or whatever transformation is required.

Copy and Paste

Selections can be used in copy and paste or cut and paste operations. Moving a selection from one part of an image to another is effectively the same as using the ordinary Cut and Paste options in the Edit menu. Use the Copy and Paste functions if you need to duplicate the selection while leaving the original intact. The Copy and Paste method is also used to add elements of one photograph to another image. This was the method used to add the dinghy into the image of Figure 2.7 that featured in chapter two. The dinghy had to be scaled down slightly and rotated a little in order to make it fit well into the image, and it is usually necessary to apply some transformations when copying material from one image to another.

Essentially the same method was used with the outsize pigeons of Figure 2.8, again in chapter two. This time three copy and paste operations were used, one for each pigeon. The three pigeons were produced from the same source material, but the scaling is different for each one. Also, different transformations were used for each copy in an attempt to make them look a bit different. A perfectionist would have altered the reflections in the river to match the added pigeons, but with joke images it is not always best to be too pedantic.

Note that something like this will not work well if (say) the pigeon is viewed from above in the original scene but from below in the doctored image. In this example the pigeon was viewed slightly from below in the original image, and this viewpoint has been maintained with the copies in the doctored image. Similar lighting is also important in the source and destination images. The light is predominantly from the right in the source and destination images, giving reasonably plausible results.

Stitching

Stitching, in a digital imaging context, is where two or more complete images are combined to form one large image. In other words, you take a photograph of (say) a landscape in two overlapping sections, which are then joined to make one (hopefully) seamless image. While this is not the quickest and most convenient method of taking photographs, and can not be applied to all types of photograph, it does have some definite advantages.

One of them is that by combining two photographs you are effectively increasing the resolution of your camera. Even allowing for a loss where the two images overlap, a 1.3 million pixel camera can produce 2.3 million pixel images, a 2.2 million pixel camera can produce 4 million pixel images, and so on. If you can normally print pictures to a maximum of about A5, using the stitching method it should be possible to produce something approaching full A4 prints.

Another advantage is that it gives wide-angle pictures from a camera that does not have a wide-angle lens, or even wider angle pictures from one that does. Few digital cameras have zoom lenses that can go wider than the equivalent of about 35 millimetres on a 35-millimetre camera.

This gives only a slightly wider angle of view than a standard lens. This is a big drawback if your main interest is landscapes and seascapes. Stitching two photographs together enables very wide-angle photographs to be produced.

The reason many photographers opt for the stitching technique is that they wish to take panoramic shots. Many cameras, digital or otherwise, have a special mode for panoramic photography. Unfortunately, all this does is to remove (typically) the top and bottom thirds of the image. This gives so-called "letterbox" format images, but the angle of coverage

Fig.7.37 The left half of the image

is not very great. In fact the vertical angle of coverage is very restricted. Stitching together two or three photographs produces a "letterbox" format print and gives a massive angle of view.

Stitching methods

Some cameras have a special mode for stitching photographs together, and others are supplied with a special utility program for this purpose. Some image editing programs now have this feature, or you can undertake the process manually using practically any image editing program. The manual approach leaves you in full control of the process, but stitching photographs together is much more difficult than most people imagine. The basic process is to first enlarge the canvas of one

Fig.7.38 And the right section

Fig.7.39 The manually joined version of the image

image so that there is space to accommodate the other image or images. The first image to be added to the existing one is opened, and it is selected in its entirety. In Photoshop Elements this is achieved by selecting All from the Select menu. The Copy and Paste facilities are then used in the normal way to copy the selected image onto the base image. The selection is moved around on the base image until a perfect match is found.

Unfortunately, in practice it is very unusual for a perfect match to be possible. Where it can be achieved it generally takes a great deal of trial and error, and a lot of time. There are various causes for a lack of a perfect match where the images overlap. You may have moved slightly between shots, and the fact that the camera angle has to change from one shot to the next can give perspective problems. The horizon might slope fractionally one way in one photograph and the other way in the next one. There will often be a slight but noticeable difference in exposure

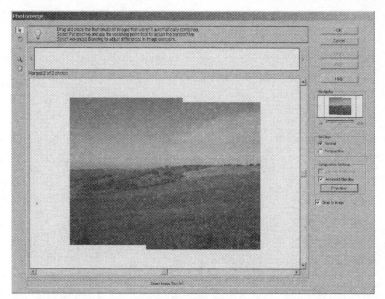

Fig.7.40 Stitching two images together in Photoshop Elements 2

from one image to the next, although this problem can be rectified before trying to stitch the images together.

Figure 3.37 and Figure 3.38 show two photographs having a generous overlap so that they could be easily stitched together manually. Joining them actually proved to be quite awkward. This is not surprising as there are plenty of objects in the photographs that are not very far away from the camera. In general the stitching process is easier if the nearest objects are well into the distance. Figure 7.39 shows the manually joined version of the photograph, which is reasonably convincing. However, a good match at the edges was never achieved, and retouching was used to hide an otherwise obvious join. The join is about one third of the way in from the left-hand side.

Automation

To use the automated stitching facility of Photoshop Elements, start by going to the Edit menu and selecting the Create Photomerge option. Operate the Browse button in the new window that appears and then select the files that you wish to use in the stitched image. Then operate

Fig.7.41 The join is visible in the plain area of sky

Fig.7.42 Some manual retouching has hidden the join

Fig.7.43 The automatically stitched version of Fig.7.39

the OK button to start the merging process. After a delay while the program does some processing a window like the one of Figure 7.40 will appear. The slider control below the Navigator panel can be used to zoom in on the combined image so that it can be searched for imperfections at the join or joins. A pan control is available from the toolbar in the top right-hand corner of the window.

It is merely necessary to operate the OK button if the program has successfully stitched the images together. If there is a problem you can remove the tick from the Snap to Image textbox and then use the tools to manually position the images, and if necessary apply rotation to one or more of the constituent images. Alternatively, more automated help can be produced by ticking the Advanced Blending and (or) Perspective checkboxes. The Advanced Blending function does an automatic equivalent of manual retouching to hide the join or joins. The Perspective function adjusts the images to take into account the change in camera angle from one section to the next.

Figure 7.41 show the combined image produced by the automated stitching process, after cropping to remove the rough edges. The two images have been fitted together very expertly, but the difference in the exposure of the two prints has left an obvious join in the plain area of sky. Darkening the right-hand image prior to the merging process would probably have avoided this, but it was easily smoothed out using some retouching with the Clone tool set at about 50 percent opacity (Figure 7.42). Figure 7.43 shows an automatically stitched equivalent of Figure 7.39, and the automated version is actually the more accurate of the two.

Points to remember

It is possible to get good results from most images by applying any processing to the entire image. However, with some images it is better to apply selective processing. For example, an excessively bright sky can be selected and darkened with no risk of rendering the rest of the picture too dark.

Objects can be selected and then moved to a different part of the image. This leaves a blank space where the selection used to be, but it can usually be filled in using normal retouching techniques. Scaling or other transformations are sometimes needed in order to make the relocated material fit in plausibly with the rest of the image.

Selections can be copied and pasted from one image to another. This type of thing is often used to produce fake photographs of people with their favourite pop or film stars, visual joke images, etc. Although simple in theory, it can sometimes be difficult to get reasonably convincing results. Scaling and other transformations are often required.

Most image editing programs have a number of different selection tools. The simplest ones offer no help to the user, who must drag rectangles or other shapes onto the image, or simply draw around the area that must be selected. Magnetic selection tools provide a degree of automation.

The user draws close to the outline of the selection, and the tool searches for an outline to snap to. Fully automatic systems search for adjacent pixels of a similar colour.

It is usually necessary to do a certain amount of tweaking to the parameters of the automatic and semiautomatic selection modes in order to obtain good results. A high tolerance setting results in an automatic system selecting practically everything. A low tolerance setting results in next to nothing being selected. Try to find a good compromise, but if necessary build up the selection using a low tolerance setting.

In practice it is often necessary to use two or more selection tools in order to obtain accurate results. It can also be necessary to use different selection modes. One mode enables selections to be gradually built up using an additive process. Another mode enables areas selected in error to be removed from the selection.

Panoramic pictures, etc., can be produced by joining two or more pictures together. While simple in theory it is often difficult to get convincing results in practice. It is much easier using a utility program specifically designed for this purpose, or the automated help available from some image editing software.

Using brushes

Brush off

Image editing programs are ideal for retouching jobs on photographs, such as painting out bits of pictures that you do not like, repairing damage in old prints, and so on. Retouching photographs is not exactly new, and it has probably been around for almost as long as there have been photographs. However, it is much easier to achieve good results using the digital version, and the range of possibilities is larger.

With conventional retouching the photograph is altered using special paints and inks. These can be applied using conventional brushes or an airbrush. The direct equivalent of this with Photoshop is to mix the desired colours and then paint them onto the image using the various brush tools. The trouble with this approach is that photographs do not usually have large areas of one colour. There are usually colour graduations and plain areas usually have more texture than is apparent at first glance. A lack of graduations and texture can make the retouched areas stand out like the proverbial "sore thumb". The simple painting approach can work well with small areas, but it takes a lot of effort and skill to produce the textures to make larger areas look convincing.

The photograph of Big Ben (Figure 8.1) provides a good example of a photograph that is easily retouched using any of the normal techniques. Make your initial experiments with something fairly straightforward such as this. One slight problem with this photograph is the bits of the Parliament building that are intruding into the picture in a few places at the bottom of the picture. You might like it this way, but they slightly spoil the otherwise very simple composition and are an unwanted distraction. Being at the edge of the picture and against a virtually plain background, painting out these objects is about as easy as retouching photographs gets. It is made easier by the fact that the resolution of the photograph is not very high, and the individual pixels are clearly visible

Fig.8.1 The original version of the image

even using a modest amount of zoom. In general, the higher the resolution of an image the more carefully it has to be retouched.

Brush size is often important with retouching work, but all the more so with the simple painting technique. In this case the plainness of the background makes it less important as there are no textures to paint in. There is actually a hint of texture in the background, but this is due to camera "noise" and is not inherent in the scene. It is so slight the painting over each object with a single colour should give convincing results.

The ordinary brush tool is used for this type of retouching. It is accessed via the sixth button down in the left-hand column of the Toolbox. A wide range of preset brush styles and sizes are available from the Brush menu in the Options bar. This becomes available in the Options bar when any brush or brush type tool is selected. The default size of this menu is quite small, but it can be dragged to a larger size via the triangle in the bottom right-hand corner. Having a larger range of brushes displayed avoids excessive scrolling of the options. Figure 8.2 shows some lines drawn using a few of the brushes from this menu. As will be apparent from this, more than just simple brushes of various widths are available. Some of the brushes produce special effects or try to mimic natural media such as chalks and crayons.

It is a good idea to produce a blank page using the New option from the File menu and then try some of the brushes. Note that the width of any brush can be altered via the Size textbox just to the right of the Brushes menu. Left-clicking the triangle just to the right of this textbox enables the brush size to be adjusted via a slider control. A submenu can be

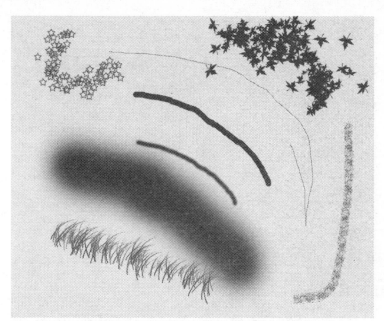

Fig.8.2 Brushstrokes made using brushes of various types

produced by left-clicking the small button in the top right-hand corner of the menu. Some of the options alter the way the menu is presented, such as giving a text only version, but most users prefer the default style. Alternative brush sets are available, and loading one of these results in the menu changing to suit new brushes.

It is worth taking some time to experiment with the preset brush sets. However, the brushes in the default set are perfectly adequate for most photographic retouching work. The default brushes are divided into three main groups, and one of these is the type that produces well defined lines with "clean" edges. The largest group produce simple lines but with fuzzy edges. The third group produce textures and effects. The brushes with blurred edges are good for retouching images, as the fuzzy edges often help blend the newly added material with the original image. This is particularly important with an image such as the one being processed here, where any abrupt change in colour will be readily apparent on the plain areas being retouched, even if the change is very small.

Fig.8.3 The retouched version of the Big Ben image

Figure 8.3 shows the image with all the offending objects painted out. I did things the hard way and mixed the colour used to paint over each object. The easy way is to use the Eyedropper facility of the Color Picker, selecting an area just to one side of the object to be removed. There is some variation in the colour of the sky from one object to the next, so a different colour had to be used for each object. With this type of thing it is important to zoom in on the area being altered so that you can see exactly what you are doing. This helps to avoid leaving to odd pixel unchanged and accidentally painting over edges that should be left unchanged.

Fig.8.4 The original image, complete with part of a dinghy

Getting artistic

It is possible to paint out objects on something other than a plain background, but it is more time consuming and requires more skill. The photograph of Figure 8.4 is slightly spoiled by part of a dinghy that is intruding at the bottom right-hand edge. It could be removed by cropping the bottom of the photograph, and this might work quite well. The alternative is to paint some sea over the top of the dinghy, which has the advantage of leaving the basic composition intact.

The obvious problem with this second approach is that it is necessary to paint in some convincing textures that will look like an area of sea. It helps a great deal if you are reasonably artistic. Another problem is that you do not know what should fill the area vacated by the removed object. Fortunately, neither does anyone else, so it provided it looks reasonably plausible there is no problem. Retouching does not have to be right, but it does have to look right. You have to allow yourself a certain amount of artistic licence when doing this type of thing.

The first step is to paint over the offending material with a colour that blends in well with the surrounding area. This gives a good basis to

Fig.8.5 The dinghy has been covered with a uniform colour

Fig.8.6 Some textures have been added to make it more convincing

*Fig.8.7 The original image. The dinghy in the foreground should look
      familiar (see Fig.2.7)*

work on. Painting textures directly onto the existing material is likely to
prove rather confusing, making the process much more difficult. Figure
8.5 shows the photograph with the dinghy painted out. In Figure 8.6 I
have painted in some likely looking textures, using the surrounding area
as a guide. The colours were copied from the surrounding material using
the Color Picker and the Eyedropper tool, and this helps to blend the
new material into the picture. The end result is reasonably convincing.

Fig.8.8 The dinghy on the right is to be removed

Cloning

There is a much easier way of handling this type of thing, which is to copy existing material over the object or objects you wish to remove. This is probably the only practical solution in cases where there is a great deal of fine texture in the surrounding area. Painting such textures is certainly possible, but it takes huge amounts of time carefully building up the textures using a tiny brush. Suppose that the dinghy about halfway up the right edge of Figure 8.7 is to be removed. The zoomed view of the area (Figure 8.8) shows that there is a large amount of fine detail in the surrounding area, which would make the normal painting technique very time consuming. On the other hand, there is plenty of material in the surrounding area that can be copied over the dinghy.

Photoshop Elements provides a special type of brush for copying material from one area to another, and this is called the Clone Stamp tool, but it is usually just referred to as the Clone tool. It is accessed via the second button up in the left-hand column of the Toolbox. The Clone tool excels at painting over unwanted objects or blemishes by copying from surrounding areas. We are all familiar with the problem of trees in the background seeming to grow out of the heads of people in the foreground. This type of problem can actually occur with all sorts of photographs. The Clone tool is ideal for dealing with this type of thing, or with any similar changes.

Painting using the Cloning tool is similar to using the ordinary Brush tool, but there are some important differences. As normal, a suitable brush has to be selected. Filling large areas is quicker using a large brush, but a small brush is often needed for filling in fiddly little areas. Accordingly, it is often a matter of starting with a large brush and moving down to a small one for the final touches. In this case the area involved is not particularly large or small, and there are no awkward little areas to fill. Consequently, a medium size brush is all that is required.

With a normal brush you "paint" on the screen by dragging the brush. In other words, you hold down the left mouse button while moving the mouse. The same method is used with the Clone tool, but an error message will be produced if you try to use it without first indicating what you wish to clone. You do this by first placing the pointer at the centre of the material you wish to clone and pressing the Alt key. Incidentally, when using any form of brush tool the pointer is actually an outline of the brush. You can therefore see the exact size and shape of the selected brush. When you press the Alt key, the pointer will change to a sort of crosshairs sight. Drag the pointer to the centre of the area that will be retouched, release the left mouse button, and then release the Alt key.

By doing this you are indicating an offset to Photoshop Elements. If you dragged the mouse 70 pixels up and 42 pixels to the left, then it will "paint" using material 70 pixels down and 42 pixels to the right of the brush. You are not restricted to copying to and from the areas indicated when setting the offset. It is possible to paint anywhere on the screen using this offset, but with the proviso that the source must be somewhere on the image. If the position of the brush is such that the source area is taken beyond the edge of the image, there is nothing to clone and nothing is "painted" onto the screen.

It is necessary to apply some common sense when using the Clone tool. Look at the image to find a source that will convincingly cover the object or blemish that is to be removed. In general it is best to use source material that is quite close to the area that will be covered. Material from further afield often looks as though it is suitable, but when you try it there are problems. In most images there are variations in the general level of brightness from one area to another. This can result in the cloned material

Fig.8.9 The retouched version of the image

being noticeably lighter or darker than its immediate surroundings. Like everything else in a photograph, textures and patterns tend to get smaller as they recede into the distance. If a pattern is obviously larger or smaller than its surroundings it will look like a patched area of the photograph.

The direction of any pattern is another important consideration. In this example the pattern is fairly random, which makes it easy to get good

Fig.8.10 The retouching here was done using the Clone tool

results. In the previous example the pattern in the sea ran horizontally throughout, which would give a wide choice of source material using the clone method. There will often be variations though, and a common example is where a portrait has a blemish in the subject's hair. The lines in the hair will run in various directions, and the blemish must be patched using cloned material that runs at something very close to the correct angle. Again, material close to the blemish is more likely to give convincing results than material copied from further afield. Copy in the direction of any lines in an attempt to make them run straight through the cloned area without any unnatural breaks.

It is often necessary to copy from more than one source in order to produce convincing results. Even when dealing with background material, copying a large amount from one area to another can produce a fairly obvious duplication. Some photographers are not keen on cloning techniques because of this. There is something to be said for using multiple sources even when it is not necessary to make a small amount of source material fill a large area. Apart from avoiding obvious duplication, using more than one source often produces more convincing results anyway.

Fig.8.11 The characters in the background are to be removed

The multiple source technique was used in Figure 8.9, where the dinghy was painted out in a matter of seconds. Figure 8.10 shows the photograph used in the previous example, but this time it has been retouched using the Clone tool. Again, it took only a matter of seconds to complete the task, and the end result is at least as convincing as the painted version.

Tricky situations

The more complicated the underlying material, the more difficult it is to paint-out objects from an image. This is the same whether you use conventional retouching techniques or the cloning method. Figure 8.11 shows a highly zoomed view of the beach scene used in an earlier example. You may feel that the people and the dog in the background add to the liveliness of the scene or that they just clutter things up and ruin the composition. Here we will assume that they must be removed, and this is a bit trickier than in the previous examples. The characters to be removed are in front of various types of material, including the wharf, waves, wet sand, and foam. Each character is in front of more than one type of background material.

Fig.8.12 The figure on the left, and her shadow, have been removed

Simply painting out each character with a single type of background material is clearly not going to give plausible results. The right kind of material has to be used in each area that is painted with cloned material. With the figure on the left for example, a band of foam passes through the middle of the figure. A white area of foam must therefore be copied across this area to give a continuous line of foam. The head and upper body are in front of an ordinary area of sea, so ordinary sea is therefore copied over this area. The legs are in front of wet sand, so an area of wet sand must be copied over them. There is a shadow here as well, and it is important to remove this as well. The final image will look a little strange if it is covered with ghostly shadows of invisible people!

Figure 8.12 shows the zoomed view with the figure on the left removed, and Figure 8.13 shows the finished image with all the unwanted characters removed. If you did not know that the picture had been altered it is unlikely that you would ever guess. The cloned material has been added sympathetically so that it blends in well with existing material, leaving no obviously glitches where the cloned and original material meets. Note that it is generally easier to blend cloned material into an image using a fuzzy edged brush and that obvious joins are often left if a type having a "hard" edge is used.

Fig.8.13 The finished image with all the background characters removed.

It is not always practical to remove unwanted objects from a picture. Sometimes the material in the background will be too complex and exacting for simple cloning techniques to work convincingly. It is better to leave objects in the image rather than remove them in a way that is unconvincing.

Expanding images

The Clone tool can be used to expand an image. Probably the most common use of this technique is where an image has been rotated to correct a sloping horizon. The easy solution to removing the four triangular blank areas produced by doing this is to crop the image, but this also results in some of the image

Fig.8.14 The rotated image, complete with blank areas

itself being removed. The alternative is to add some likely looking cloned material into the blank areas, or to use a mixture of cloning and cropping. Figure 8.14 shows the rotation example used in a previous chapter. In the version of Figure 8.15 the blank areas produced by rotating the image

have been filled with cloned material so that nothing from the original image has been lost.

Essentially the same technique can be used to make minor adjustments to the composition of a picture. Figure 8.16 shows the modified beach scene photograph, but it has a strip of extra material added down the right-hand edge. In the original version

Fig.8.15 The retouched version of Fig.8.14

Fig.8.16 The widened version of Fig.8.13

the two running figures were rather too close to the edge of the picture, and were virtually going off the edge of the image. Adding a few millimetres down the right-hand edge has effectively moved them into the picture, giving a more viewer-friendly composition. Of course, the first step with this technique is to resize the canvas so that a few millimetres are added at the appropriate edge of the image. The Clone tool is then used to fill the vacant strip.

The technique for adding the new material is basically the same as the one used for painting out unwanted objects. The angle used when

Fig.8.17 Here the buoy on the left is in its original position

cloning should be such that any lines at the edge of the picture are carried seamlessly through into the newly added area. In other areas try to vary the angle so that obvious duplication is avoided. Being realistic about it, no more than a few percent can be added to each edge without the copying process becoming obvious, but that is often enough to tidy up what would otherwise be slightly rough composition.

Duplicate flaws

When using the clone tool it is important to bear in mind that is copies from the image as it is when you start each cloning operation. This point is demonstrated by Figure 8.17 and 8.18. Figure 8.17 shows the original picture, complete with a mooring buoy on the left-hand side of the picture. In Figure 8.18 it has been painted out using material copied just to the right of its original position. However, I have continued painting towards the left, and the buoy has reappeared to the left of its original position. Even though the object was not visible on the screen when it was cloned, it was still in the computer's memory, and it was still copied to the new position.

Fig.8.18 Here the cloning process has moved the buoy to the left rather than just removing it

Of course, this could be useful if you need to move something slightly, but it also means that in most situations there is a definite limit on the amount of material that can be cloned in a single operation. The smaller the offset used, the smaller the amount that can be copied without cloning the object you are trying to cover. Results are often best with a small offset, but a large offset has the advantage of enabling each operation to clone more material. A compromise therefore has to be sought. If circumstances force the use of a small offset, it is still possible to use a small amount of source material to fill a large area. However, it has to be done in several clone operations rather than one large one.

It is desirable to clone material in as few operations as possible as this makes it quick and easy to produce seamless results. In practice this is not an option if a small offset is used, and copying large areas runs the risk of making the use of cloning too obvious. Due care has to be taken when using numerous small cloning operations to fill a large area. It is easier to end up with odd looking repeating patterns than it is to produce convincing results. Varying the direction and size of the offset helps to avoid or at least disguise any repeating patterns.

Fig.8.19 The cloud has been cloned from one image to another

Alignment option

When trying to make a small amount of source material go a long way it can be useful to remove the tick in the Alignment checkbox of the Options bar. As already explained, the Clone tool normally operates using the offset indicated by pressing the Alt key and dragging the pointer. This offset is used wherever you "paint" on the screen. It can be changed at any time by pressing the Alt key and dragging the pointer again, but it can be tedious and time consuming if numerous changes are required.

Things operate rather differently with the Alignment option switched off. Before using the Clone tool it is merely necessary to press the Alt key and then left-click on the centre of the area that you wish to copy from. Each time you start painting with the Clone tool it will start copying from the point that you indicated. In effect, a new offset is indicated and used each time you start using the Clone tool. Simply press the Alt key and left-click on another point in order copy from a different part of the image. Obviously this method can be very useful when it is necessary to copy the same object to various points on the image.

Note that the Clone tool is not restricted to copying from one part of an image to another. With two images loaded into Photoshop it is possible to set a start position for the copying in one image and a destination point in another image. This provides an offset in the usual way, and material can then be copied from one picture to another. In Figure 8.19 this method has been used to copy a cloud from the beach scene to a photograph of HMS Belfast. This type of thing will often work quite well, but copying most types of object from one image to another is less straightforward than you might expect. Errors of scale are fine for visual jokes, but you have to be careful not to inadvertently produce a joke image. The Copy and Paste method is often better as it permits scaling and other transformations.

With any form of copying there can be problems with different types of lighting. The final image will look a bit odd if the copied object is backlit but the main scene is lit from the front, or vice versa. Another problem is that an added object might not look right unless it is accompanied by an added shadow. Whatever method of copying is used, this type of thing is often less than convincing. Things like filling small blemishes using material from another print and copying a cloud to an otherwise cloudless sky are usually successful, but it can be difficult to obtain good results when trying anything more ambitious. It can be done, but you have to be careful with the choice of source material, and the cut and paste method is usually better.

When undertaking any complex cloning it is a good idea to save the image at various stages in the development of the work. If things start to go awry it is then easy to go back to an earlier stage where things were progressing nicely. It is just a matter of using the Save As facility in the File menu to save the image under different names, such as Image-1, Image-2, Image-3, and so on. Unwanted versions can be deleted once you have finished processing the image. Of course, the History palette enables the image to be taken back 20 steps without the use of snapshots, but you can soon find that more than 20 cloning operations have been used.

Layers

With the All Layers checkbox ticked it is possible to copy from any visible layer to the current layer. This checkbox is not ticked by default, and it is then only possible to copy from the current layer. Certain operations can be a bit confusing for newcomers to Photoshop Elements, and other photo-editing software, since they automatically produce a new layer.

Paste operations produce new layers, and each piece of text that is added is automatically placed onto its own layer. Without realising it, you can soon have quite a large number of layers that Photoshop has generated. As a consequence of this, you find that most of the image can not be edited, or so it appears anyway.

The point of using one layer per element in the image is that it makes it easy to edit each element separately. For example, text or pasted material can be moved by selecting the correct layer and then dragging it using the Move tool (the one at the top of the right-hand column in the Toolbox). There is no need to bother about selecting the material that must be moved, since there is nothing else on that layer. Move the entire layer and you move the required elements in the image. There is no need to heal gaps left when the material is moved, because it does not leave any.

Think of layers in terms of each one being on a separate piece of transparent film, with the pieces of film laid one on top of the other. Material on a piece of film near the top of the pile will obscure some of the material on lower layers. If the layer is moved to one side, the obscured material can be seen, but a different part of the image is obscured on the lower layers. Hence objects can be moved around without the need to fill in any gaps left by the changes. If an object is cut from an image it will still leave a "hole", but once it is pasted onto a new layer it can be moved around without damaging the underlying image. Layers give tremendous freedom, and they are a feature of most graphics software.

Automatically generated layers can give beginners problems because the new layer becomes the current one, and it is not possible to edit anything on another layer. Attempts to do so either have no effect or produce error messages. Normally it is only possible to edit the current layer. In the case of a cloning operation, it is normally only possible to clone from and to the current layer. With the All Layers checkbox ticked it is possible to copy from any layer, but it is still only possible to add cloned material to the current layer.

Much image editing can be done without the use of layers, but with certain types of editing their use is clearly mandatory. The Layers palette is used to control the layers, and it can be activated by operating the Layers tab in the Options bar or selecting Layers from the Window menu. The Layers palette has a list of all the layers in the image, and initially there is just one that is called Background. Any layers that are added by text or paste operations are added above any existing layers, and they are called Layer 1, Layer 2, Layer 3, and so on (Figure 8.20). The position of a layer

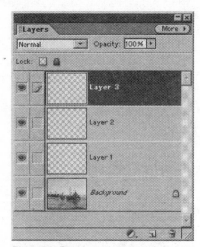

Fig.8.20 The Layers palette. Layer 3 is currently selected

in the list is the same as its position in the image. For example, Layer 2 is on top of Layer 1 and the Background layer. Anything on Layer 2 therefore covers these lower layers. Similarly, anything on Layer 3 would obstruct the view of Layer 2 and the lower layers.

It is possible to move a layer to a new position in the list, and the image, by dragging its name in the list to a new position. Note that the layers are not automatically renamed, and Layer 5 retains that name even though it is only three positions above the Background layer. It is the position in the list that counts, and not the names. As pointed out previously, it is only possible to edit the current layer. It is merely necessary to left-click on a layer's name in the list in order to make it the current layer and editable. There are eye icons in the left-hand column of the list. Left-clicking on an eye icon makes the relevant layer invisible, and left-clicking again makes it reappear. It is often necessary to switch off upper layers so that lower ones can be seen properly for editing purposes.

It is possible to manually generate a new layer by selecting New and then Layer from the Layer menu. A small dialogue box will appear, and you can then alter the name of the layer or accept the default name. Alternatively, operate the Create Layer button at the bottom of the Layers palette. This is the middle button. The current layer can be deleted by selecting Delete Layer from the Layer menu. Any layer can be deleted by dragging its entry to the Delete Layer button at the bottom of the Layers palette. This is the right-hand button. Note that there must always be at least one layer in an image, so it is impossible to delete a layer if it is the only one present.

As implemented in Photoshop Elements, layers are a fairly involved topic. However, for most purposes you only need to be able to select the required layer, control the visibility of layers, and alter the positions of layers. As explained previously, these are all easily achieved via the Layers palette.

Mode menu

Returning to the subject of the Clone tool, the Mode menu (Figure 8.21) gives a long list of alternatives to straightforward cloning, and this is available with any brush tool selected. Some of these are fairly obvious in the way that they function, while others are something less than obvious in this respect. The best way to get to grips with them is to go through the complete list, trying them one by one.

The Luminosity option is quite useful, and it simply applies the luminosity values of the cloned material while retaining the colour values of the original image. The Color option has the opposite effect, with the luminosity values of the original image being

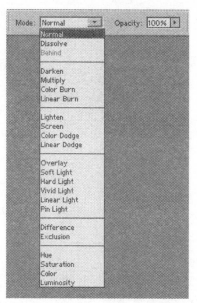

Fig.8.21 The numerous options of the mode menu

retained and only the colour being copied. This can produce some good ghostly effects. In fact a number of the options produce ghostly effects. Try the Soft Light, Lighten, and Darken options for example.

The Opacity control might be better termed the Transparency control, and it gives normal operation at 100 percent and an invisible copy at zero percent. It is sometimes possible to blend the cloned material into the original more convincingly if less than 100 percent opacity is used. With the Alignment option used it is possible to set a low opacity value and gradually build up the cloned material to the required strength by repeatedly copying it. One slight problem in using less than 100 percent opacity is that it can result in textures in the cloned area of the image being smoothed out. This is almost certain to occur if the cloned material is brought up to the required opacity by copying it from more than one source. There tends to be a sort of averaging process that will certainly alter textures and can lose them altogether.

Note that simply placing the brush over an area and holding down the left mouse button will not result in the image gradually building up. It is the number of times that the brush is swept over an area that determines

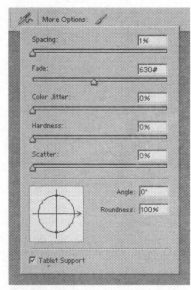

Fig.8.22 The extra brush options

the strength of the cloned image. You can get this build-up effect with some image editing programs via the Airbrush tool, and it is a very useful facility. This method gives the greatest control over the mixing of the original and cloned material, but it requires a bit more skill to fully utilize its potential. It is especially useful if you are using a pointing device that is not pressure sensitive, and otherwise provides little control over the flow of paint.

There are additional variations available from the Further Options button in the Options bar. Operating this button produces the control panel of Figure 8.22, and it is a good idea to experiment with the settings. In Figure 8.23 the strokes at the top and on the right are respectively the fuzzy edged and normal varieties. The Hardness control determines the hardness or softness at the edges of brushstrokes. The second and third strokes from the top were produced using the Scatter and Spacing controls respectively. The brushstroke at the bottom used the Color Jitter facility. The stroke on the left was produced using the Fade facility. The effects can be combined to produce further options. For most retouching work the normal and fuzzy edged brushes will suffice, but there is a vast range of alternatives available should you need them.

Dodge and Burn

Dodge and burn are two terms used when making photographic prints by hand. Dodging is when card masks or the operator's hands are used to block light from the enlarger to prevent it from reaching certain parts of the photographic paper. This in only done for part of the exposure, and its purpose is to reduce the exposure to parts of the print. Burning is the opposite process, where the print is exposed normally, and then extra exposure is used on certain parts of the print. On the face of it, burning makes areas lighter, and dodging makes them darker. It is

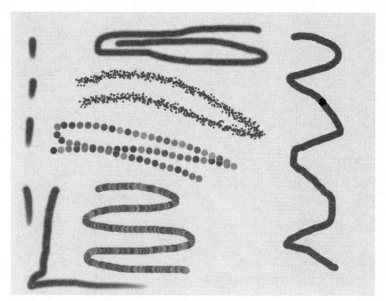

Fig.8.23 Some of the available brush effects

actually the other way around though, because the prints are normally made from photographic negatives onto negative printing paper. Therefore, burning makes areas darker and dodging makes them lighter.

Where you need to lighten or darken a large area it is usually better to select that area and then process it using the Levels facility or the ordinary Brightness and Contrast controls. The Dodge and Burn tools are normally used where one or several relatively small areas must be processed. Figures 8.24 and 8.25 show the "before" and "after" versions of an image where the Burn tool has been used to darken some of the cloud areas to make them look more menacing and dramatic. The Burn tool is ideal for this type of thing.

You will often find that the effect of the Burn tool is too strong, but its effect can be reduced via the Exposure control on the Options bar. To reduce the effect, use a lower setting than the default value of 50 percent. A setting of about 15 to 20 percent is usually sufficient. It might occasionally be better to have the Burn tool provide a stronger effect by increasing the exposure value. The Range menu in the Options bar permits the burning to be applied principally to the shadows, mid tones,

Fig.8.24 The original version of the image

Fig.8.25 Here some of the clouds have been darkened using the Burn tool

or highlights. An increase in contrast can be produced by applying burning to the shadow areas.

The Dodge tool has the same controls as the Burn type and is much the same in use except, of course, it lightens rather than darkens. The main use for the Dodge tool is in lightening excessively dark shadow areas. Strong shadows tend to be a problem whenever the light is provided by a single source, such

Fig.8.26 The "before" image

as the sun on a cloudless day. This can give problems with things like a shadow under the bride's nose making it look like she has a moustache! Modern films have good colour saturation, but this seems to have been achieved at the expense of ever higher levels of contrast. Consequently, digital images produced by scanning prints, negatives, or transparencies often have a definite lack of detail in the shadow areas.

Moderate use of the Dodge tool will sometimes help to bring out a little more detail in the shadows, and will prevent shadow areas from looking excessively "heavy". Figure 8.26 shows part of a photograph of some fishing boats in a seascape. The photographs in this book have been subjected to a certain amount of contrast reduction in order to accommodate the printing process, so the shadows on the original image are even darker than those in Figure 8.26. In Figure 8.27 some lightening of the shadows has been applied using the Dodge tool. Avoid excessive use of the Dodge tool, as it will provide rather washed out colours. The opposite is true of the Burn tool, which will produce oversaturated colours if you are not careful.

Fig.8.27 The "after" version

It is not a good idea to immediately opt for the Dodge tool when dealing with excessively dark areas. As demonstrated previously, some processing using the Levels or

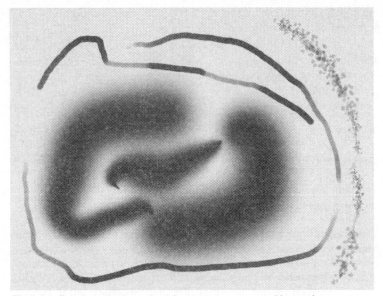

Fig.8.28 Brushstrokes made using a pressure sensitive stylus

Curves facilities will usually provide good overall brightness and avoid this type of problem. The Dodge tool is best for localised problems that can not be fixed using these facilities. Also, bear in mind that an area can be selected, and adjustments to brightness, contrast, and colour balance can then be exclusively applied to that area.

Sponge tool

The Sponge tool is grouped with the Dodge and burn tools, and it is often used in conjunction with them. This is a useful tool in its own right though. In its normal (Desaturate) mode the Sponge tool reduces saturation, or weakens colours in other words. I presume the name of this tool is derived from the small sponges that watercolorists sometimes use to remove paint from the paper, giving weaker colours. Darkening an area using the Burn tool often results in excessively strong colours and the Sponge tool will correct this problem. Of course, it can be used wherever an image has problems with over bright colours.

The Mode menu gives the option of setting the Sponge tool to the Saturate mode, where it has the opposite effect to normal. In other words, it

*Fig.8.29 The Options bar for the Magnetic Lasso tool has a Pen
Pressure option*

increases the colour saturation. Lightening areas using the Dodge tool
often results in washed-out colours, and the Saturate mode can be used
to correct this problem. It can also be used wherever there is a localised
problem with weak colours. Overall problems with colour saturation are
more easily corrected using the Hue/Saturation feature.

Pressure sensitive

If you are using a graphics tablet with Photoshop it is very likely that it
will be pressure sensitive. This facility can be used to good effect with
Photoshop Elements' brush tools, and the pressure sensitivity can be
used in a variety of ways. Figure 8.28 shows some brush strokes
produced using a pressure sensitive stylus. With some strokes the
pressure controls the width of the stroke while with others it controls the
flow of "paint". As one of the strokes demonstrates, it is still possible to
produces straightforward strokes at maximum width (or whatever), and
you are not forced into producing fancy brushstrokes when using a
pressure sensitive device.

The facilities available from graphics tablets vary from one unit to another.
Units designed primarily for use with CAD systems are often large but
may lack pressure sensitivity. For use with image editing programs these
tablets are still better than a mouse, but a smaller unit that does have
pressure sensitivity is a much better choice. Some graphics tablets go
beyond pressure sensitivity and permit the angle of the pen to control
certain aspects of brushstrokes. The documentation supplied with the
tablet should provide details of the facilities available, and how to use
them with popular graphics programs, including Photoshop Elements.

With the tablet correctly installed, additional options will be available when
using the appropriate tools. Pressure information can be used with some
tools that do not really fall into the brush category. Figure 8.29 shows
the options bar with the Magnetic Lasso tool selected, and there is a Pen
Pressure checkbox. The Edge Width value decreases with increasing
pressure when this option is ticked.

Fig.8.30 The Selection Brush was used to "fine tune" this selection

Selection Brush tool

The Selection Brush tool is accessed via the third button from the top in the left-hand column of the Toolbox. It operates much like the ordinary Brush tool, but it is a selection that is painted onto the image. The usual marquee or marquees appear to indicate what has been selected. This is a purely manual method of producing selections, but you can zoom-in and selected bits of the image pixel by pixel if necessary. This gives the ultimate in selection accuracy, but it can be quite slow. However, it is possible to mix this method with other types of selection, and doing so will often speed things up.

In Figure 8.30 the petals of the rosebud were largely selected using the Magic Wand tool, with the selection then being expanded using the Selection Brush tool. Slightly too much has been selected on the top right-hand edge, but this is easily corrected. Do not use the eraser tool to trim back selections. It will erase the image in the normal way and will not alter the selection. The Selection Brush tool has two modes that are selected via the Mode menu in the Options Bar (Figure 8.31). The Selection mode is used by default, and the area you paint over becomes

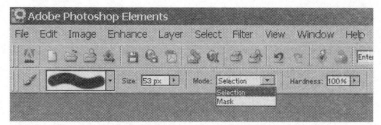

Fig.8.31 The Selection Brush tool has two modes of operation

a selection in this mode. The other mode is the Mask type, and the area you paint on the screen is a mask, and everything else is selected.

A slightly overdone selection can be trimmed back by switching to the Mask mode. The selected area is then covered by a red overlay and the masked area is shown normally (Figure 8.32). You then simply paint over the area you wish to deselect and switch back to the Selection mode when you have finished. If you paint a mask rather than a selection, it can be trimmed back by temporarily switching to the Selection mode.

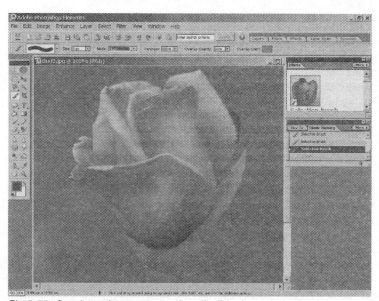

Fig.8.32 A red overlay appears when the Mask mode is used

Fig.8.33 The selection has been trimmed back where there were errors and then extended to include the leaves and stem

Of course, the Inverse function in the Select menu operates with selections and masks produced using the Selection Brush tool, so you can paint a selection and change it to a mask (or vice versa) using this function.

It is useful to bear in mind that any selection can be edited by switching to the Selection Brush tool and then using the appropriate mode to add to or reduce the selection. This is usually the easiest method of making fine adjustments to selections. The red overlay used in the Mask mode is not appropriate for all images, but an Overlay Color button appears at the right end of the Options bar when this mode is selected. Operating this button produces the usual Color Picker window where any desired colour can be chosen. There is also an Overlay Opacity setting in the Options bar, and this can be used to control the strength of the overlay.

Figure 8.33 shows the rosebud image with the selection trimmed back and then extended to include the stem and leaves. The selection can then be used in the normal way. In Figure 8.34 it has been inverted and then the original background has been replaced with a graduated type.

Paint Bucket tool

The Paint Bucket and Graduation tools are not strictly speaking brush tools, but they are often used to paint new backgrounds onto images, as in a previous example (see Figure 7.32). It is therefore reasonable to group them with the brush tools. The Paint Bucket tool applies a single colour to the image (the current foreground colour), but not with the same direct control that is possible using a brush. The Paint Bucket and Graduation tools are

Fig.8.34 A new background has been added to the image

both examples of tools that provide flood fills. In other words, they instantly fill the selected area.

One way of using the Paint Bucket tool is to select an area via the usual selection tools, delete the contents of the selection by pressing the Delete key, and then left-click somewhere within the selection using the Paint Bucket tool. The selection will then be filled with the currently selected foreground colour. Although this tool is mainly used for painting backgrounds, it is the foreground and not the background colour that it uses.

It may not be necessary to make a selection before using this tool, as it has some ability to selectively fill areas. It works in a way that is very much like the Magic Wand tool, and it seeks out pixels of a similar colour to the one that you left-click on with the tool. Like the Magic Wand tool it normally looks for a single area, but it will look for any pixels of an appropriate colour if the Contiguous checkbox is not ticked. Also in

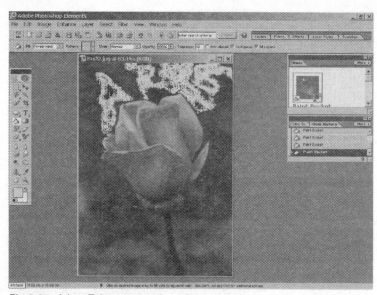

Fig.8.35 A low Tolerance setting often produces scrappy results

Fig.8.36 A high Tolerance setting usually selects too much

common with the Magic Wand tool, it has a Tolerance setting that determines the range of colours that will be replaced. The higher the Tolerance setting, the less discriminating it becomes.

If the main subject stands out well from a fairly plain background it might be possible to replace the background using a single click of the Paint Bucket tool. In most cases it is not as simple as this, and it will be necessary to use multiple clicks to gradually cover the appropriate area. Using a low Tolerance

Fig.8.37 The Soft Light option produced this background effect

setting helps to avoid having the paint bleed into the wrong areas, but it can also produce numerous islands that would take a long time to fill individually (Figure 8.35). Using a high Tolerance setting gives greater coverage with fewer islands, but runs the risk of the paint flowing into the wrong areas. In Figure 8.36 for example, some of the stem and the lower part of the rosebud have been filled because they were a similar colour to the background.

Usually the best tactic is to use a medium setting of around 30 and use multiple selections. If a few islands are produced they can be retouched using the ordinary Brush tool. Unless the main subject stands out really well from the background it is probably best to use the normal tools and techniques to select the background, which can then be replaced easily and with certainty.

Note that the Mode menu provides the same options that are available when using the Brush tool. It is therefore possible to paint with effects

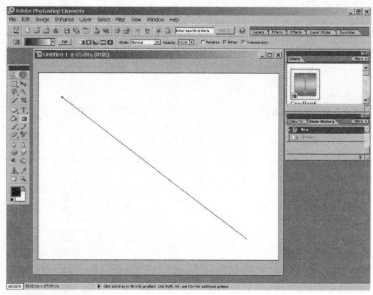

Fig.8.38 Adding the control line for a graduated fill

rather than a single colour. In Figure 8.37 the Soft Light option was used when filling the background. The effect is severely watered down by the conversion from colour to greyscale, but it gives an idea of the types of thing that can be achieved.

Gradient tool

The Gradient tool has no built-in selectivity, so making a selection first and the applying the paint is the only option when using this tool. It provides a graduated fill that starts at the current foreground colour and finishes at the current background colour. In Figure 8.38 the first point was placed by left-clicking near the top left-hand corner of the screen and then the pointer was dragged towards the diagonally opposite corner. A "rubber band" line is produced between the first point and the current position of the pointer.

Releasing the mouse button at the second point produced the result shown in Figure 8.39. The foreground and background colours were black and white respectively, so these are the start and finish colours in

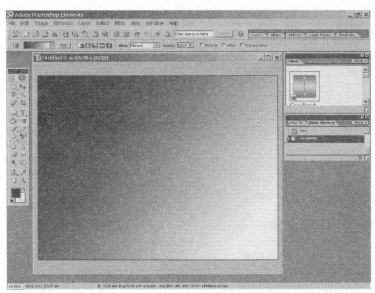

Fig.8.39 The fill produced by the control line of Fig.8.38

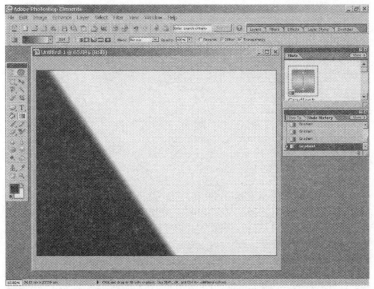

Fig.8.40 The transition from one colour to the other can be abrupt

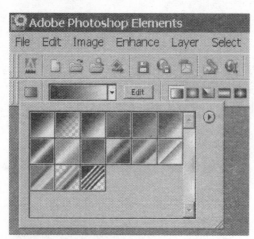

Fig.8.41 *Preset graduated fills are available from this pop-down menu*

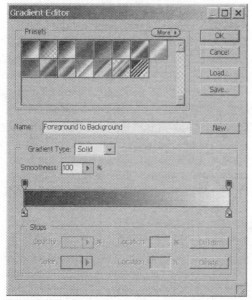

Fig.8.42 *You can design your own fills using the Gradient Editor*

the graduated fill. Note that the direction of the graduation follows the angle of the line in Figure 8.38. The graduation occurs within the two guide points placed on the image. Anything beyond these points is set to the foreground or background colour, as appropriate. Setting the two points very close together gives a very rapid change from the foreground colour to the background colour, as in Figure 8.40.

There are some preset graduations available from a pop - down menu on the options bar (Figure 8.41). The current gradient can be added to this menu by operating the triangular button near the top right-hand corner of the window and choosing New from the popup menu that appears. Add a name for the graduation in the dialogue box that appears and then operate the OK

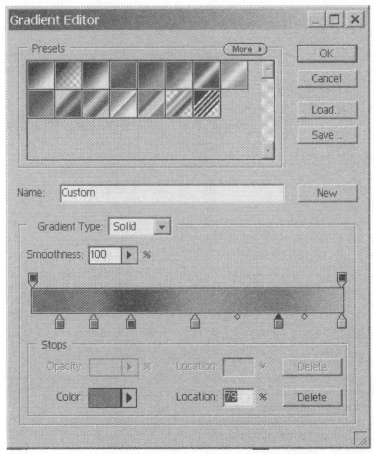

Fig.8.43 A complex gradient fill set up on the Gradient Editor

button. A thumbnail of the new graduation should then be added to the menu.

Complex graduations can be produced by left-clicking on the thumbnail of the current graduation in the Options bar. This produces the control panel of Figure 8.42. Left-click below the gradient bar in order to add a new colour at that point on the bar. The markers beneath the bar can be slid into new positions so it is easy to make fine adjustments to the

Fig.8.44 This background uses the gradient setup of Fig.8.43

graduations. A marker can be removed by left-clicking on it to select it and then operating the Delete button. Alternatively, just drag it away from the gradient bar. The colour provided by a marker can be altered using the Eyedropper tool to select a colour from an image.

*Fig.8.45 A radial gradient can produce a simple but effective
background*

To mix a colour, select the appropriate marker and then left-click the
colour button near the bottom left-hand corner of the window.
Alternatively, double-click the appropriate marker. Either way, the

standard Color Picker will be launched and the required colour can then be selected in the usual way. When a marker is selected, a smaller marker appears on each side it. These minor markers control the point at which the middle colours occur, and they can be dragged to new positions to distort the graduations. With the Smoothness setting at 100 percent there is the usual gradual and smooth change from one colour to the next. With lower settings there is a faster rate of change close to each of the main markers.

Figure 8.43 shows a complex gradient set up in the Gradient Editor, and Figure 8.44 shows it in use as a background. There are plenty more options available when producing graduated fills. Selecting Noise from the Gradient Type menu of the Gradient editor produces complex and usually quite psychedelic gradients. The Options bar offers several alternatives to the linear graduations that are produced by default. The radial gradient is probably the most useful, and Figure 8.45 shows a gradient of this type used as a background for the rosebud photograph. Plain backgrounds have their uses, but in general a simple graduated background works better. Be careful when using complex gradients as they can tend to distract the viewer from the main subject rather than helping to show it off to good effect.

Points to remember

Retouching can be used to remove unwanted objects from an image, such as a tree in the background that appears to be growing out of someone's head, passers by encroaching into a family group, or rubbish spoiling a beauty spot. It can also be used to cover imperfections in images such as scratches and chips in old prints.

It is possible to use the standard Brush tool for retouching, but it can be difficult to get convincing results. Most pictures contain complex graduations and textures that can be difficult to produce even if you are a reasonably talented artist.

Retouching using the Clone tool is usually much quicker and easier than traditional retouching methods. You can paint using textures "borrowed" from other parts of the image or even from another image. It is still necessary to exercise a certain amount of skill in order to get the new material to blend in properly with the existing material.

Be careful when using repeated cloning to fill a large area from a small amount of source material. This tends to produce repeating patterns that render the cloned material implausible. Using different offsets or switching off the Alignment option can help to avoid this sort of thing.

The Selection Brush tool can be used to paint selections or masks onto and image. This can be time consuming, but it gives total control over the selection process and therefore offers perfect accuracy if you are prepared to take the time and effort. It can also be used to modify and perfect existing selections.

The Paint Bucket tool can be used to flood an area with a single colour, which can be useful for producing plain backgrounds. It has built-in selectivity that operates in essentially the same way as the Magic Wand tool, but it is often better to use the selection tools to make a selection in the normal way, delete the selection, and then fill the area using the Paint Bucket tool.

With a photograph of a single object, such as an item for sale in an Internet auction, replacing the background with a simple graduated type usually shows off the object to good effect. Many image editing programs can produce complex graduated fills, but these can be a distraction if you are not careful.

Filters

What is a filter?

When you get involved with image editing software it is not long before
you encounter the term "filter". In conventional photography a filter is a
piece of glass or plastic that is fixed in front of the lens. Sometimes the
purpose of the filter is to correct a potential defect in the photograph,
such as removing the strong orange cast that occurs when taking pictures
under tungsten lighting using an ordinary daylight film. More usually it is
to provide an effect of some kind, such as a soft focus or a fog effect.

Fig.9.1 The non-filtered version of the cat image

Filters for conventional photography fall into the "love them or hate them" category. Some photographers use them for practically every photograph while others will not let them near their cameras.

Filters in their digital form have probably gained wider acceptance than the conventional variety, but they still fall into the "love them or hate them" category. The range of filters available for conventional photography is quite large, but the range of effects obtainable is actually rather limited. The range of filter effects that can be produced using digital techniques is truly vast, and conventional photography simply can not compete in this respect.

Some digital filters are designed to improve images, including filters that attempt to sharpen slightly blurred images. Most are in the special effects category though, and provide soft focus effects, various types of blurring, and clever distortions. A third type of filter adds what is normally termed artistic filtering. In other words, the filtering is designed to make a photograph look like a drawing or painting. Most of these filters try to make the image look like a particular type of drawing or painting, such as a watercolour painting or a pencil sketch.

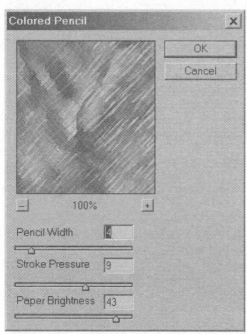

Fig.9.2 There are three controls for the Colored Pencil filter

The number of filters available varies considerably from one image editing program to another. The more simple programs have few if any, while the upmarket programs such as Photoshop have dozens built-in and the ability to take more in the form of plug-ins. I am not sure if Photoshop

Fig.9.3 A light Stroke Pressure setting was used for this image

Elements has the complete range of filters included with the full version of Photoshop, but it certainly has all the main categories in the Filter menu, and the submenus appear to be fully populated. Filters that sharpen, blur, and distort are all available, together with a useful range of artistic filters. In their digital form filters are well worth a try, and when used sensibly they can produce some beautiful results.

Artistic filtering

Even those having little interest in filter effects would be well advised to spend a little time experimenting with a selection of artistic filters. It is quite good fun and you might just find some effects that will produce some really good results. Some of the most effective artistic filters are designed to effectively turn a photograph into a sketch. Figure 9.1 shows a photograph of the furry friend who likes to sleep on my computer monitor during the winter months. Strong textures like those in his fur are often good candidates for drawing or painting effects. For this

Fig.9.4 A heavier Stroke Pressure setting was used for this version

example I selected the Colored Pencil filter, which is in the Artistic submenu of the Filter menu. This produced the control panel of Figure 9.2, where there are three sliders that can be used to vary the effect. This is typical of the Photoshop Elements filters, but different filters require different controls.

The names of the controls give good clues to their functions, but in the end it is down to the "suck it and see" method. In this case there is a Paper Brightness control. The paper shows through in areas of high luminosity, so the image looks more or less normal using a high value. Setting this slider near zero gives black paper, and therefore black highlights! The Pencil Width setting determines the width of the lines used, with higher values giving broader lines. This effectively acts as a definition control, since wider lines reduce definition. Most of the artistic filters have a control that is broadly similar in its effect. The third control is for Stroke Pressure, and this gives weak colours at low settings and strong colours at high settings.

Figures 9.3 and 9.4 show filtered versions of Figure 9.1. A lighter Stroke Pressure setting has been used in Figure 9.3, together with finer lines.

This gives a less heavy effect than the version of Figure 9.4. If I did not know that these images had been produced from a colour photograph I think that I might be fooled into thinking that they were genuine drawings. In the greyscale reproduction used here, Figure 9.4 does a reasonable imitation of a drawing done with a graphite stick or something similar. Figure 9.3 looks more like a drawing done using a graphite pencil.

Fig.9.5 The Colored Pencil filter has not worked well with this picture

It is worth experimenting with the controls to get the exact effect you require. The sketched look does not work well with all subjects though. Figure 9.5 shows the rosebud photograph after processing by the Colored Pencil filter. It does not work very well in the greyscale version shown here, and looks like nothing much at all in the original colour version. Sketching filters generally work best with images that contain plenty of texture and lines.

Preview

Note that the image does not respond to changes in the controls until the OK button is operated and the filtering is applied. Even using a fast computer it usually takes several seconds for the effect to be applied to the image. However, there is a small preview section in the control panel that shows part of the image, and this does respond to the controls in real-time, or as close as Photoshop Elements and your computer can

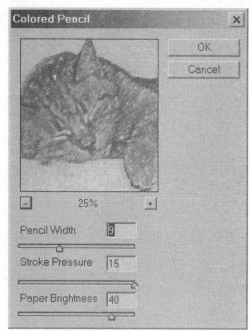

Fig.9.6 The scale of the preview panel can be changed

get to real-time operation. At a scale of 100 percent it is only possible for the preview panel to show a small part of the image.

It can be useful to use a lower scale in order to show more of the image (Figure 9.6). The preview resolution is relatively low, but it gives a good overall impression of what the filtered image will look like. Use the small + button below the preview image to increase the scale, or the – button to reduce it. It is possible to pan around the image by placing the pointer over the preview panel. The pointer then changes to the pan (hand) icon, and the image can be dragged in the normal way.

Some of the simpler filters do actually permit the effect to be applied to the image in real-time. The preview panel is still available, but where possible it is much better to tick the Preview checkbox and view the changes on the image itself. A few of the more complex filters lack any form of preview facility. It is then a matter of using trial and error, with the aid of the Undo facility, until the desired effect is obtained.

Some of the other artistic filters can be used to give a sketched effect, and the Rough Pastels filter is worth trying for this type of thing. Figure 9.7 shows the sleeping cat image after processing with this filter. This filter has several controls and it is worthwhile experimenting with them in order to obtain the best effect. The Dry Brush filter is another useful one, and as its name suggests, it gives more of a painted than a sketched look. Figure 9.8 shows the cat image after processing with this filter.

Fig.9.7 The Rough Pastels filter was used for this image

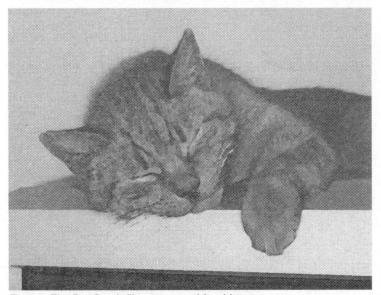

Fig.9.8 The Dry Brush filter was used for this one

Fig.9.9 The Golden Hinde image prior to filtering

The Cutout filter is an interesting one that can produce some attractive results. It effectively reduces the image to areas of solid colour, giving an effect rather like a collage made by gluing pieces of coloured paper onto a piece of board. The controls can be set to show a certain amount of detail, so it is not only usable with images that already consist of large and fairly obvious shapes. In general though, it works best with that type of image. Figures 9.9 to 9.12 show "before" and "after" versions for a couple of pictures.

The controls for this filter enable the number of colours (levels), and two others govern how closely the edges of areas are followed. Greatly simplifying an image will sometimes produce an image that is still to a large extent recognisable from the original (Figure 9.13). In other cases it takes things down to such a simplified level that the original is largely lost and an abstract image is produced. This is demonstrated by Figure 9.14 and 9.15 where the simplified image is not really recognisable as anything at all. If you wish to convert a photograph into an abstract image it is worthwhile experimenting with the controls in order to produce

Fig.9.10 The Golden Hinde with Cutout filtering applied

Fig.9.11 The "before" version of this image

Fig.9.12 The "after" version with Cutout filtering applied

Fig.9.13 Although greatly simplified, the image is still recognisable

Fig.9.14 Another "before" version

Fig.9.15 This greatly simplified version does not really look like anything at all, and does not work too well as abstract art

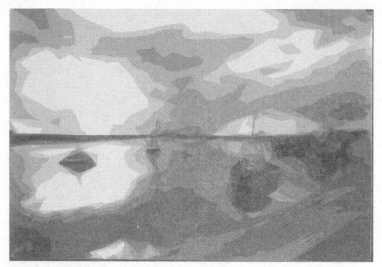

Fig.9.16 This image works better than the version of Fig.9.15

the best effect. The image of Figure 9.15 does not really work too well as an abstract design, but the version of Figure 9.16 works quite well.

Editing

Because the image is reduced to solid areas of just a few colours, it is quite easy to make changes to an image that has been processed using the Cutout filter. The areas of colour produced by the filtering can be filled with a different colour using the Paint Bucket tool, the shapes are easily edited using the Brush tool, and so on. Replacing some of the solid fills with gradients can produce some interesting results. This filter is popular for turning photographs into simple designs for use on home-made greetings cards and that general type of thing. It is certainly worth giving this filter a thorough testing, since you will probably find lots of uses for it.

The Watercolor filter is possibly the best of the artistic filters if you need to produce a painting effect from a photograph. Quite a good watercolour effect can be obtained after a little trial and error with the controls. Figure 9.17 shows the fishing boat picture used in a previous example, but with some added watercolour filtering. It is worth trying the Paint Daubs filter,

Fig.9.17 Watercolour filtering has been applied to this image

Fig.9.18 This image already has a painterly quality

Fig.9.19 Paint Daubs filtering enhances the painterly qualities

which actually offers a range of effects via the Brush Type menu at the bottom of its control panel. The Simple option from this menu gives quite a good painterly effect, as shown by the "before" and "after" images of Figures 9.18 and 9.19.

There are further artistic style filters available from the Brush Strokes submenu. The image of Figure 9.20 was processed using the Splatter filter in Figure 9.21 and the Sprayed Strokes filter in Figure 9.22. There are some more extreme filters available in this submenu, including the popular Sumi-e filter (Figure 9.23). It is well worth exploring both this submenu and the Artistic submenu if you are interested in producing painting and drawing effects, plus a few effects that are a bit more potent.

Yet more artistic filters are available via the Sketch submenu, but their usefulness is perhaps a bit limited as they produce black and white images. Nevertheless, some interesting and effective results can be produced using these filters. Figures 9.24 to 9.26 respectively show images produced with the aid of the Conte Crayon, Photocopy, and Graphic Pen filters. The latter can do a remarkably good imitation of a genuine pen and ink drawing.

Fig.9.20 *The non-filtered version of the squirrel photograph*

Fig.9.21 *The Splatter filter has been used for this version*

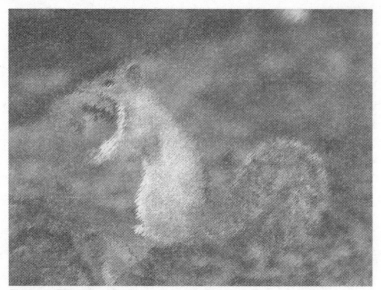

Fig.9.22 This effect was produced by Sprayed Strokes filtering

Fig.9.23 The popular Sumi-e filter can produce some odd effects

Fig.9.24 *The Conte Crayon filter has produced a pleasing effect*

Fig.9.25 *The Photocopy filter retains outlines and some textures*

Fig.9.26 The Graphic Pen filter produces some nice effects

It is worth experimenting with the Impressionistic Brush tool, which is an alternative available from the button that provides the standard Brush tool. It is not possible to "paint" on the screen with this brush, and its effect to scramble the material already in the image. It produces some rather extreme effects unless a very small brush size is set. This tool is fine if you wish to apply a painterly effect to a small part of an image, or wish to render some text illegible a bit more artistically than simply blanking it out. In general it is better to use the filters where artistic filtering is needed.

Oversize printing

It is perhaps worth mentioning that the normal rules about print sizes do not really apply when an artistic filter has been applied to an image. A lack of detail in a large print is not usually of any importance when an artistic filter has been applied, since most of these filters actually reduce the amount of detail in the picture. Each case has to be taken on its own merits, but in most instances a large amount of detail is not required and can be counterproductive. The idea of most artistic filtering is to reduce the picture to simple shapes that only hint at or completely ignore fine detail.

There are no strict rules for the maximum size of print once an artistic filter has been applied, and it is a matter of using your judgement. A doubling or trebling on each dimension is usually acceptable, and will often look much better than a print at the normal size for that resolution. In general, the more detail the filtering removes, the larger the maximum acceptable print size. With filtering that reduces a picture to a few simple shapes it is often possible to print an acceptable poster size picture. Unfortunately, this type of thing is well beyond the capabilities of ordinary inkjet printers unless you are prepared to print the picture in sections and then join them together.

Of course, when printing a filtered picture large it is usually a good idea to boost the number of pixels so that it is not possible to see individual pixels on the finished print. I suppose it is possible that large pixels could improve the effect, but in most cases it has completely the opposite effect. The large pixels just give a confused effect. There are actually special textured inkjet papers available that give a "canvas" look to printouts, so that they look more like the real thing. Like any specialist paper the prices are quite high, but it might be worth the additional expense if you are particularly interested in this aspect of things.

Blurring

Photoshop Elements has a range of blur filters, and it is also possible to produce blurring using other tools such as the appropriately named Blur tool and the Smudge tool. The latter providing a much stronger blurring effect than the former. On the face of it, tools and filters to make your images less sharp are the last thing that you need. However, blurring all or part of an image can be beneficial. Photographers have for many years used soft focus filters that provide a mixture of a sharp image and a seriously out of focus image. This type of thing is particularly popular for portraits, where the overall effect is quite pleasing and wrinkles and other skin blemishes miraculously disappear.

Sports photographers often use powerful telephoto lenses that have wide apertures, and this combination gives an extremely narrow depth of field. Also, the out of focus areas tend to be well and truly out of focus. These factors are normally deemed an advantage rather than a drawback. Sports photographers could have frequent problems with objects in the background seeming to be growing from the heads of the sports persons,

Fig.9.27 This version has the original background

or more unfortunate places. With the backgrounds completely out of
focus this does not occur. The backgrounds are often so out of focus
that they are purely abstract and it is not possible to make out individual

Fig.9.28 The Smudge tool has not produced the right effect for the background of this image

objects. This lack of distraction helps to focus attention on the main subject.

Fig.9.29 A lower Strength setting has produced a better result

The squirrel photograph of Figure 9.27 was taken using a powerful telephoto lens, but with the lens well stopped down. The background is well out of focus, but it is still a bit distracting. It is more distracting in the

Fig.9.30   The bird tends to merge into the complex background

original colour version than in the greyscale conversion, due to the bright greens on the tree trunks. These stand out from the rest of the image, which is otherwise composed almost entirely of browns and greys. Blurring the background while leaving the squirrel and the tree intact is not difficult using Photoshop Elements. The first step was to mask the squirrel and the trunk of the tree so that the background could be blurred without altering these areas. Any of the normal selection methods could be used, but in this case I found it easiest to select the squirrel and tree trunk using the Selection Brush tool in the Mask mode.

The next task is to blur the background on the Background layer. There are several ways of doing this, but the obvious one of selecting Blur from the Blur submenu is unlikely to have much effect. The Blur option is designed to give a slight blurring of material that is quite sharp. Its effect on the parts of images that are already blurred is quite small. The Blur More option provides a stronger effect, but it is still inadequate for this task.

The Gaussian Blur option provides a variable degree of blurring and would certainly do the job, but when used strongly it tends to produce featureless results. In some cases an almost plain background is just

Fig.9.31 A very strong blurring effect can be applied

what is needed, but was not really what I was looking for in this case. The Smudge tool provides better results. When using this tool the image is effectively comprised of wet paint which the smudge tool moves around. When used at maximum strength it provides some lively results (Figure 9.28), but it is not really appropriate for this image. Reducing the Strength setting in the Options bar to about 20 percent gives better results (Figure 9.29), and has produced the desired effect.

Gaussian Blur

The Gaussian Blur option mentioned previously is useful for adding anything from a slight blurring to a very strong effect like viewing things through ground glass. It is excellent for blurring backgrounds, and in this example it is the background of the photograph shown in Figure 9.30 that will be blurred. In terms of sharpness, contrast, etc., the photograph is reasonable as it stands. The problem is that the bird's head is mingling into the cockle shells in the background. In the original colour version the bird appears to be completely headless! Another problem is that the strong contrasts and textures in the cockleshells

Fig.9.32 A much weaker blurring effect is adequate in this case

slightly overpower the main subject, which is a turnstone incidentally. High contrast backgrounds with masses of fine detail can tend to make the main subject appear to have slightly "soft" focussing even though it is actually quite sharp.

Strictly speaking it is not the foreground that will be processed, since the shells are in the foreground, middle ground, and background, and they will all be blurred. It is everything except the turnstone that has to be given the blurring treatment. I started by selecting the outline of the turnstone using the Magnetic Lasso tool, and then refined it slightly using the Selection Brush tool. The Inverse option in the Select menu was then used to select everything outside the outline. It was then just a matter of applying the required amount of Gaussian Blur filtering.

This filter permits the effect to be previewed on the image, and very strong blurring can be applied if desired (Figure 9.31). In this case it is something a bit more subtle that is required, and Figure 9.32 shows the finished image. Particularly in the original colour image, the bird stands out from the background much better. There were still some dark areas in the background that merged into the bird's head, but these were lightened with the Burn tool.

Fig.9.33 *Some of the shells around the bird's legs have been left unfiltered*

The blurring effect is often more convincing if some of the background material is left unchanged. In the example of Figure 9.33 a patch of shells around the bird's feet was included in the mask. This gives an abrupt transition from the blurred area of background to the unchanged material, but this can be smoothed over using the Blur tool around the edges of the sharp background material.

Bear in mind that blurring is not the only way of dealing with overbearing backgrounds. A reduction in contrast is a useful alternative, and this method has been used with the image shown in Figure 9.34. The contrast in the turnstone has been increased using the Auto Contrast facility. This has worked quite well with the greyscale version of the image, and in my opinion at any rate; it works better than the blurred version. With the colour images though, it is usually the blurring that gives the best result. If a plain background is needed, it can be produced by reducing the contrast to zero. This has been done in Figure 9.35 by using the same setting for the lower set of slider controls in the Levels window. Move the sliders to the left for a darker grey, or to the right for a lighter grey. Alternatively, with the textures removed from the background it is easy to add any desired colour using the Paint Bucket tool, or a graduated background using the Gradient tool.

Fig.9.34 A reduction in contrast offers an alternative to blurring

Fig.9.35 The background is easily reduced to a shade of grey

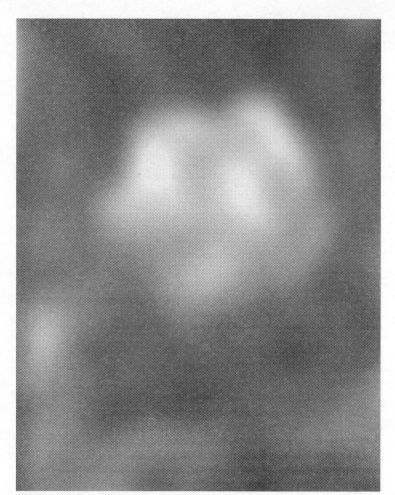

Fig.9.36 The blurred image must be well and truly blurred

Soft focus

The Gaussian Blur filter is useful for adding a soft focus effect. It is important to realise that a soft focus effect is not the same as simply blurring the image slightly. Simply adding some Gaussian Blur filtering produces a blurred image and not a soft focus effect. A soft focus effect

Fig.9.37 A very subtle soft-focus effect can be applied

is produced by having a mixture of a sharp image and one that is very blurred. Photographers often improvise soft focus filters by smearing Vaseline onto a plain glass filter, with the degree of softness being varied by using more or less Vaseline, as required. A popular method in the early days of photography was to use a diffraction grating, which usually meant taping material from a pair of stockings over the lens!

Fig.9.38 Less fading of the blurred image gives a stronger effect

Both of these methods give the required combination of a blurred image and a sharp one, but lack precise control. Using Photoshop Elements it is easy to use any degree of soft focussing. By keeping a copy of the sharp image it is possible to change your mind and use a less soft effect, which is something that can not be done if the filtering is used when the picture is taken. For this example the soft focussing effect will be added

Fig.9.39 A very "soft" effect is produced with a small amount of fading

to the rosebud photograph, and the first step is to apply the Gaussian Blur filtering. This is obtained via the Blur submenu of the Filter menu.

Using too little blur filtering is a common error when adding a soft focus effect. If any detail is still visible in the blurred image, mixing it with the sharp image produces a blurred image rather than a proper soft focus effect. It is preferable to have the broad areas of colour retained from the original image, but all detail must be lost in the blurring. Do not take the filtering so far that a virtually plain image is produced. Adding a totally blurred image with a sharp one tends to produce a very marked loss of contrast even with a relatively weak soft focus effect. Something like the degree of filtering shown in Figure 9.36 should give good results.

The usual technique for obtaining a soft focus effect, and the one that will be used here, is to add the blurred image on a layer above the sharp image. By altering the transparency of the blurred image it is possible to control the strength of the soft focus effect. The first step is therefore to duplicate the image on a second layer. Select Duplicate Layer from the Layer menu, and give the new layer an appropriate name in the small dialogue box that appears. Operate the OK button to produce the new layer. The new layer is then processed using the Gaussian Blur filter, making sure that a suitably large amount of blurring is used.

With the blurring added to the new layer it is very easy to mix it with the sharp image. Operate the Layers tab at the right end of the Options bar and then adjust the Transparency slider control to obtain the desired effect. Greater fading provides a weaker effect. Fig.9.37 shows the rose image with a weak effect, while in Figure 9.38 the fading has been reduced slightly to obtain a slightly "softer" effect. In Figure 9.39 only a small amount of fading has been used and a very "soft" image has been obtained.

Smart Blur

The Smart Blur filter is a very useful one that often provides a good alternative to soft focus effects. Its basic effect is to blur the image apart from the edges it detects. This form of filtering is much used by portraitists because of its ability to remove fine marks and patterns, and thus "take years off" the sitter. It can be used in most situations where a smoother and softer appearance is required. There are two slider controls for this filter (Figure 9.40), and a preview panel, but no option to preview the effect on the image itself.

The Threshold control determines the degree of contrast required for Photoshop Elements to deem something an edge. Few outlines are produced using a high setting, while practically everything is taken as an outline at low settings. The Mode menu has two options that permit the outlines to be viewed on the preview panel. In one mode only the outlines are shown, and in the other mode the outlines are overlaid on the normal image. It is obviously important that all the main outlines are detected, but there can also be some unwanted effects if too many are detected. In most cases it is best to select one of the outline preview modes and adjust the threshold control so that only the main outlines are detected.

The Radius control effectively governs the amount of blurring that is added, and it is just a matter of adjusting it for what is felt to be the best effect. Some of the filters, including the Smart Blur type, have three quality settings (Low, Medium, and High). With low

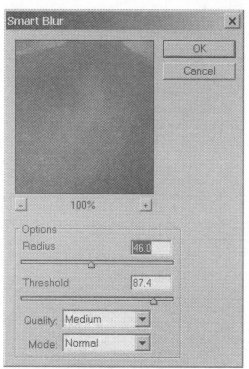

Fig.9.40 The Smart Blur window

resolution images it will probably not make too much difference which one is used, and with higher resolution images there might still be little difference between the Medium and High settings. However, the time taken to calculate the changes to the image does vary considerably from one setting to the next. Even with a fast computer it can take quite a long time to make the calculations when the High setting is used.

Figure 9.41 shows the Smart Blur filtering added to the rosebud. The main edges have been identified correctly and quite a good effect has been produced. Objects tend to look as though they are made from china or porcelain when this filtering is used in large amounts, so use it in moderation unless this is the effect you require. Paradoxically, slightly "soft" images often look sharper when this form of blur filtering is applied.

Fig.9.41 The Smart Blur filter produces an interesting alternative to the soft-focus type

This happens because the edges are retained but the slightly blurred details become blurred so much that they disappear. Photoshop Elements provides better ways to deal with "soft" images though.

Fig.9.42 Motion Blur filtering has produced the first supersonic snail

Sharp filtering

I would guess that anyone who has put a film through a camera has taken a photograph that is something less than completely sharp. The most obvious reason for a lack of sharpness is that the camera was not focussed correctly, but there are other causes. Some cameras are better than others, and some lenses are certainly much better than others. With some cheap cameras it does not make much difference whether the camera is focussed well or badly. The results are poor either way!

What is termed "camera shake" is certainly a major cause of blurred photographs. Many people jerk the camera as they take each photograph, which can significantly reduce the sharpness even when using a fast shutter speed. Fast moving subjects taken using an inadequate shutter speed is another common cause of blurred images. Sometimes the blurring can be largely avoided by panning with the movement. This will usually blur the background, but this helps to give an impression of speed. The Photoshop Elements Motion Blur filter can

Fig.9.43 The non-filtered picture of the vixen

be applied to a background to give the same effect. In Figure 9.42 the snail has been stretched slightly to make it more streamlined, a small amount of Motion Blur filtering has also been added to the snail, and a large amount has been added to the background. The result is the world's first snail capable of going from 0 to 60mph in less than five seconds!

Another common problem is inadequate depth of field. Wide apertures enable fast shutter speeds to be used, but will usually result in relatively little being genuinely in focus, particularly with telephoto lenses. With a portrait you focus on the subject's eyes and they are properly in focus on the photograph, but the nose and ears are not. As already explained, limited depth of field can have its advantages, but only in the right circumstances. In many instances it is preferable to have as much depth of field as possible.

Blurring an image is easy enough, but sharpening is a different matter. Filtering can certainly make slightly "soft" images look much more acceptable, and it can also increase the apparent depth of field in

Fig.9.44 The Sharpen filter has only a limited effect

photographs that are a bit lacking in this respect. If a photograph is well and truly blurred it would be naïve to expect filtering to turn it into a perfect photograph. Even the systems using supercomputers to process images from space can not do that. Sharpness filtering also tends to be ineffective with serious camera shake of the type that produces a double-image effect. Using sharpness filtering on images of this type simply gives you two sharper images!

Options

There are four types of sharpening available from the Sharpen submenu, and the first of these is the straightforward Sharpen option. This operates by looking for variations in colour and tone, and it increases the contrast between adjacent pixels where suitable variations are found. All simple methods of image sharpening use essentially the same method, and are really just providing localised increases in contrast. This can give the illusion of greater sharpness, and I suppose that in a way the image is

*Fig.9.45 Using the Sharpen edges filter produces a further
improvement*

genuinely sharper, but missing detail can not be put back in by sharpness
filtering.

The photograph of a vixen shown in Figure 9.43 is a good example of
the type of image that can benefit from sharpening. It was taken through
a window, which has slightly taken the edge off the sharpness. The
definition is not that bad and there is a hint of detail in the fur. However,
depth of field is lacking and no part of the image is "bitingly" sharp.

Figure 9.44 shows the effect of using the Sharpen filter. The change is
something less than dramatic, but as viewed on the screen of my monitor
anyway, there is a definite improvement in the apparent sharpness of the
image, particularly in the fur on the top of her head. The effect of the
Sharpen filter is relatively mild, but stronger or additional filtering can be
used. The Sharpen Edges filter, as its name implies, is primarily intended
for giving more clearly defined edges, such as the edges of furniture and
buildings. This it does very well, but when used in conjunction with the

Fig.9.46 The Sharpen More filter produces a stronger effect

Sharpen filter it will often give a useful improvement in the general sharpness without taking things "over the top".

Figure 9.45 shows the photograph with the Sharpen and Sharpen Edges filtering applied. There is only a subtle difference between this and the version that only has the Sharpen filtering applied, but the combined effect filtering is quite impressive with the image viewed on a monitor in the Actual Pixels mode. Unlike the original image, it looks acceptably sharp and it still looks quite natural. Large amounts of sharpening can be applied by using the Sharpen filer two or three times, or by using the Sharpen More filter. Figure 9.46 shows the image with the original sharpening removed and the Sharpen More filter applied.

In this case the use of the Sharpen More filter looks quite impressive, but with some images it is somewhat less impressive. It can add a slightly "brittle" and artificial look with patterns of light pixels appearing in places. Using anything beyond the Sharpen More filter more or less guarantees some rather odd looking results with most images. Unfortunately, sharpening is needed most when an image is reproduced relatively large, but it is when a sharpened image is viewed large that the filtering becomes more obvious. Always use the minimum amount of filtering that provides acceptable sharpness.

Unsharp Mask

The three types of sharpness filtering described so far are handy for those needing a quick and easy solution to a blurred image, but they provide no real control over the filtering. The same is not true of the Unsharp Mask filter, which has the customary three controls and preview option (Figure 9.47). The top control is used to set the required amount of filtering, and it covers a range of 1 to 500 percent. A Radius value is set using the middle control, and this controls the number of surrounding pixels that are altered by the sharpening. It is normally necessary to use a low value here in order to obtain an acceptable effect. A low value is particularly important with an image such as the one used here, which has masses of fine detail. A high value tends to give a glowing effect around the edges of objects or where there is a lot of fine detail (Figure 9.48), and it can also produce oversaturated colours. Set the value too low and no significant sharpening is obtained.

Fig.9.47 The Unsharp Mask window

Fig.9.48 A high Radius value can produce some odd effects

The third slider control sets the Threshold, which is the difference needed between pixels before the sharpening will be applied. High values result in Photoshop finding few areas to sharpen. With a low value the filtering is applied almost everywhere on the image, which usually results in patterns of dots starting to emerge from previously plain areas of the image. It can take a fair amount of juggling with the three controls in order to obtain the best results, but it should be possible to obtain a reasonably sharp looking picture provided the original image contains an adequate amount of detail. Figure 9.49 shows the vixen photograph after processing using the Unsharp Mask filter. This is perhaps a fraction over the top, but it shows the type of improvement that can be achieved.

Many professional users head straight for the Unsharp Mask filter when editing any image. No matter how sharp an image is to start with, it is always possible to make it look "crisper" using this facility, or the similar facilities available in other image editing programs. Whether it is desirable to do so is another matter. For low definition images that will be used on the Internet there is perhaps a good case to be made for emphasising

Fig.9.49 The Unsharp Mask filter has produced a considerable improvement in this case

the fine details which might otherwise be lost. I habitually use sharpening on web images, but not images that will be printed. There is no harm in trying a sharpening filter on every image, but there is no point in applying the filtering unless you genuinely like the effect.

The rest

There are many other filters in Photoshop Elements, but these are mostly out and out special effects types. The available effects include distortion filters that produce such things as "fisheye" lens effects, glass distortions, and so on. The Stylise menu has some of the more extreme filters, including the popular Solarize and Glowing Edges. These are shown in Figures 9.50 and 9.51 respectively. They actually work quite well in greyscale, but the Glowing Edges effect is much more potent with colour reproduction. There is plenty to experiment with if you are into this type of thing.

Fig.9.50 Even in greyscale the solarize filter produces some spectacular results

Fig.9.51 This image was produced using the Glowing Edges filter. You
get an idea of the effect here, but it is much more
spectacular in colour

Points to remember

Artistic filters are used to make a photograph look like a painting or a sketch. A wide range of effects are available including filters that imitate water colours, crayon and pencil drawings, and oil paintings. A further range of filters produce similar effects to charcoal drawings, pen and ink sketches, and other monochrome drawing mediums.

Artistic filters work best when they are applied to images that are appropriate for that type of medium. Pastel, pencil, and similar filters work best with images that contain plenty of lines and textures that can be built up from lines. It can be difficult to get this type of filtering to work well with images that have lots of smooth gradients, but these images often work well with watercolour and other painting filters.

Blur filtering is mainly applied to "busy" backgrounds that are otherwise a distraction, or where the main subject tends to blend into the background. Reducing the contrast in a background can be used in the same way, and can sometimes be more effective.

It is usually possible to print images much larger than normal when artistic filtering has been used. A lack of detail in the print is usually of no importance with this type of thing, so the normal rules about maximum print size do not apply. However, boost the number of pixels in the image to avoid jumbo pixels on the prints.

A soft-focus effect is not produced by blurring an image. A soft-focus effect is produced by combining a sharp image with one that is very blurred. The strength of the effect can be varied by altering the relative strength of the blurred image. The more transparent the blurred image is made, the weaker the soft-focus effect obtained.

The Smart Blur filter offers a useful alternative to a soft-focus effect when it is necessary to soften textures. It leaves edges unchanged but blurs everything else. It is often used with portraits to reduce wrinkles and skin blemishes.

Using a sharpen filter can greatly improve the appearance of an image, producing an apparent increase in the sharpness and the depth of field. However, a sharpen filter can not add any detail to an image, and the effect is only worthwhile if a reasonable amount of detail is present in the image.

Adding text

Text and layers

It is often desirable to add text to an image, but in the past this was not really a strong point of most image editing programs. Photoshop was relatively weak in this respect until quite recently, but it now offers an excellent range of text facilities, and most of these also available in Photoshop Elements 2. There are vertical and horizontal versions of the Type tool and the same versions of the Type Mask tool are available. The normal type tools produce text in the current foreground colour, but this can be overridden by selecting a different colour from the Options bar.

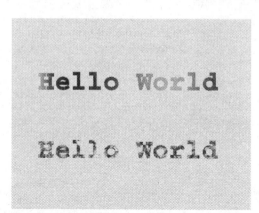

Fig.10.1 Mask text can be filled with gradients and textures from images

The mask versions of the Type tool produce masks that can be used in the usual ways, and in Figure 10.1 the mask at the top has been filled with a gradient. The lower mask was used over the section of a photograph where there was a stone wall. Text can be produced in this way on one image and then transferred to another using the Copy and Paste facilities.

Photoshop Elements places each piece of normal text on its own layer, but text masks are simply placed on the current layer. While normal text is left on its own layer it is readily edited, but there are some restrictions on the way it can be treated. In particular, filters have no effect on text unless it is "simplified". This is the Photoshop Elements term for converting it into a normal image comprised of pixels. Rasterize and render are two alternative terms for this process. A warning message appears if you try to apply a filter to a normal text layer. Operate the OK button to go ahead and simplify the layer.

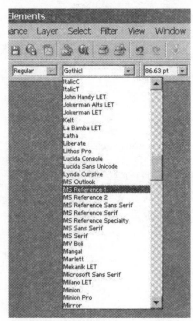

Fig.10.2 A full range of fonts is available

Note that when a text layer is merged with the main image using the Merge Layers function, the text layer will be simplified in the process. Once converted to pixels it is possible to apply filters or any of the other processes that can be used with images, but normal text editing is not possible. Make sure the text is correct before you rasterize it, or use any function that will result in it being rasterized. Some of the more up-market image editing programs have a built-in spelling checker that helps to avoid embarrassing mistakes. This feature is not present in most low-cost image editing programs, including Photoshop Elements. Check the spelling by other means prior to simplifying a text layer or merging it with the main image.

Text options

There are a number of choices available from the Options bar when one of the Type tools is selected. These are mostly the sort of thing that you find in word processors or any programs that handle text. One of the buttons near the right end of the Options bar is an exception, and this toggles the text between the vertical and horizontal modes. Any newly added text will follow the current setting of this button. Existing text can be altered by first selecting it. This operates in normal word processor fashion, with text being selected by dragging the text cursor through the

Fig.10.3 Anti-aliasing gives the text at the top a smoother appearance

characters you wish to change. The selected characters are shown in inverse video. The selected text will respond immediately to any changes in the setting of the Text Orientation button.

Towards the left end of the Options bar there is the usual font menu that lists all the available fonts (Figure 10.2). There is no preview facility so that you can see what each font looks like, but some text placed on the current layer will change to the selected font. You can quickly try out a few likely fonts.

The menu to the left of the Fonts menu provides text styles such as Regular, Italic, and Bold. The available options will probably vary slightly from one font to another. To the right of the Fonts menu is yet another menu, and this one offers a range of text sizes from 6 to 72 points. Other sizes can be obtained by typing the appropriate point size into the textbox. To change the size or style of existing text, select the type tool and the appropriate layer, and then highlight the text by dragging the cursor through it. Then select the required style and (or) text size.

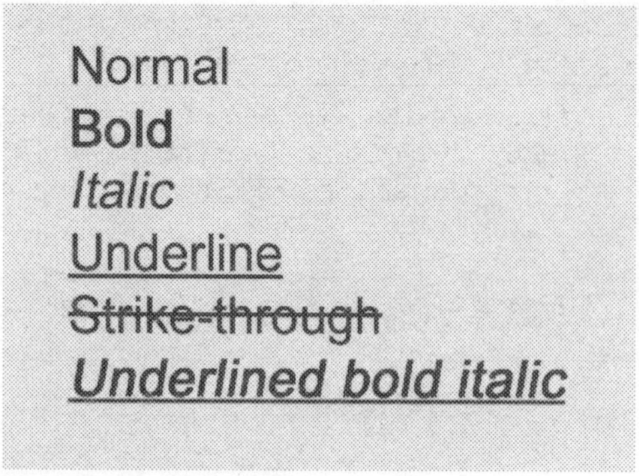

Normal

Bold

Italic

<u>Underline</u>

~~Strike-through~~

<u>***Underlined bold italic***</u>

Fig.10.4 Five text styles are available

The button to the right of the Size menu enables anti-aliasing to be switched on or off. Anti-aliasing is designed to give text a smoother appearance, and it operates by using some pixels around the edges of characters at a colour half way between those used for the text and the background. This can be seen in the zoomed view of Figure 10.3 where the text at the top has anti-aliasing and the text at the bottom has none. Apart from a better general appearance, anti-aliasing can make small text more legible. It is particularly good when it is used with fonts that have a tendency to merge adjacent letters. Anti-aliasing is often used when producing web pages, but it is generally less useful when producing printed pages.

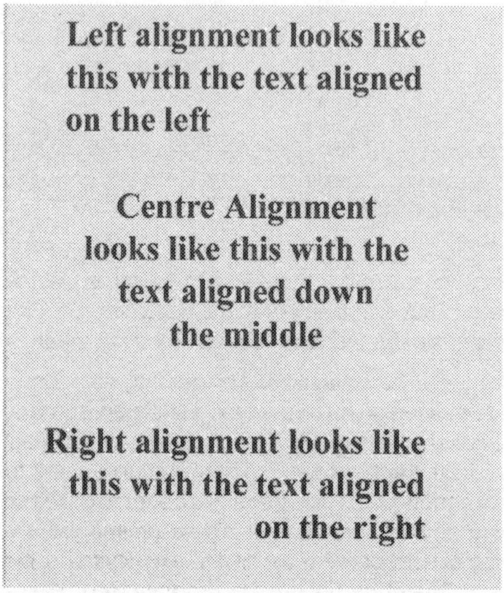

Next along to the right there are four buttons that provide bold, italic, underline, and strike-through effects (Figure 10.4). These effects can be used in any combination. To the right of these there are three buttons that provide left, centre, and right alignment (Figure 10.5). Fully aligned (justified) text is not

Left alignment looks like this with the text aligned on the left

Centre Alignment looks like this with the text aligned down the middle

Right alignment looks like this with the text aligned on the right

Fig.10.5 Three alignment options are available but there is no fully justified option

available. To the right of this is the button that is used to set the text colour, and operating this button produces the standard Color Picker.

The next button is used to produce warped text, and operating it produces a small dialogue box (Figure 10.6). This offers a choice of 15 types of warped text from the Style menu, but the range is effectively much larger because there are three slider controls that permit wide variations within each style. Figure 10.7 includes four examples of warped text. The usual types of warped text are available, including text in various arcs, flag style text, and twisted text. It is well worth taking some time to experiment with the various options available here. If you need something a bit more artistic than plain text, the warped text feature is the place to go. The two buttons at the right end of the

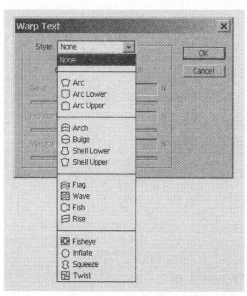

Fig.10.6 There are 15 types of warped text

Options bar simply enable the current text editing to be cancelled or committed to the image. Note that by moving from the text tool to another tool you are effectively operating the Commit button.

Photoshop Elements does not have facilities for dealing with large amounts of text, and this is not a feature of many image editing programs. It can be useful to have extensive features for handling text, but in most cases it would be doing things the hard way. Where it is necessary to merge images with large amounts of text it is generally better to produce and format the text in a word processor and then import the images into the text file. These days most word processors have the ability to import image files of various types. The other option is to produce the text in a word processor, adjust the pictures using an image editor, and then

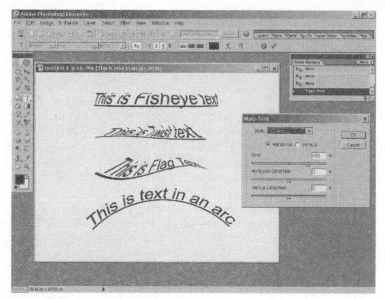

Fig.10.7 Four examples of warped text

combine the two using a desktop publishing program. This was the method used to produce this book, and it is the way that most books, magazines, etc., are produced these days.

Adding text

The users of programs such as Photoshop Elements probably have little need for combining their images with large amounts of text. If you just need to add the odd line of text, or perhaps two or three entirely separate lines of text, then they can be typed direct onto the image. Just select the appropriate Type tool, left-click on the image at the point where you need the text, and start typing. Left aligned text will be added to the right of the starting point, right aligned text is added on the left, and centre aligned text is added equally on both sides. The pointer is a vertical line when it is placed over text, indicating that the text can be selected and edited in normal word processor fashion. Of course, the pointer is a horizontal line when it is placed over vertical text.

Away from the text it changes to the Move pointer, and it is then possible to drag the text to a new position. Where separate lines of text are added it is advisable to place them on individual layers so that they can be positioned independently. Having placed the first line of text, select the Background layer by left-clicking on its entry in the Layers palette. Next, left-click on the image at the point where the next line of text is to be added, and a new text layer will be generated automatically. Add the line of text, selected the Background layer again, and so on until all the text has been entered. Alternatively, just add the new layers manually by selecting New from the Layer menu followed by Layer from the submenu.

Drop shadow

It is the ability of Photoshop Elements to produce fancy text that is of interest to most users. The warped text effects described previously are very useful for this type of thing, and a huge range of effects can be produced. These effects are very popular for use in web pages, as are drop shadow headlines. Photoshop Elements has no drop shadow effect as such, but it is quite easy to produce this effect using the Transform facility and blur filtering.

To try this effect, start by adding some text to a blank page. It is best to use a fairly large text size so that the drop shadow effect can be seen very clearly. Then add the same text again, but on a different layer. With this layer still selected, and the second piece of text committed to the image, select Simplify Layer from the layer menu. With the second line of text now converted to pixels it is possible to apply the usual transformations and filtering to it.

The first task is to flip the text vertically. Operate the Move button in the top right-hand corner of the Toolbox, and a bounding box should then appear around the second line of text. Go to the Edit menu and select Rotate followed by Flip Vertical. This should give an upside-down mirror image of the text, which is then moved accurately into place beneath the first line of text. The Move tool is already selected so it is just a matter of dragging the text into position.

This provides a basic drop shadow, but it can be made to look a bit more convincing by applying other transformations, such as stretching it vertically and skewing it slightly. In doing this you are effectively adjusting the position of the light source that is producing the shadow. Some blurring can be added to make the apparent light source more diffuse. The Gaussian Blur filter is the obvious choice, since it gives excellent

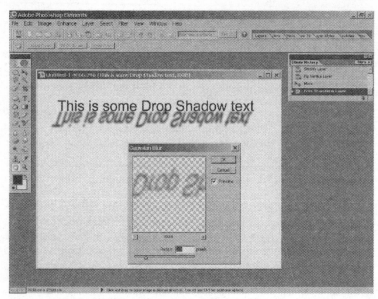

Fig.10.8 Using blurring with a drop shadow effect

control over the degree of blurring. Figure 10.8 shows the type of thing that can be produced.

Of course, the shadow does not have to be immediately below the original line of text, and if preferred it can be moved away using the Move tool. It can also be placed above the main text rather than beneath it if that is the effect you require. The type of drop shadow shown in Figure 10.9 is very popular. This does not use the vertical flipping and has the shadow text only slightly offset from the main text.

Opacity

There are other ways of altering the effect, including adjustment of the Opacity control for the layer that contains the shadow text. This controls the opacity of the shadow but not the original text, and the shadow can therefore be made paler without altering the original text (Figure 10.10). Reducing the opacity is virtually mandatory when using a drop shadow that is only slightly offset from the main text. Otherwise the two lines of text tend to merge together and become unreadable. Using a different

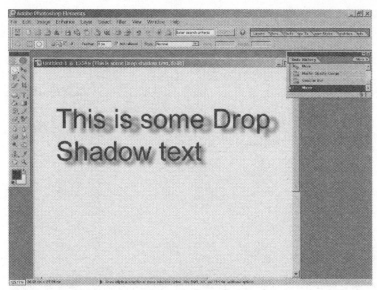

Fig.10.9 A popular type of drop shadow effect

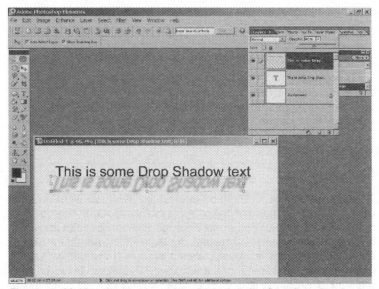

Fig.10.10 Making the shadow text paler using the Opacity control

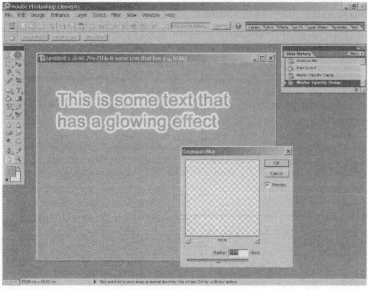

Fig.10.11 Glowing effects are easily produced

colour for the shadow text is an alternative way of avoiding this problem. It would probably not be too difficult to select the drop shadow text and alter its colour, but it makes sense to apply any change of colour when initially adding the text.

Another option is to use a well blurred shadow when it is near the main text. If the shadow is reasonably distinct it produces a double image effect that most people find unpleasant to look at. It also reduces legibility. The double image effect can still occur if the shadow has been faded and (or) it is a different colour to the main text. Blurring the shadow text to give "soft" edges is a certain way of avoiding double image problems. Obviously this is not a problem if the shadow is set well away from the text, and you then have much more freedom with shadow effects.

Text can be manipulated to produce many other effects. In Figure 10.11 the original text has been placed over an identical piece of text. The second piece of text has been converted to pixels and then blurred using the Gaussian Blur filter. This produces a sort of glowing effect around the text, and variations on the effect can be obtained by varying the amount of blur applied. Note that a suitably dark or contrasting background is needed in order to make this type of effect work properly.

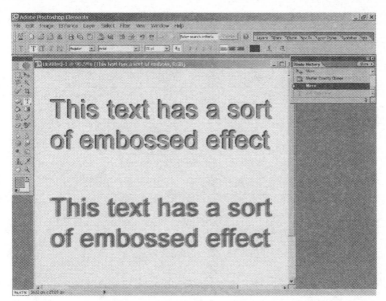

Fig.10.12 Combining two text strings can produce good effects

Embossed and other three-dimensional effects can be obtained by slightly offsetting one string of text from an identical string. In the upper piece of text in Figure 10.12 the text on the upper layer is much darker than the one on the lower layer. In the lower text in Figure 10.12 the darker text is on top but has been made slightly transparent via the Opacity setting for its layer. Metallic effects can be produced by adding mask text and then using the Gradient tool to add a suitably metal-like fill. The two pieces of text in Figure 10.13 were filled with the Copper gradient included as standard with Photoshop Elements, and a version with modified colours to give a gold effect.

Selection

Although normal selection methods do not work with text unless it is simplified, it is possible to apply some transformations without rasterizing text. First select the text by dragging the text cursor through it. The Skew and Free Transform options are then available from the Transform submenu, and it is also possible to rotate and scale the text in the normal way. The usual bounding box with handles appears around the text

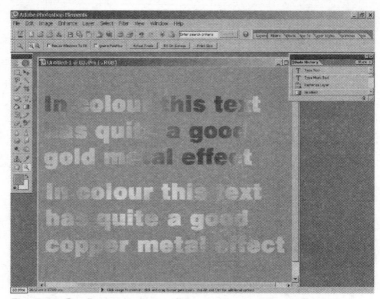

Fig.10.13 Gradients can be used to produce metal text effects

when the Skew or Free Transform option is selected. Unfortunately, the Free Transform facility is not quite as free as it might be, and it is not

Fig.10.14 Normal text can be skewed

possible to distort the text via this route. It is still useful to manipulate text in this way, and it is possible to make some useful changes via this method (Figure 10.14).

Rasterizing

As pointed out previously, in order to use the full range of Photoshop Element's clever tricks with text it is necessary to rasterize text. This converts it from text into an image comprised of pixels. The full range of transformations, filters, etc., can then be applied, but the text editing facilities are lost. This makes it important to remove any errors from the text before it is rasterized. It is rasterized by making the text's layer the

Fig.10.15 More transformations are possible with rasterized text

current one and then selecting Simplify Layer from the Layer menu. Alternatively, if you try filtering or another facility that requires the text to be rasterized, you will be asked if you wish to simplify the text so that the processing can be applied. Operate the OK button and the text will be rasterized prior to the filtering or other effect being applied. Of course, it is unnecessary to simplify text produced via a text mask, as it will already be in the form of normal pixels.

Once the text has been converted it can be selected using the normal methods and the whole range of processes becomes available. In Figure 10.15 the text has been selected and then distorted to give a sort of 3D effect, with the text seeming to recede into the distance. In Figure 10.16 some text has been added to the photograph of the speeding snail. After conversion it was skewed and a small amount of Motion Blur filtering was applied.

Captions

As explained in a previous chapter, it is possible to add a caption to a photograph via the Print Preview facility. However, this method gives no control over things like the size and position of the caption, and it is only really intended for things like adding copyright and date information to an image. Of course, captions can be placed direct onto the image, but in general it is better to add them outside the image area. It is not possible to add text outside the image, but the canvas can be enlarged in order to provide space for a caption outside the true image area.

Fig.10.16 Filtering can be added to rasterized text

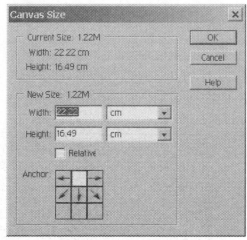

*Fig.10.17 The Canvas Size window enables
the canvas to be expanded*

In Photoshop Elements this is achieved by going to the Image menu and selecting Resize, followed by Canvas Size from the popup submenu. This produces a window like the one of Figure 10.17. By default any increase in size will be applied equally to all four edges, but this can be changed via the block of nine buttons near the bottom left-hand corner of the window.

Fig.10.18 *Text is added to the new space in the usual way*

Fig.10.19 *A full range of text effects can be used with captions*

Suppose that space is needed for a caption to be added beneath the image. The middle button in the top row would be activated, and this would prevent any space being added above the image. No space will be added at the sides because only the Height setting will be altered, and this is increased by the amount of space you wish to add beneath the image.

Operate the OK button to make the change take effect and then add the text into the blank area in the normal way. A colour or even a gradient can be added into the added space if desired. Figure 10.18 shows an image that is complete with a caption added in this way. Using this method it is possible to add text above the image, below it, or even down the sides using vertical text. The full range of text sizes, fonts, and effects are available (Figure 10.19).

Fig.10.20 The layout used when making greetings cards

On the cards

Making your own custom greetings cards is very popular, and most people value a one-off card made just for them far more than they would an expensive readymade card. There are plenty of stationery kits available for card making on an inkjet printer, but any good quality inkjet paper or thin card will do. There are also special programs for creating greetings cards, and some photo-editing programs have special facilities for this purpose. However, it is not difficult to make your own cards using the facilities available in any good image editing software.

One slight problem when making your own cards is that the normal (folded in half) variety requires printing on both sides of the paper. The design on the front of the card is on the opposite side of the paper to the greetings printed inside. It is possible to print on both sides of the paper by printing on one side and then the other, but this does not give good results with some papers. Note that most inkjet papers have a special coating on one side, and that the printing must be applied to that side only, or poor results are likely to occur.

The usual way around this problem is to use a piece of paper that is twice as large as normal and then fold it into quarters. The front and both inside pages are then on the same side of the paper (Figure 10.20). Note that the front and rear of the card are the other way up compared to the inside pages. Probably the easiest way of tackling a card is to first produce the image for the front. Having done so, double the width and height of the canvas, adding the new material to the left and above the existing image.

Fig.10.21 A completed greetings card design

Next add the appropriate greetings on the inside right panel, which is the top right-hand panel at this stage of the proceedings. Remember to rotate the text through 180 degrees. There are plenty of fancy fonts for this type of thing, including some that look like handwriting. You should then have something like Figure 10.21. Material can be added to the back and (or) left inside page of the card if desired. It is then just a matter of printing the design, folding into quarters, adding your signature, etc., and it is finished.

Finally

It is not possible to cover every facet of digital photography in a book this size, but the wide range of topics covered should at least provide an insight into the possibilities of this medium. Using the methods described herein it is possible to get the optimum technical quality from any image, add text and creative effects, and cover up blemishes or unwanted objects in images. In the end there is only one way to learn about any creative pastime, and that is to spend time exploring the possibilities.

Points to remember

Most image editing programs are not designed to handle anything more than a few lines of text. Where it is necessary to combine images with large amounts of text it is generally better to load the images into a word processor or to combine the words and images in a desktop publishing program.

The standard text features should be available from an image editor, such as various types of alignment, the full range of installed fonts, a wide range of sizes, and styles such as italic and underline.

It is often possible to apply a useful range of effects to text, but it is normally necessary to convert text into pixels in order to add filtering and certain transformations. The normal text editing facilities are lost once the text is converted into pixels, so make sure that there are no errors in the text before converting it to pixels.

Various types of drop shadow and many other effects can be obtained by using two identical strings of text with processing such as Gaussian Blur filtering being applied to one of both text strings. Some image editors have built in facilities for producing special effects with text.

Many image editing programs have facilities for fitting text to an arc, and can provide more sophisticated forms of distortion such as twisted or wavy text. Be careful when using some of the more extreme distortions. They can look very good but leave the text illegible.

Captions are easily added to images, and it is just a matter of increasing the canvas size so that there is somewhere for the caption text. The full range of text sizes, effects, etc., is then available.

Index

A

abstract	282
Adjust Backlighting	177
Advanced Blending	223
advantages	29
album	79
Alignment option	245
All Layers checkbox	246
anti-aliased	205
artistic filtering	273
Auto Contrast	157, 296
Auto Levels	159

B

background	183, 212, 259
Background layer	248
backlighting	177
backup	19
batteries	32, 75
Bitmap	133
blurring	289
BMP	22
Bold	319
brightness	38, 165
browser safe	138
brush	170, 227, 250
brushstrokes	229
Burn tool	215, 251

C

Canvas Size	330
canvas size	91
caption	120, 329
cards	2, 332
CD-R	2
clipping	154
Clone Stamp tool	234
CMYK	126, 128
Color Picker	127, 144, 230
Colored Pencil filter	274

colour	56, 125, 147
Compactflash	9
composition	242
compression	11
computer	46, 53
Contiguous checkbox	204
contrast	38, 156, 165
converging verticals	111
conversion	141
Copy and Paste	217
cost	33
costs	59
Create Photomerge	221
crop marks	120
Crop tool	102, 115
cropping	104

D

data storage	10
depth of field	289
Deselect	190
Distort function	110
distortions	65
dithering	133
Dodge tool	253
dots per inch	55
download time	7
drawbacks	45
drivers	15
drop shadow	323
Dry Brush filter	276
Duplicate Layer	302

E

Edge Contrast	198
editing	3, 80, 87
embossed	327
Enhance menu	148
EPS	22
expanding images	241
Exposure control	251

Index

Eyedropper   230
Eyedropper tool   142

F

f numbers   66
Feathering   207
Fill Flash   173
filter   42, 271
Firewire   12
fisheye   312
flare   65
flash modes   68
flipping   116
formats   19
Frequency   198
Fuzziness control   180

G

Gaussian Blur   293, 326
GIF   21
Glowing Edges   312
Gradient Editor   268
Gradient tool   212, 262, 296
graphics tablet   255
greetings cards   332
Greyscale   131
grid   101
Grow option   209

H

hard copy   117
highlights   151
histogram   154
History palette   90
HSB   126, 129
Hue/Saturation   167

I

image quality   94
importing   16
Indexed Color   136
ink cartridge   60
inkjet   60
inkjet printer   3, 57
Intersect with Selection   188
Inverse   211
Italic   319

J

Jpeg or Jpg   20

L

Lasso tool   190
layers   23, 111, 246, 317
Layers palette   247
LCD   77
lens   62
Levels   160
longevity   49

M

Macintosh   53
macro   72
Magic Wand tool   199
Magnetic Lasso tool   196
marquee   106
Marquee tool   184
mask   214
Mask mode   257
memory   2
memory card   8
mixing   125
Mode menu   249
monitor   76

N

New Selection	189
NiCad	76

O

Opacity control	249, 324
Options bar	90, 228, 318
Overlay Color	258

P

Paint Bucket tool	259
Paint Daubs filter	282
panoramic	219
paper	60
Paste	217
PCs	53
PCX	22
PDF	22
Pen Pressure option	255
Pencil Width	274
perspective	108
Photomerge	221
Photoshop Elements	88
PICT	22
pixel	96
pixels	4
pixilation	7
Png	21
Polygonal Lasso tool	192
pressure sensitive	254
preview	275
primary colours	56, 128
printer	3
printers	55
printing	288
PSD	23

R

radial gradient	267
Radius value	311
rasterizing	328
RAW	23
rechargeable	75
Red Eye Brush tool	171
red-eye	169
Remove Color	181
Replace Color	179
resolution	7, 46, 93
retouching	227
RGB	126
rotation	98
Rough Pastels filter	276
RS232C	12

S

saturation	152, 172
Selection Brush tool	256
Selection menu	206
selections	183
shadows	151
Sharp filtering	305
Sharpen Edges	309
Sharpen More	309
Similar	210
Sketch submenu	284
sloping horizon	100
SLR	1, 45
Smart Blur	302
Smartmedia	8
Smudge tool	294
soft focus	208, 298
Soft Light	261
software	3, 78
Solarize	312
Sony Memory Stick	9
speed	58
speed rating	67
Sponge tool	254

Sprayed Strokes filter	284
stitching	218
storage	54
stretching	114
Stroke Pressure	274
Style menu	188, 321
Subtraction mode	187
swatches	141

T

telephoto	63
text	317
Text Orientation	319
text size	319
thumbnail	150
TIFF or TIF	21
Tolerance setting	261
tolerance setting	202
TWAIN	14
Type tool	322

U

Unsharp Mask	310
USB	13

V

Variations	148

W

warped text	321
web page	3
web safe	138
wide angle	63

Z

zoom range	64